Oh, the doors you will open!
SCHOOL BUS

Twists and Turns

Senior Authors

Isabel L. Beck • Roger C. Farr • Dorothy S. Strickland

Authors

Alma Flor Ada • Roxanne F. Hudson • Margaret G. McKeown
Robin C. Scarcella • Julie A. Washington

Consultants

F. Isabel Campoy • Tyrone C. Howard • David A. Monti

www.harcourtschool.com

Printed in the United States of America

ISBN 10: 0-15-369853-5
ISBN 13: 978-0-15-369853-8

3 4 5 6 7 8 9 10 048 17 16 15 14 13 12 11 10 09 08

Twists and Turns

www.harcourtschool.com

Theme 1
School Days

Contents

Social Studies

Language Arts

Lesson 3

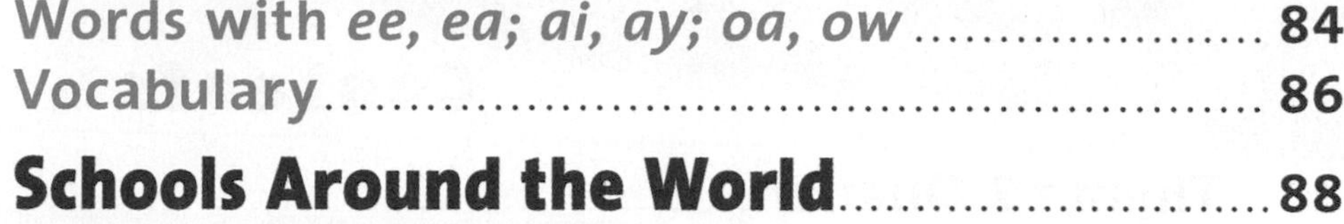

Science

Science

Lesson 4

Science

Social Studies

Lesson 5 Theme Review

Theme 2

Together We Can

Contents

Science

Social Studies

Language Arts

Theme 3
As We Grow

Contents

Comprehension Strategies

Strategies for Reading

A **strategy** is a plan for doing something well. You may use strategies before, during, and after reading.

Before You Read

- **Preview the text** by looking at the title, headings, and photographs or art.
- **Access prior knowledge** by thinking about what you already know.
- **Predict** what the text will be about and what you might learn from it. Then **set a purpose** for reading.

While You Read

Think about what you understand and do not understand. Use the comprehension strategies on page 11 to help you read and understand.

After You Read

Talk with a classmate about which strategies you used and why you used them.

Strategies to Use During Reading

- **Use Story Structure** Keep track of the characters, setting, and plot events to help you understand a story.
- **Summarize** Pause as you read to think about the most important ideas in the text.
- **Ask and Answer Questions** Ask yourself and others questions about what you read. Answer questions your teacher asks to better understand.
- **Use Graphic Organizers** Use charts and diagrams to help you read.
- **Monitor Comprehension** When you do not understand what you read, use one of these fix-up strategies.
    - **Reread**
    - **Read Ahead**
    - **Adjust Reading Rate**
    - **Self-Correct**

READING-WRITING CONNECTION

	Lesson 1	Lesson 2
SELECTION TITLES	**Ruby the Copycat** The Singing Marvel	**The Day Eddie Met the Author** Good Books, Good Times; Surprise
Comprehension Strategy	Use Graphic Organizers	Use Graphic Organizers
Focus Skill	Characters and Setting	Characters and Setting

rage

Theme 1 School Days

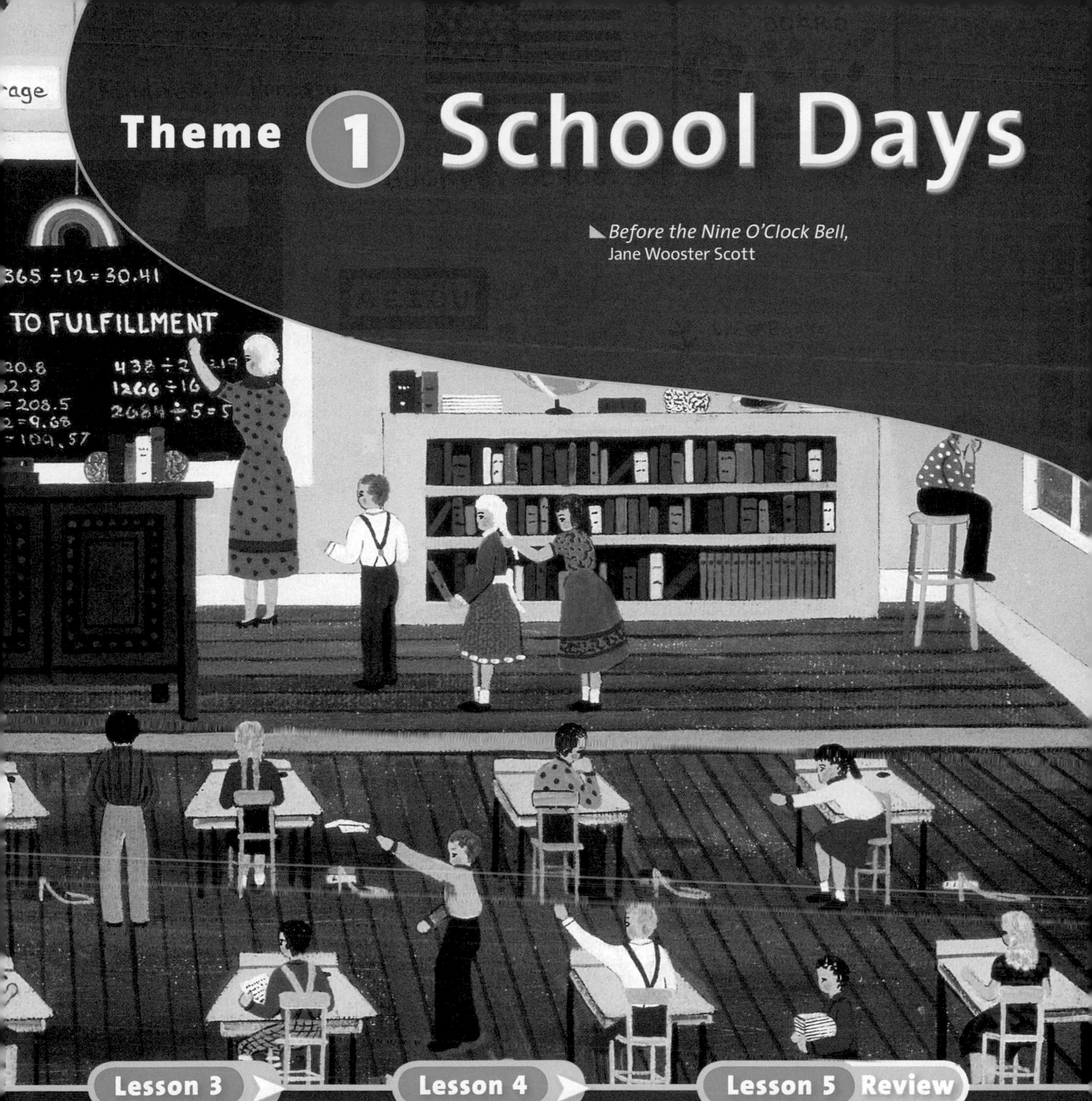

365 ÷ 12 = 30.41

TO FULFILLMENT

Before the Nine O'Clock Bell,
Jane Wooster Scott

CONTENTS

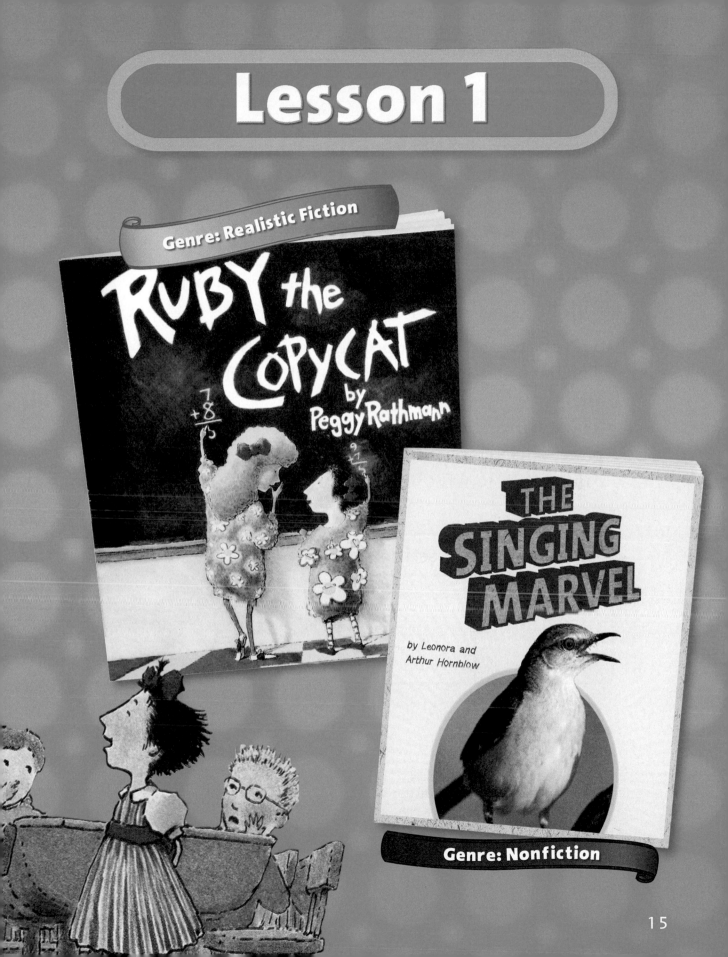

Lesson 1

Genre: Realistic Fiction

RUBY the COPYCAT
by Peggy Rathmann

Genre: Nonfiction

Focus Skill

Characters and Setting

Every story has important elements, or parts, including characters, setting, and plot.

- The **characters** are the people or animals in the story. The things characters say and do tell you what they are like.
- The **setting** is where and when the story takes place. Where and when a story takes place can be clues to what will happen.

Characters	Setting

Tip

Identifying the characters and setting in a story will help you understand what you read. It will also give you clues about what is important in the story.

Read the story below, and look at the chart. What do you know about the main character and the setting?

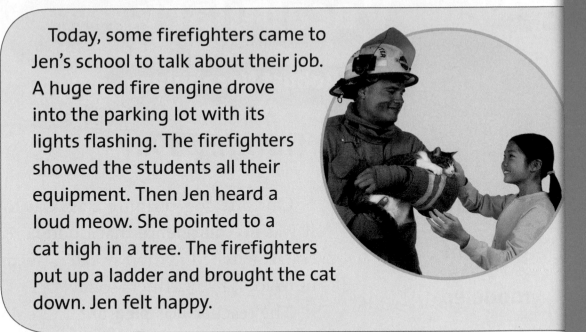

Today, some firefighters came to Jen's school to talk about their job. A huge red fire engine drove into the parking lot with its lights flashing. The firefighters showed the students all their equipment. Then Jen heard a loud meow. She pointed to a cat high in a tree. The firefighters put up a ladder and brought the cat down. Jen felt happy.

Characters	Setting
• Jen •	• school •

Try This!

Look back at the story. What does Jen do that shows she is helpful? Why is the setting important?

www.harcourtschool.com/storytown

Vocabulary

Build Robust Vocabulary

- coincidence
- pleasant
- modeled
- murmured
- loyal
- recited

Training Day

Our first dog-training class was today. It was no **coincidence** that Buddy's red collar matched my red sweater. I wanted us to look like partners today!

The teacher was **pleasant** and calm. We watched as she **modeled** the first command. "Sit!" she said. She held her hand just above her dog's head. As he looked up at her hand, he sat down. "Good dog," she said. I copied her command, but Buddy wouldn't sit!

Buddy and I practiced the "sit" command all morning. In class, I was the first person to try the command. "Sit," I **murmured**. Buddy looked at me and stood.

"Speak firmly," the teacher said. "Your dog is **loyal** and wants to obey you."

"Sit!" I said. Buddy sat! "Good dog!" I said. We learned more commands. As I **recited** each one, Buddy seemed to know what to do. I was very proud of him!

www.harcourtschool.com/reading

Word Detective

Your mission this week is to look for Vocabulary Words in library books that you read for fun. Each time you see a Vocabulary Word, write it in your vocabulary journal. Don't forget to tell where you found each word.

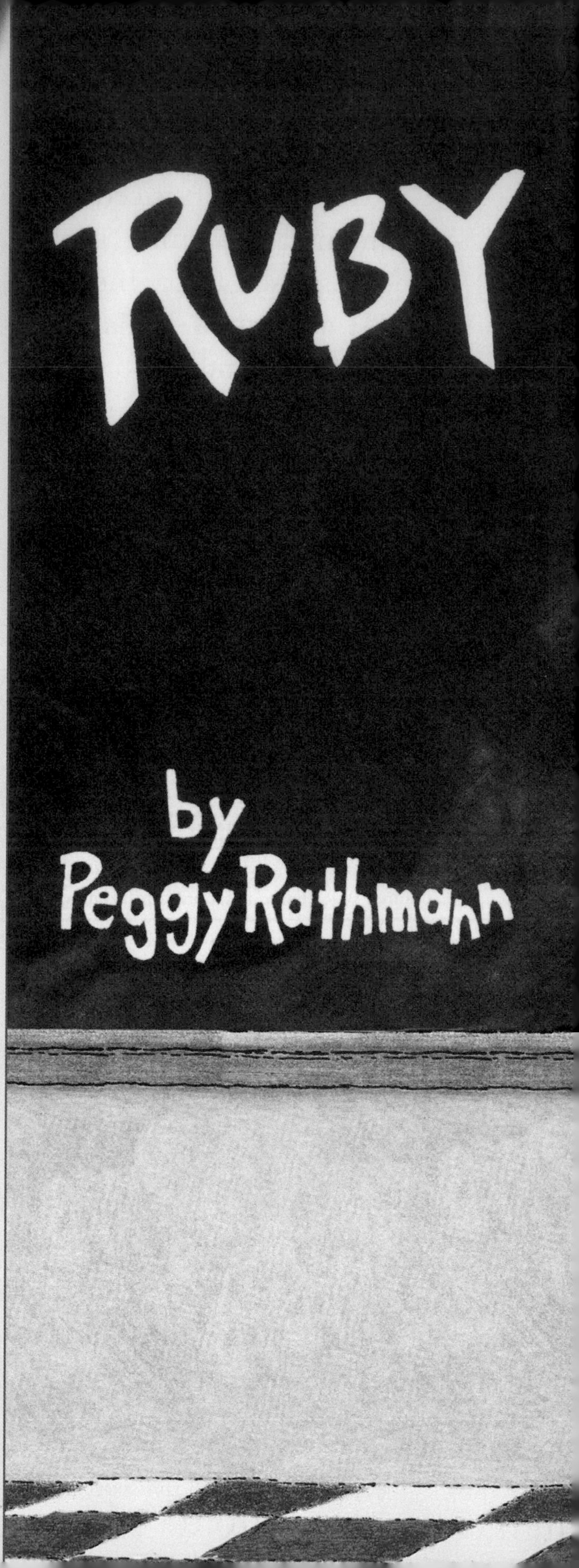

Genre Study

3ELA-6-E3-16

Realistic fiction tells about characters and settings that are like people and places in real life. Look for

- a beginning, a middle, and an end.
- characters and a setting that could be real.

Characters	Setting

Comprehension Strategy

3ELA-7-E1-17

Use graphic organizers like the one above to tell about the characters and setting.

LOUISIANA GRADE-LEVEL EXPECTATIONS—3ELA-6-E3-16 define characteristics of types of literature; 3ELA-7-E1-17 demonstrate understanding of information

RUBY

by Peggy Rathmann

the COPYCAT

Monday was Ruby's first day in Miss Hart's class.

"Class, this is Ruby," announced Miss Hart.

"Ruby, you may use the empty desk behind Angela. Angela is the girl with the pretty red bow in her hair."

Angela smiled at Ruby.

Ruby smiled at Angela's bow and tiptoed to her seat.

"I hope everyone had a pleasant weekend," said Miss Hart. "Does anyone have something to share?"

"I was the flower girl at my sister's wedding," said Angela.

"That's exciting," said Miss Hart.

Ruby raised her hand halfway. "I was the flower girl at my sister's wedding, too."

"What a coincidence!" said Miss Hart.

Angela turned and smiled at Ruby.

Ruby smiled at the top of Angela's head.

"Class, please take out your reading books," said Miss Hart.

At lunchtime, Ruby hopped all the way home on one foot.

When Ruby came back to school, she was wearing a red bow in her hair. She slid into her seat behind Angela.

"I like your bow," whispered Angela.

"I like yours, too," whispered Ruby.

"Class, please take out your math books," said Miss Hart.

On Tuesday morning, Angela wore a sweater with daisies on it.

At lunchtime, Ruby hopped home sideways.

When Ruby came back to school after lunch, she was wearing a sweater with daisies on it.

"I like your sweater," whispered Angela.

"I like yours, too," whispered Ruby.

On Wednesday, Angela wore a hand-painted T-shirt with matching sneakers.

After lunch, Ruby hopped back to school wearing a hand-painted T-shirt with matching sneakers.

"Why are you sitting like that?" whispered Angela.

"Wet paint," said Ruby.

On Thursday morning, during Sharing Time, Angela modeled the flower girl dress she wore at her sister's wedding.

Ruby modeled her flower girl dress, too, right after lunch.

Angela didn't whisper anything.

By coincidence, on Friday morning, both girls wore red-and-lavender-striped dresses.

At lunchtime, Angela raced home.

When Angela came back to school, she was wearing black.

On Friday afternoon, Miss Hart asked everyone to write a short poem.

"Who would like to read first?" asked Miss Hart.

Angela raised her hand. She stood by her desk and read:

I had a cat I could not see,
Because it stayed in back of me.
It was a very loyal pet—
It's sad we never really met.

"That was very good!" said Miss Hart. "Now, who's next?" Miss Hart looked around the room. "Ruby?"

Ruby stood and recited slowly:

I had a nice pet,
Who I never met,
Because it always stayed behind me.
And I'm sure it was a cat, too.

Ruby smiled at the back of Angela's head. Someone whispered. Ruby sat down.

"What a coincidence," murmured Miss Hart.

Angela scribbled something on a piece of paper. She passed it to Ruby. The note said:

YOU COPIED ME!
I'M TELLING MISS HART!
P.S. I DO NOT LIKE YOUR HAIR THAT WAY.

Ruby buried her chin in the collar of her blouse. A big tear rolled down her nose and plopped onto the note.

When the bell rang, Miss Hart sent everyone home except Ruby.

Miss Hart closed the door of the schoolroom and sat on the edge of Ruby's desk.

"Ruby, dear," she said gently, "you don't need to copy everything Angela does. You can be anything you want to be, but be Ruby first. I like Ruby."

Miss Hart smiled at Ruby. Ruby smiled at Miss Hart's beautiful, polished fingernails.

"Have a nice weekend," said Miss Hart.

"Have a nice weekend," said Ruby.

On Monday morning, Miss Hart said, "I hope everyone had a pleasant weekend. I did! I went to the opera." Miss Hart looked around the room. "Does anyone have something to share?"

Ruby waved her hand. Glued to every finger was a pink plastic fingernail.

"I went to the opera, too!" said Ruby.

"She did not!" whispered Angela.

Miss Hart folded her hands and looked very serious.

“Ruby, dear,” said Miss Hart gently, “did you do anything else this weekend?”

Ruby peeled off a fingernail.

“I hopped,” said Ruby.

The class giggled.

Ruby’s ears turned red.

“But I did! I hopped around the picnic table ten times!” Ruby looked around the room. “Watch!”

Ruby sprang from her desk.
She hopped forward.

She hopped backward.

She hopped sideways
with both eyes shut.

The class cheered and clapped their hands to the beat of Ruby's feet. Ruby was the best hopper they had ever seen.

Miss Hart turned on the tape player and said, "Follow the leader! Do the Ruby Hop!"

So Ruby led the class around the room, while everyone copied *her*.

And at noon, Ruby and Angela hopped home for lunch.

Think Critically

1. What is Ruby like at the beginning of the story? What is she like at the end? Focus Skill CHARACTERS AND SETTING

2. What is the first way that Ruby copies Angela? IMPORTANT DETAILS

3. If you were Ruby, would you copy Angela? Explain. EXPRESS PERSONAL OPINIONS

4. How do you know that the author believes that everyone has something special to share? DRAW CONCLUSIONS

5. **WRITE** In what ways are Ruby and Angela the same? In what ways are they different? Use details from the story to explain your answer. SHORT RESPONSE

LOUISIANA GRADE-LEVEL EXPECTATIONS—**3ELA-1-E4-08(c)** identify character traits/feelings/motivation; **3ELA-1-E5-10** summarize main events/ideas/details; **3ELA-7-E1-17(c)** make inferences/draw conclusions; **3ELA-7-E1-17(d)** compare/contrast; **3ELA-7-E3-20** explain author's viewpoint; **3ELA-7-E4-21(e)** connect to real-life situations

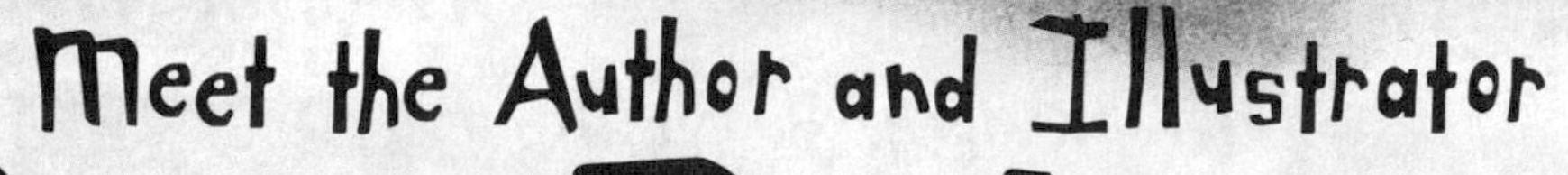

Meet the Author and Illustrator

Peggy Rathmann

Peggy Rathmann started writing and illustrating children's books while she was on a car trip. She was sitting in the back seat with her niece. For fun, she started to draw a story.

The ideas for all of Peggy Rathmann's stories come from her own life. When she was studying to be a writer, she tried to write like the other students in her class. Like Ruby, she learned that being herself was the best thing she could do.

GO online www.harcourtschool.com/storytown

Science
THE SINGING MARVEL
by Leonora and Arthur Hornblow
Expository Nonfiction

THE SINGING

from Birds Do the Strangest Things

No one wants to be a copycat! Even so, people can learn a lot by copying others. Babies learn to talk by copying their parents. Some birds can also copy the sounds of other animals. Read about one of them on the next page.

MARVEL

by Leonora and Arthur Hornblow

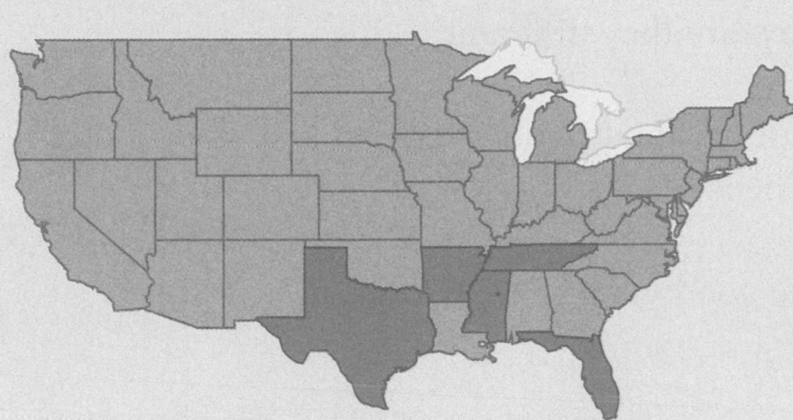

The mockingbird is the state bird of Arkansas, Florida, Mississippi, Tennessee, and Texas.

Do you want to hear the songs of many birds? Then go find a mockingbird. It can sing its own beautiful song. It can also sing the song of almost any bird it hears. It can copy other sounds. It can even copy the bark of a dog or a police officer's whistle.

It often sings all the songs and sounds it knows, one right after the other. Maybe this is its way of saying, "Listen to the mockingbird."

Connections

Comparing Texts

3ELA-1-E6-11
3ELA-7-E1-17(d)
3ELA-7-E4-21(e)

1. Think about Ruby and the mockingbird. How are they alike? How are they different?

2. What did you learn about Ruby that can help you in making new friends?

3. What are some good ways to welcome a new student to class?

Vocabulary Review

3ELA-2-E6-27

Jason recited a pleasant poem.

Word Sort

Work with a partner. Sort the Vocabulary Words into two groups. Decide whether each word is a *character trait* or a *character action.* Compare your sorted words with your partner, and take turns explaining why you put each word where you did. Then choose one word from each category and write a sentence that uses both words.

- coincidence
- pleasant
- modeled
- murmured
- loyal
- recited

Fluency Practice 3ELA-1-E3-07

Partner Reading

Choose your favorite paragraph from "Ruby the Copycat." With a partner, take turns reading your paragraphs aloud. If you make a mistake, reread the sentence until you can say it correctly. Tell your partner what you liked about how he or she read.

Writing 3ELA-7-E1-17 3ELA-7-E3-20 3ELA-2-E6-27

Write a Notebook Entry

Write about the ideas in "Ruby the Copycat." Tell what the author wanted you to learn by reading the story. Use the graphic organizer to help you remember what happened in the story.

My Writing Checklist

Writing Trait → Ideas

- ✔ I use a graphic organizer to help remember information about the characters and the story.
- ✔ I write my ideas about what the author wanted me to learn.

Characters	Setting

LOUISIANA GRADE-LEVEL EXPECTATIONS—3ELA-1-E3-07 adjust reading speed; 3ELA-1-E6-11 connect to prior knowledge; 3ELA-7-E1-17 demonstrate understanding of information; 3ELA-7-E1-17(d) compare/contrast; 3ELA-7-E3-20 explain author's viewpoint; 3ELA-7-E4-21(e) connect to real-life situations; 3ELA-2-E6-27 write for various purposes

Reading-Writing Connection

Personal Narrative

A **personal narrative** is a story that you tell about yourself. After reading "Ruby the Copycat," I wrote about my experience as a new student.

Student Writing Model

New-School Jitters
by Tamiko

It just wasn't fair! I had been such a good student back home in Japan. Now I hardly knew what the teacher was saying. It was my first morning in an American school, and I felt alone.

First, my teacher introduced me. Then I bowed to the class, and my classmates giggled. What were they laughing at?

At lunch, I ate alone. Later that day, the teacher called my name. I didn't know what she was asking. I put my head down and cried. A nice girl named Nadia helped me.

Today I speak English well, and I'm doing great at school. Best of all, Nadia is my best friend!

Writing Trait

IDEAS
A good personal narrative considers audience and purpose. In this case, the purpose is to show what it is like to be a new student.

Writing Trait

ORGANIZATION
Transition words such as *first, next, after,* and *later* help connect ideas in personal narratives.

Here's how I write a personal narrative.

1. **I brainstorm ideas for writing. I do this by making a list of experiences I have had.**

Playing soccer
First day at school
Learning to ride my bike
Celebrating holidays

2. **I think about whom I want to read my writing. I also think about my purpose. I choose one idea to write about.**

Playing soccer
First day at school
Learning to ride my bike
Celebrating holidays

3. **I begin to plan my writing. I make notes by using a web.**

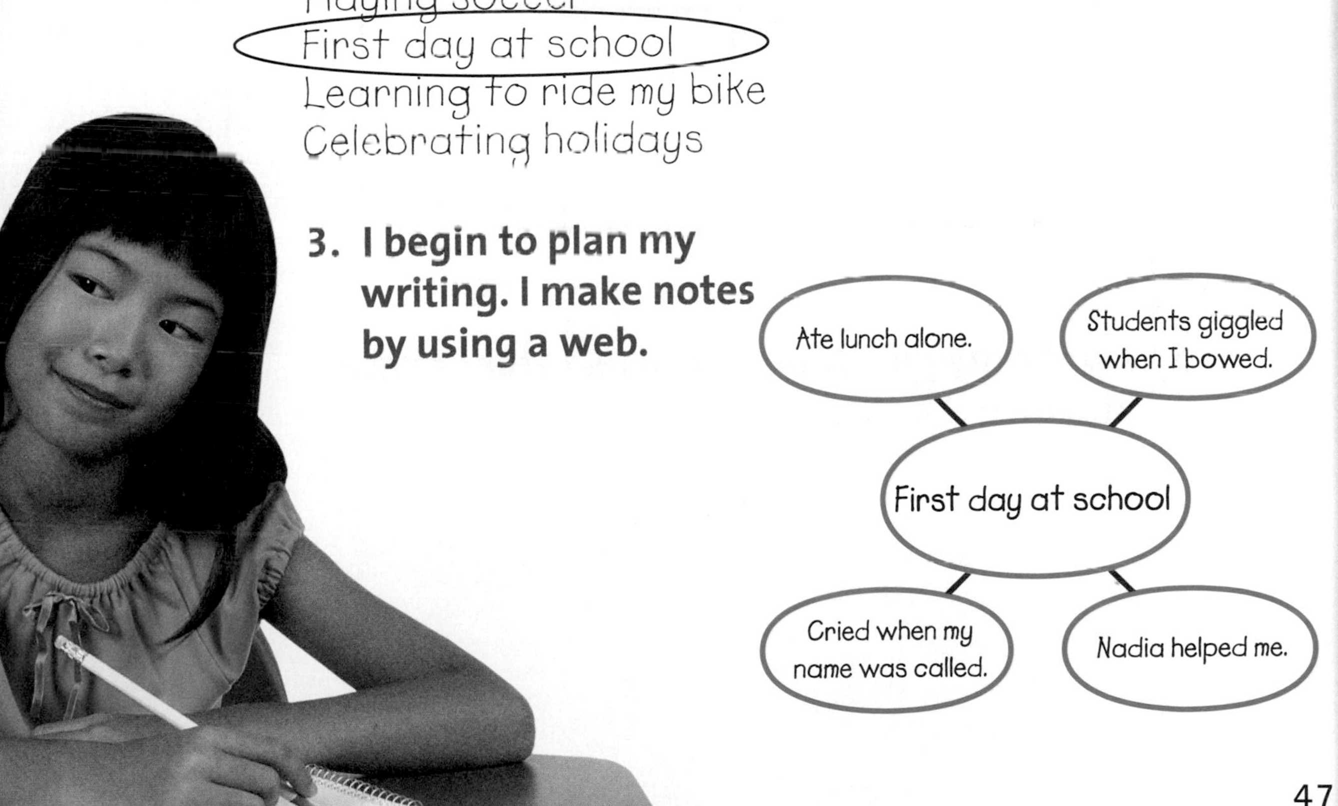

4. **I organize my writing into a beginning, middle, and end.**

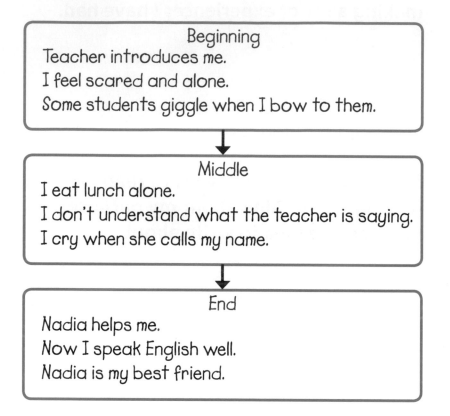

Beginning
Teacher introduces me. I feel scared and alone. Some students giggle when I bow to them.

↓

Middle
I eat lunch alone. I don't understand what the teacher is saying. I cry when she calls my name.

↓

End
Nadia helps me. Now I speak English well. Nadia is my best friend.

5. **I write my personal narrative. Later I revise it and give it a title.**

Here is a checklist I use when I write a personal narrative. You can use it when you write one, too.

Checklist for Writing a Personal Narrative

- ☐ I choose an audience and a purpose for writing.
- ☐ My personal narrative tells about an interesting experience I have had.
- ☐ I write my narrative in an order that makes sense, such as time order.
- ☐ To connect my ideas and paragraphs, I use transition words such as *first, next, later,* and *last*.
- ☐ I include my thoughts and feelings.
- ☐ I use a variety of sentence types.

CONTENTS

Lesson 2

Genre: Realistic Fiction
THE DAY
EDDIE
MET THE AUTHOR
by Louise Borden
illustrated by Will Terry
Good Books, Good Times!
Surprise
by Beverly McLoughland
illustrated by Jui Ishida
Genre: Poetry

Characters and Setting

Remember that the characters and setting are two important parts of a story.

- What a **character** says or does gives clues to what the character is like.
- The **setting** can give clues to what might happen. Different parts of a story may have different settings. Pay attention to how the setting affects a story. Could the same story events happen in a different time or place?

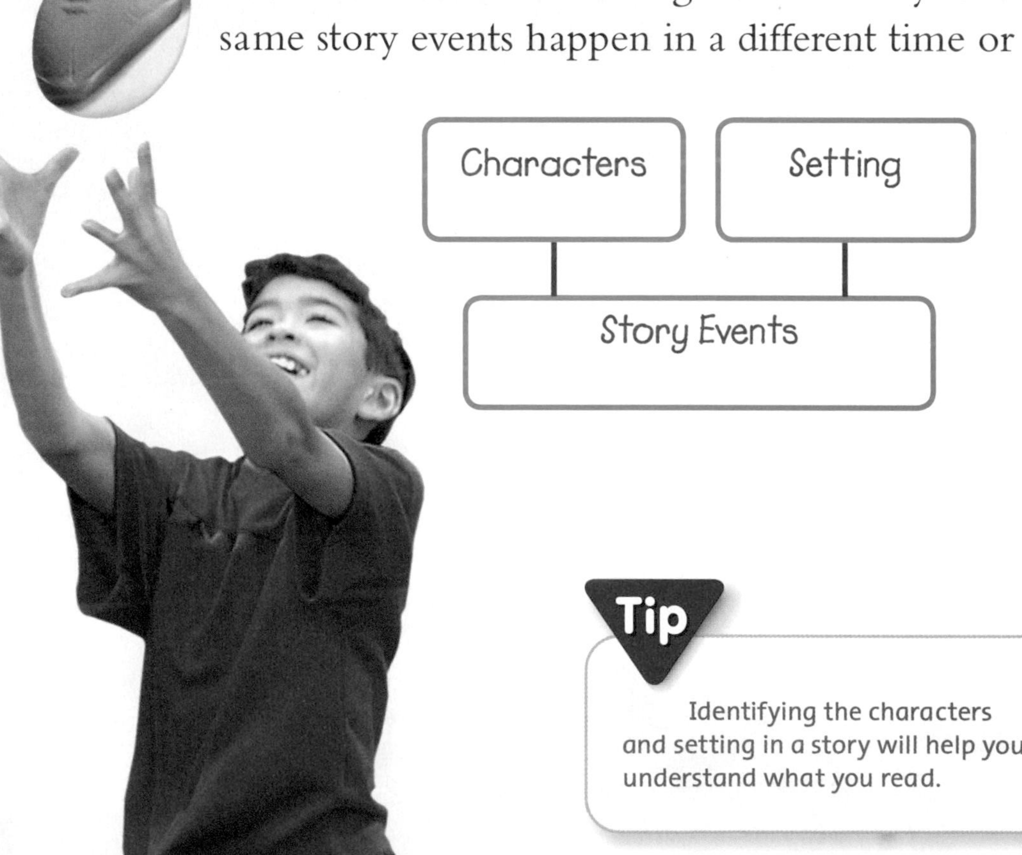

Tip

Identifying the characters and setting in a story will help you understand what you read.

Read the story, and look at the story map. Tell details about the characters and setting.

Stan wanted to do everything his older brother, Bill, did. Bill was playing catch on the playground with his friend Mike. They were throwing a football.

"May I play?" Stan asked.

"Sure, if you can catch it," Bill said. He threw the ball high in the air. Stan ran and held his hands together. The ball landed right in his hands!

"Nice catch," Bill said. "You can join us."

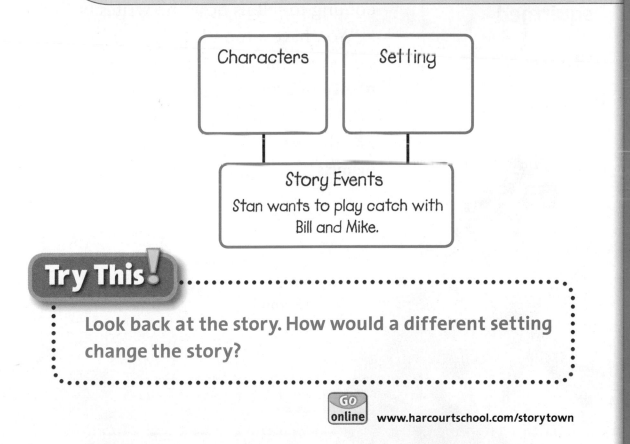

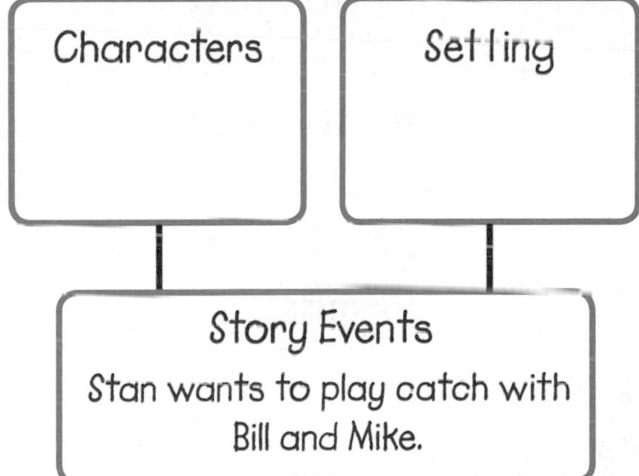

Try This!

Look back at the story. How would a different setting change the story?

www.harcourtschool.com/storytown

Vocabulary

Build Robust Vocabulary

- assembly
- plenty
- dismiss
- squirmed
- patchwork
- autographed

Author in the School

September 25

At this week's school **assembly**, we heard exciting news. Principal García said that we will be having a special visitor. An author, Amy Hill, will be coming to tell us how she writes books!

"You have a month before the visit," said the principal. "That should give you **plenty** of time to read some of Ms. Hill's books. You can decide which book you like the best." Then Mr. García began to **dismiss** each class.

None of the students **squirmed** or talked during the assembly.

September 28

The school library has a display of Amy Hill's books. There are more than twenty different titles to choose from! One library table looks like a **patchwork** quilt of book covers.

The library is also having a contest. Students have to guess which book Ms. Hill will choose to read first during her visit. Winners will receive an **autographed** copy of Ms. Hill's latest book.

The library has many copies of each title, so everyone will have a chance to read them.

www.harcourtschool.com/storytown

Word Scribe

Your mission this week is to use Vocabulary Words in your writing. For example, you could write about your favorite assembly. Read what you write to a classmate.

LOUISIANA GRADE-LEVEL EXPECTATIONS—3ELA-2-E6-27 write for various purposes

3ELA-6-E3-16

Genre Study

Realistic fiction is a story that can happen in real life. Look for

- a setting that is real or could be real.
- characters who behave like real people.

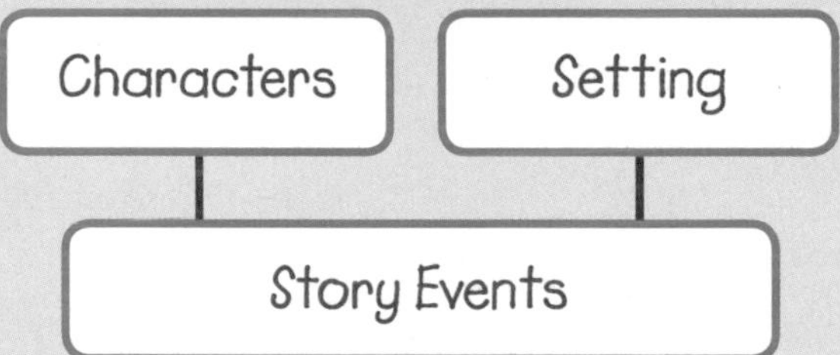

3ELA-7-E1-17

Comprehension Strategy

Use graphic organizers like the one above to tell about the characters and setting.

LOUISIANA GRADE-LEVEL EXPECTATIONS—3ELA-6-E3-16 define characteristics of types of literature; 3ELA-7-E1-17 demonstrate understanding of information

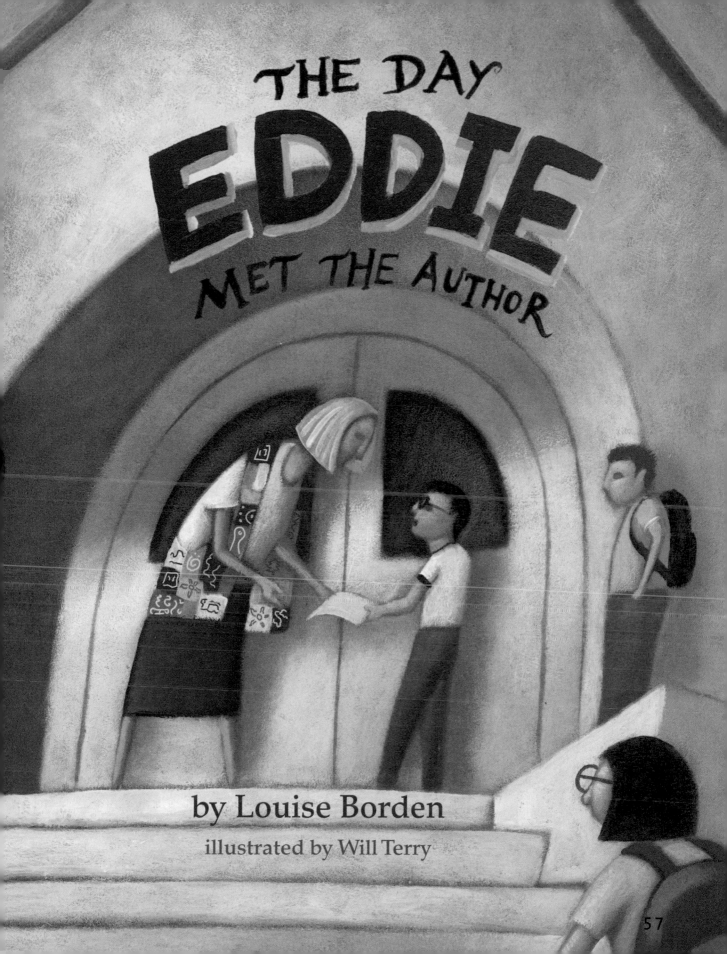

THE DAY EDDIE MET THE AUTHOR

by Louise Borden

illustrated by Will Terry

Tuesday, October 10th was going to be a great day for Eddie and his class. It was the day a real author was coming to Riverside Elementary School. Eddie had been waiting, waiting, waiting. . . . The whole school had been waiting. Especially Eddie's teacher, Mrs. Morrow. She *loved* real authors. She loved how real authors made the words flow, and how the words sounded just right, and went with pictures in their own way.

Mrs. Morrow said she couldn't live without books and the wonderful stories in them. She said third graders had their own stories to tell: "We are all authors with important stories inside us." Eddie chewed on his pencil and thought hard. How could *his* stories ever be like a real author's?

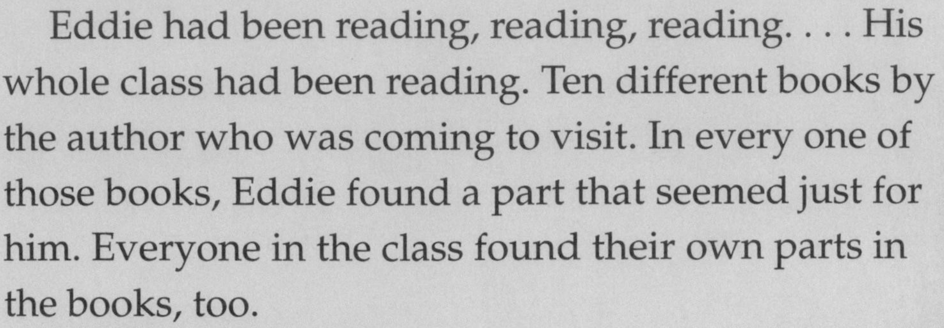

Eddie had been reading, reading, reading. . . . His whole class had been reading. Ten different books by the author who was coming to visit. In every one of those books, Eddie found a part that seemed just for him. Everyone in the class found their own parts in the books, too.

"How does the author do that?" Eddie asked Mrs. Morrow one morning as the bell rang for recess.

"That's a great question, Eddie," his teacher said. "You'll have to ask her when she comes."

Eddie wrote down his author question on a bright yellow piece of paper and put it in his desk, right on top of his "Ideas to Write About" notebook.

"That's a question you won't want to lose," Mrs. Morrow told him with her best smile.

Eddie Lewis Grade 3
How do you write books that have parts meant for me?

At last! The big day! Mrs. Morrow wrote *Tuesday, October 10th* on the chalkboard in her best cursive.

Mrs. Morrow led her class into the gym. There was the real author! She was testing Mr. Chickerella's microphone and getting ready for the assembly. Arthur was setting up chairs for the teachers.

Eddie checked out the author from head to foot. He thought real authors would look different from everybody else.

This author just looked like a teacher or a mom.

Eddie sat between two of his classmates and he sat up straight. The author was wearing a vest that was a patchwork of pictures from some of her books. Eddie looked to find his favorite one—there it was! There were whispers in the audience. Then Mr. Chickerella welcomed their special guest. No one in Mrs. Morrow's class talked or squirmed, not even Tyler Mason. Everyone was ready to listen, and the author began:

"I can tell you've all had your noses in my books. . . . I've been reading your wonderful writing in the school hallways, and seen your terrific illustrations. . . ."

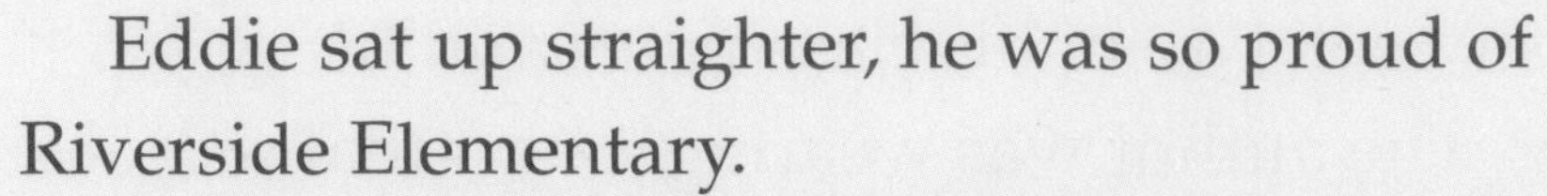

Eddie sat up straighter, he was so proud of Riverside Elementary.

"Some of you may be wondering how to become a writer. The best way to become a writer is to be a reader. . . ."

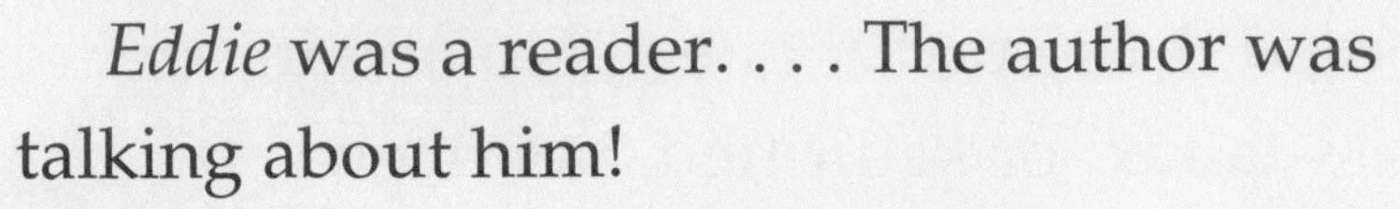

Eddie was a reader. . . . The author was talking about him!

The minutes of the assembly zoomed by. Eddie never wanted it to end. Today he felt like a real writer.

Finally it was time for questions and answers. Eddie put his hand up, fast as lightning, but there were other hands in front of him and behind him, and on both sides. Everyone wanted the author to call on them. Eddie waved his yellow paper in the air. His question was important. Mrs. Morrow had said it was not a question to lose.

"How long have you been a writer?"
"How old are you?"
"Have you autographed our books yet?"
"Which book is your favorite book?"

"Do you ever run out of ideas?"
"How old are your kids?"
"Which book was the hardest to write?"

No one asked the question that Eddie wanted answered. But the assembly was over, and Eddie hadn't been called on. Mr. Chickerella began to dismiss the second and third graders. Eddie's question! His important question on the most exciting day of the school year! He wanted to know the answer.

Eddie read the words he had written on his yellow paper.

Slowly Eddie folded up his question and put it back in his pocket. Suddenly he felt a grown-up's hand on his shoulder. But it wasn't Mrs. Morrow. Or Mr. Chickerella. It was the author! She was standing right next to Eddie in the third-grade line, asking him his name. Then she said:

"I saw your hand up in the assembly, waving a yellow paper. I knew you had an important question to ask . . . but we ran out of time. . ."

The third graders began to crowd around Eddie and the author. Mrs. Morrow shushed everyone as the author unfolded the yellow paper and read Eddie's words out loud.

"Now *that* is a thinking question, Eddie!" the author said.

Her smile was like a big, warm hug. Eddie felt as tall as a grown-up standing in his third-grade line.

Everyone was quiet while the author put her hand on her chin and thought about Eddie's question. Maybe everyone was thinking about the parts of the author's books that seemed like they were meant just for them. That's what Eddie was thinking about.

Eddie Lewis
Grade 3
How do you write
books that have parts
meant for

Then the author said: "Eddie, if you write about parts of yourself, I bet your reader will have some of those parts, too. I guess that's a small answer to the big question you asked. And by the way, I've always loved the name Eddie. . . . Someday I may use it when I'm writing a book. . . ."

Eddie looked at Mrs. Morrow and gave her a wide smile. Now maybe *his* stories could be like the author's. And he would try to write from his heart.

On the afternoon of Tuesday, October 10, Eddie began a rough draft of a new story during Mrs. Morrow's writing workshop. He didn't know how it would end, but he had plenty to write about from what had happened that day. He already knew a title to use. He'd written it in his notebook as soon as he got back to the classroom:

Think CRITICALLY

1. How does Eddie feel before the assembly? How can you tell? CHARACTERS AND SETTING

2. How does the author make Eddie and the setting seem realistic? AUTHOR'S CRAFT

3. Who would you most like to have as a visitor to your school? Explain your reasons. EXPRESS PERSONAL OPINIONS

4. What does Eddie do during the assembly that shows he is excited about asking his question? CHARACTERS' EMOTIONS

5. **WRITE** Write about a time someone taught you something important. Describe what you learned. SHORT RESPONSE

LOUISIANA GRADE-LEVEL EXPECTATIONS—3ELA-1-E4-08 identify story elements; 3ELA-1-E4-08(c) identify character traits/feelings/motivation; 3ELA-1-E6-11 connect to prior knowledge; 3ELA-2-E4-25 write paragraphs with description/narration

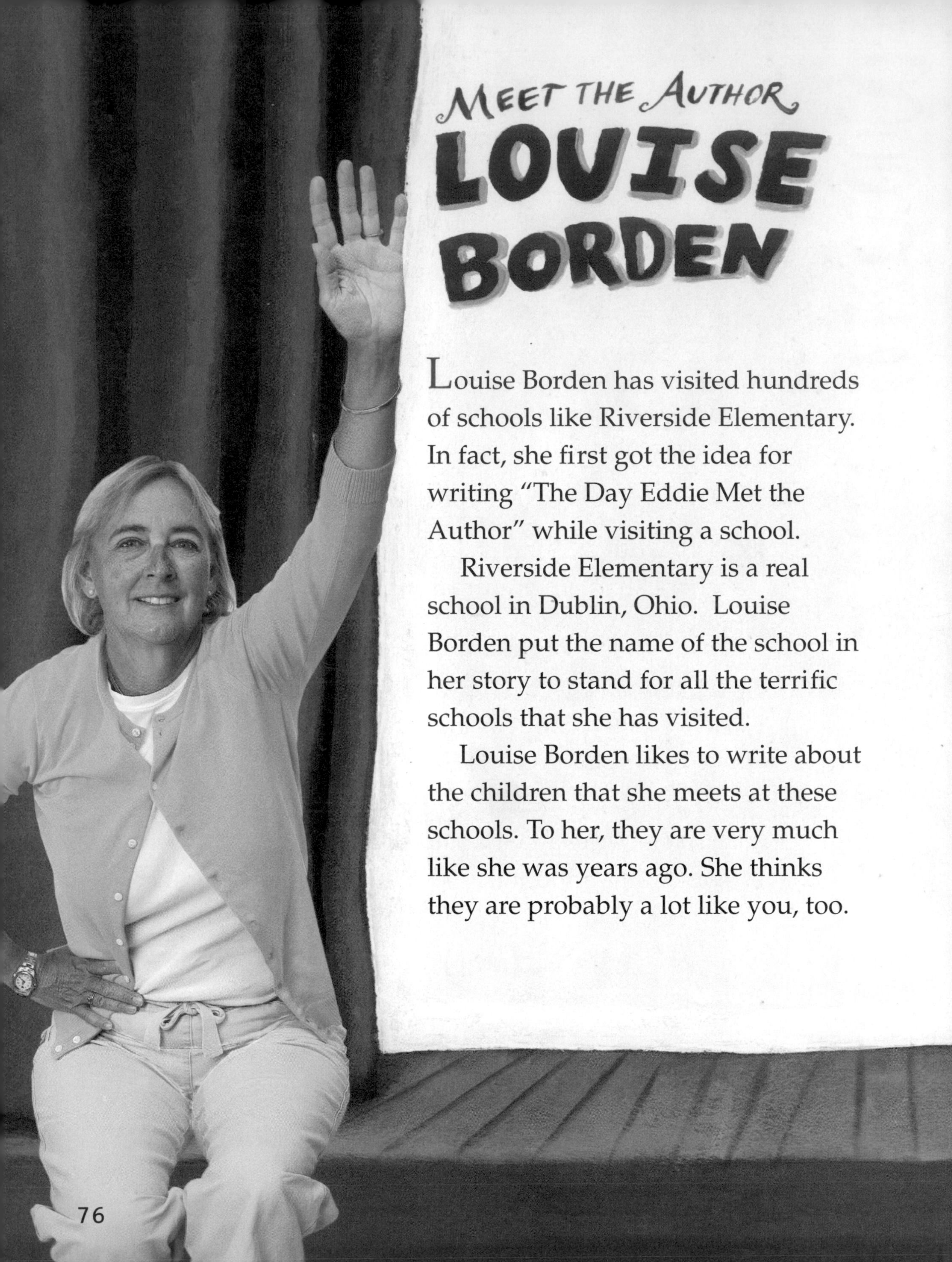

Meet the Author Louise Borden

Louise Borden has visited hundreds of schools like Riverside Elementary. In fact, she first got the idea for writing "The Day Eddie Met the Author" while visiting a school.

Riverside Elementary is a real school in Dublin, Ohio. Louise Borden put the name of the school in her story to stand for all the terrific schools that she has visited.

Louise Borden likes to write about the children that she meets at these schools. To her, they are very much like she was years ago. She thinks they are probably a lot like you, too.

MEET THE ILLUSTRATOR
WILL TERRY

As a child, Will Terry enjoyed sports and playing the cello. Once in a while, he doodled and drew pictures, too. However, he really discovered his love for drawing and painting when he went to college. He's been doing it ever since.

Will Terry likes to try out different colors and shapes when he illustrates. He also likes to create funny characters.

When he's not drawing, Will Terry enjoys snowboarding, backpacking, and mountain biking with his family.

www.harcourtschool.com/storytown

Good Books, Good Times!

Good books.
Good times.
Good stories.
Good rhymes.
Good beginnings.
Good ends.
Good people.
Good friends.
Good fiction.
Good facts.
Good adventures.
Good acts.
Good stories.
Good rhymes.
Good books.
Good times.

by Lee Bennett Hopkins
illustrated by Jui Ishida

Surprise

The biggest
Surprise
On the library shelf
Is when you suddenly
Find yourself
Inside a book—
(The *hidden* you)
You wonder how
The author knew.

by Beverly McLoughland
illustrated by Jui Ishida

Connections

Comparing Texts

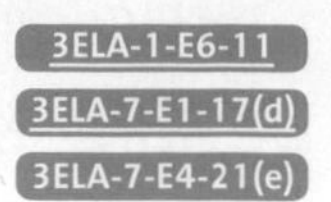

1. Compare the author's opinion about books in "The Day Eddie Met the Author" to the poet's opinion in "Surprise."

2. Have you ever felt as excited as Eddie? Explain your answer.

3. How do you think authors can help children become better writers?

Vocabulary Review

3ELA-2-E6-27

The baby squirmed under the patchwork blanket.

Word Pairs

Work with a partner. Write each Vocabulary Word on a card. Place the cards face down. Take turns flipping over two cards and writing a sentence that uses both words. Read your sentences to your partner and decide whether the Vocabulary Words are used correctly.

- assembly
- plenty
- dismiss
- squirmed
- patchwork
- autographed

Fluency Practice 3ELA-1-E3-07

Readers' Theater

Meet with a group. Choose a section of the story that has dialogue. Then choose roles, including a narrator. Practice reading the section aloud. If you make a mistake, reread until you can read your part correctly. When the group is ready, perform for the class.

Writing 3ELA-2-E3-24(b)

Plan a Narrative

Plan a narrative about a day something happy and exciting happens at school. Make sure to describe the characters well and include a clear setting. Describe the events that make the day exciting.

My Writing Checklist

Writing Trait → Ideas

- ✔ I use a graphic organizer to think about my ideas.
- ✔ I choose a character and setting that can be described clearly.

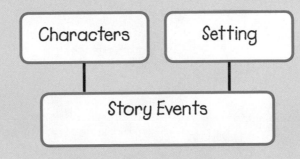

Characters	Setting

Story Events

CONTENTS

Lesson 3

Genre: Expository Nonfiction

Around the World

Schools

Keys to the Universe

by Francisco X. Alarcón

illustrated by Maya Christina Gonzalez

Genre: Poetry

Phonics Skill

Words with *ee, ea; ai, ay; oa, ow*

Some letter pairs can stand for a long vowel sound.

- The letters *ee* and *ea* can stand for the long *e* sound you hear in *seed* and *dream*.
- The letters *ai* and *ay* can stand for the long *a* sound you hear in *rain* and *pay*.
- The letters *oa* and *ow* can stand for the long *o* sound you hear in *coat* and *row*.

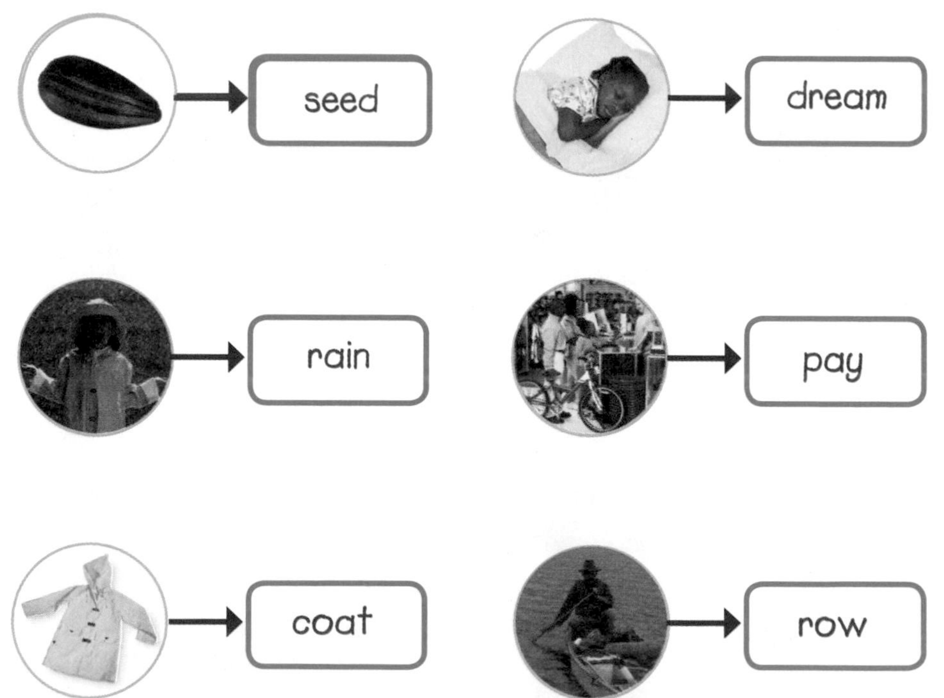

Read each sentence. Think about the vowel sound in the underlined word. Tell in which column of the chart the word goes.

1. Vicky had two long braids.
2. Can you tie a bow on the package?
3. Be careful when you cross the stream.
4. Ben weeded the garden.
5. Our new kitten is very playful.
6. We saw many boats on the water.

Words with Long *e*	Words with Long *a*	Words with Long *o*

Try This!

Look back at "Ruby the Copycat." Find words with these long vowel pairs. Tell where they go in the chart.

www.harcourtschool.com/storytown

Vocabulary

Build Robust Vocabulary

- chores
- certain
- resources
- culture
- tutor
- uniforms

Schoolyard Treats

You may think that a market is the best place to get your food. Some children have other ideas. They grow their own food while at school!

At the Edible Schoolyard in California, the children have outdoor **chores** to do. Every morning they choose a **certain** job, such as weeding or planting. They work in the garden for about an hour and a half. After the class, they talk about their day's work.

Good soil, water, and sunlight are **resources** for a healthy garden.

In Miami, Florida, a few elementary schools are part of the Plant 1000 Gardens Project. The schools' **culture** supports a love of nature. In the gardens, the children plant tomatoes and other vegetables. A volunteer **tutor** from a nearby farm helps them. After they pick the crops, the children cook and eat the tasty foods they grew.

These projects make learning exciting. When the children grow up, some of them may have their own gardens or work as chefs.

Chefs wear hats as part of their **uniforms**.

www.harcourtschool.com/storytown

Word Champion

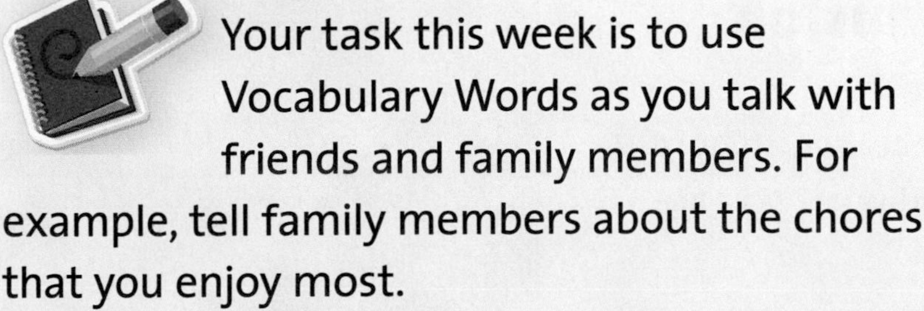

Your task this week is to use Vocabulary Words as you talk with friends and family members. For example, tell family members about the chores that you enjoy most.

3ELA-6-E3-16

Genre Study

Expository nonfiction gives information about a topic. Look for

- text divided into sections.
- headings that tell about each section.

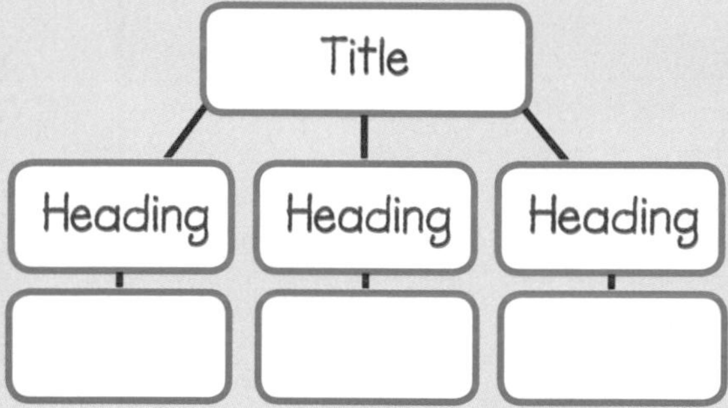

3ELA-1-E6-11
3ELA-7-E1-17

Comprehension Strategy

Use prior knowledge to help you understand what you are reading.

LOUISIANA GRADE-LEVEL EXPECTATIONS—3ELA-1-E6-11 connect to prior knowledge; **3ELA-6-E3-16** define characteristics of types of literature; **3ELA-7-E1-17** demonstrate understanding of information

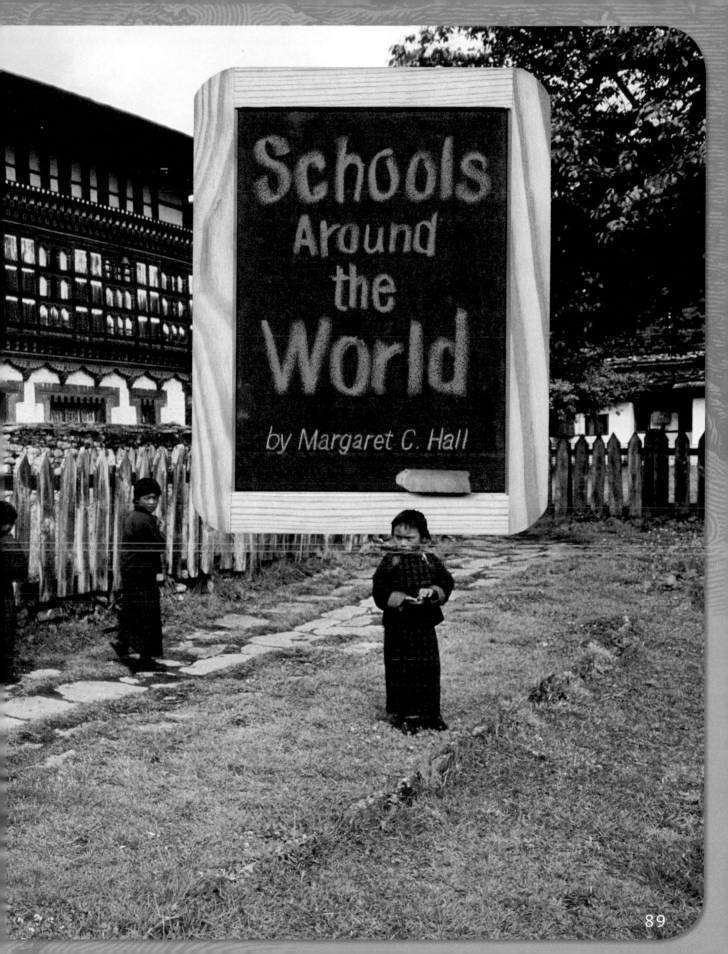

Schools Around the World

by Margaret C. Hall

Schools Around the World

All around the world, children go to school. Some children spend most of their day at school. Others spend only a few hours there.

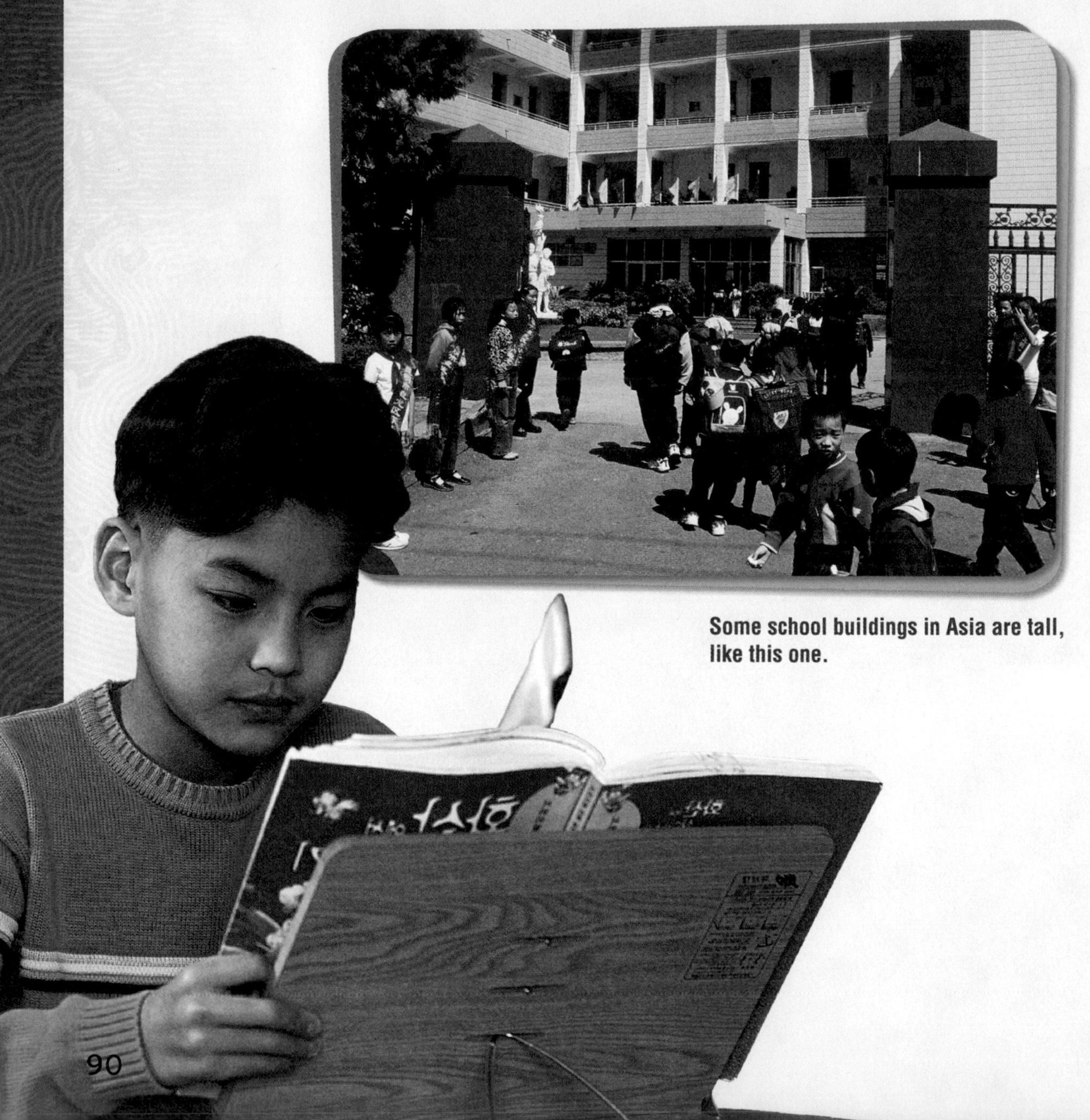

Some school buildings in Asia are tall, like this one.

These students in an American classroom start their day by saying the Pledge of Allegiance.

Schools are different in different parts of the world. But they are all the same in one way. Schools are where children go to learn.

AMAZING SCHOOL FACTS

A long time ago, a German man started a new kind of school. He thought that small children should grow like flowers in a garden. He called his school kindergarten. *The word means "children's garden" in German.*

These students in Tibet, China are about to start their morning classes.

School Buildings

The kind of school buildings children have depends on where they live. It depends on the climate and the resources of their community.

School buildings can be large or small. They can be made from many different materials. Some children even go to school outside or in buildings with no walls.

AMAZING SCHOOL FACTS

Schools have been around for thousands of years. The first schools were started to teach children about their culture.

Getting to School

Children travel to school in many different ways. The kind of transportation they use depends on where they live. It also depends on how far they have to go.

Many children walk or ride bicycles to school. Others ride in cars, on buses, or on a train. Some children go to school by boat.

AMAZING SCHOOL FACTS

In some places, children live too far away from their school to go there. Teachers give lessons over the radio or by using computers that are hooked up to the school.

School Clothing

Children around the world wear different kinds of clothing to school. What they wear often depends on the climate where they live. It also depends on what season it is.

In some schools, the students all dress alike. They wear uniforms. Students from different schools have different uniforms.

▲ **Students at this girls' school in Panama wear blue skirts and sweaters as part of their uniforms.**

These students in Germany are learning science on a class trip with their teachers.

The School Day

All around the world, teachers help students learn new things. Children do some schoolwork in groups. They do other schoolwork on their own.

Most children eat lunch or a snack at school. They may also have time to play. At many schools, children take class trips, too.

This teacher answers a question for his student at a school in Cuba.

Learning to Read and Write

One important job for teachers is to help children learn to read and write. Students learn to read and write in many different languages.

The language children use at school depends on where they live. Some children study their own language and another language, too.

At an American school overseas, students study a map of Europe.

Other Lessons

Children learn many things at school. All around the world, they study math and science. They learn about their own country and other countries, too.

Many children around the world study art and music in school. They may also learn how to use a computer.

These students in Great Britain practice playing music at school.

In this school in Japan, students help serve lunch.

School Chores

Most children have chores to do at school. They help to keep the classroom neat and clean. They may even help to set up the classroom every day.

In some places, children work to keep the schoolyard neat and clean. Some children may serve lunch to one another.

This teacher gives extra help to students after school.

After School

Some children go to school even after the school day is over. They may have a tutor to help them with the subjects that are harder for them.

Some children have other lessons after school. They study things they cannot learn in school. They may learn about dance, music, or their own culture.

These boys in Israel learn about their culture.

Students at this boarding school eat, study, and live together.

Special Schools

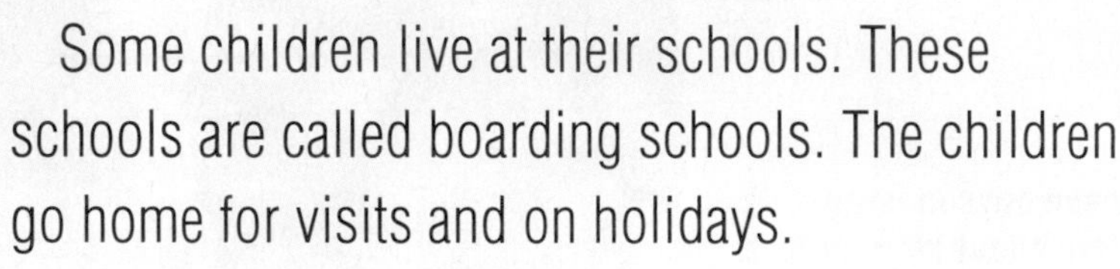

Some children live at their schools. These schools are called boarding schools. The children go home for visits and on holidays.

This girl cannot see. She goes to a school where she can learn to read and write in a special way. People who are blind read with their fingers. They use a system of raised dots called Braille.

Home Schooling

A home can also be a school. Some parents teach their children at home. They want to decide exactly what their children will learn.

People at schools will often help parents plan home lessons for their children. Many children who study at home go to a school for gym or art classes.

This mother is teaching her daughter at home.

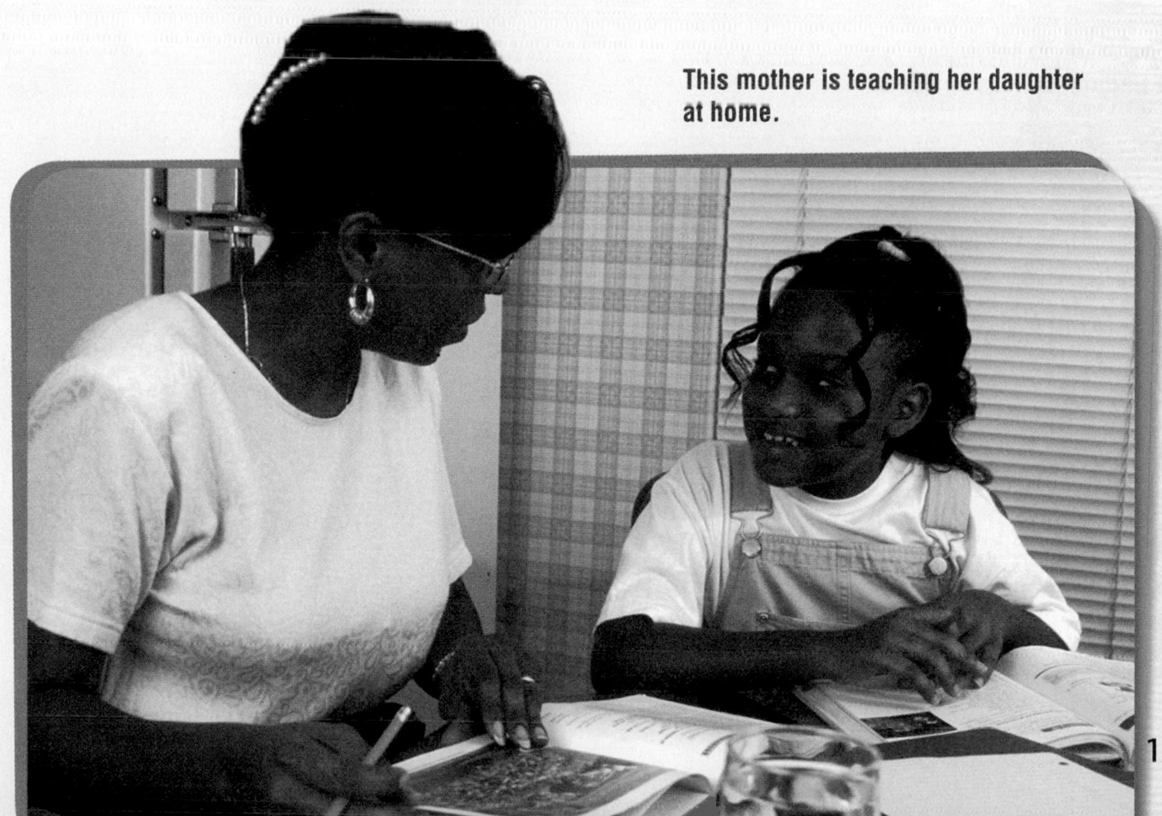

School and Work

Some children work as performers. They spend part of their day practicing the work that they do. They spend the rest of the day studying regular school subjects.

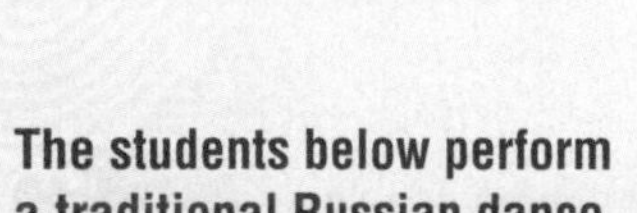

The students below perform a traditional Russian dance.

AMAZING SCHOOL FACTS

One of the subjects that was taught in ancient Greece was gymnastics. The ancient Greeks thought gymnastics was just as important to learn as math or reading!

This boy is learning gymnastics.

Older Students

These women in India go to school at night.

Many people go to school even after they are adults. They may go to college. Or, they may go to a trade school to learn how to do a certain job.

Adults also take classes for fun. They study different languages and learn how to do things. No matter how old students are, they go to school to learn.

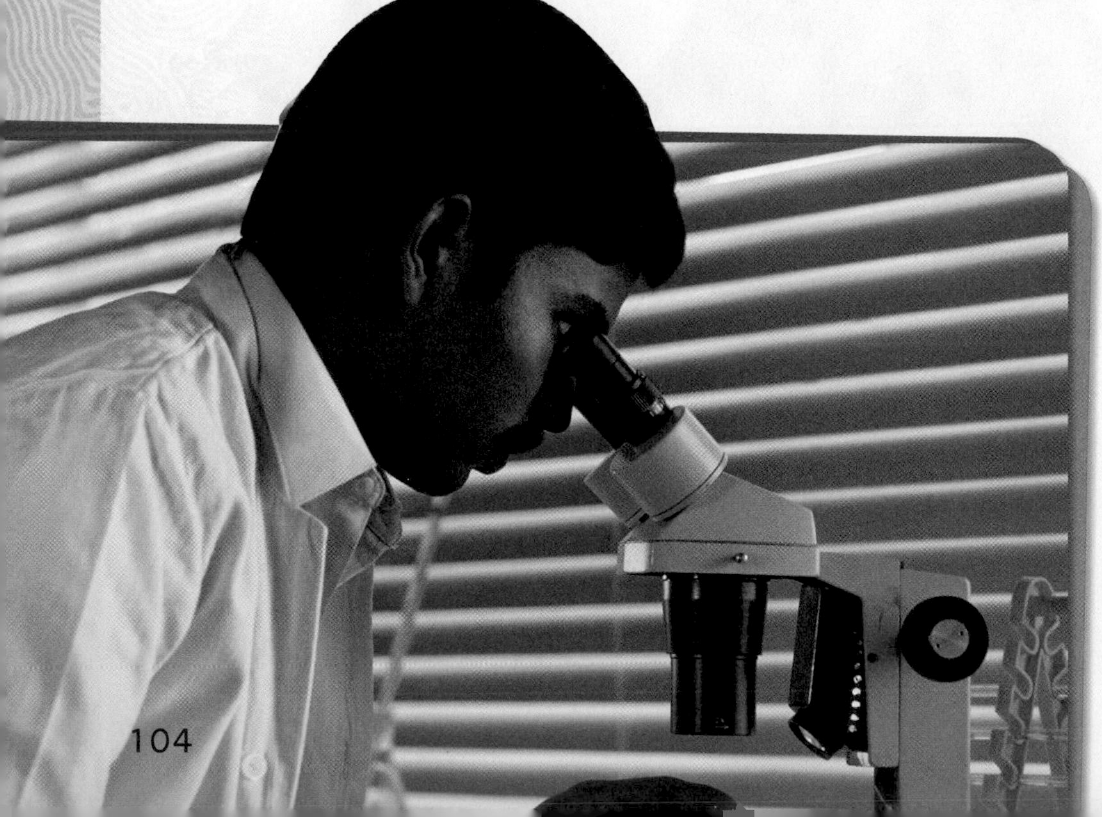

1. Look back at the heading on page 92. How does the heading help you predict what you might read about?

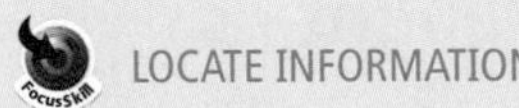
LOCATE INFORMATION

2. What are some things that children learn about at school?
IMPORTANT DETAILS

3. Which school that you read about would you most like to visit? Explain. EXPRESS PERSONAL OPINIONS

4. Does the author give information about schools or try to convince you that one school is best? Explain. AUTHOR'S PURPOSE

5. **WRITE** How is your school similar to other schools you read about? How is it different? Use information and details from the article to support your answer.
EXTENDED RESPONSE

LOUISIANA GRADE-LEVEL EXPECTATIONS—**3ELA-1-E5-10** summarize main events/ideas/details; **3ELA-7-E3-19** identify author's purpose; **3ELA-7-E4-21** apply basic reasoning skills; **3ELA-2-E1-22** write organized paragraphs; **3ELA-2-E1-22(c)** use supporting details; **3ELA-5-E1-45(b)** use printed resources

Keys to the Universe

by Francisco X. Alarcón
illustrated by Maya Christina Gonzalez

My Grandpa
Pancho
taught us

my brothers
my sisters
and me

our first
letters
in Spanish

his living
room was
our classroom
"and these are
the true keys
to the universe"

he'd tell us
pointing to
the letters

of the alphabet
on the makeshift
blackboard

Bb
Z
O
E
e
ñ

Connections

Comparing Texts

3ELA-7-E1-17(d)
3ELA-7-E4-21(e)

1. In what ways is the living room in "Keys to the Universe" like the schools described in "Schools Around the World"?

2. What did you learn about schools that surprised you?

3. What did you learn about the world from reading about different schools?

Vocabulary Review

Word Webs

Work with a partner. Choose two Vocabulary Words and create a word web for each word. Put the Vocabulary Word in the center of the web. Then write words that are related to the Vocabulary Word in your web. Discuss the word webs with your partner.

food — culture — songs

- chores
- certain
- resources
- culture
- tutor
- uniforms

Fluency Practice 3ELA-1-E3-07

Repeated Reading

Choose a section of "Schools Around the World." Read the passage aloud, using a stopwatch to time yourself. Set a goal to improve your time. Repeat the reading until you meet the goal. Do not increase your speed until you read with few or no errors.

Writing 3ELA-2-E4-25

Write a Description

Write a description of your school for a student in another country. Tell about your school. Use "Schools Around the World" to help you. Include a main idea and details that describe the sights, sounds, and smells around the school.

My Writing Checklist

Writing Trait — Organization

- ✔ I use a graphic organizer to plan my writing.
- ✔ I use transitions to connect my ideas.
- ✔ I include a main idea and sensory details.

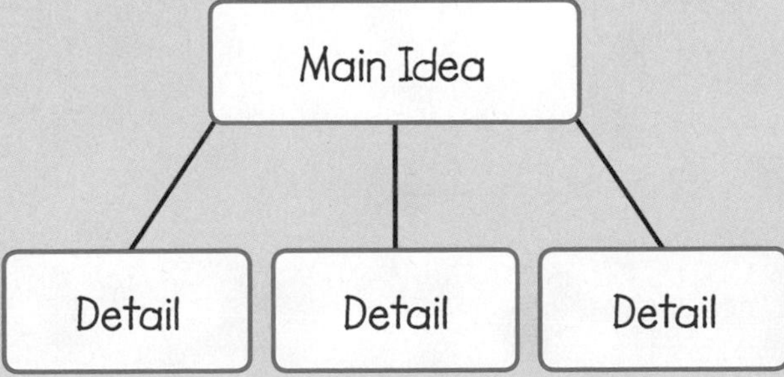

LOUISIANA GRADE-LEVEL EXPECTATIONS—3ELA-1-E3-07 adjust reading speed; 3ELA-7-E1-17(d) compare/contrast; 3ELA-7-E4-21(e) connect to real-life situations; 3ELA-2-E4-25 write paragraphs with description/narration

CONTENTS

Lesson 4

Genre: Biography

Ellen Ochoa, Astronaut

by Janet Michaels

What's in the News?

PARK SCHOOL NEWSLETTER

Fall

Number 3

Upcoming Events

September 21–23
Book Fair

October 1
Fall Concert

October 6
Family Breakfast

October 15
Astronaut Amy Jackson Visits

October 25
Art Contest

October 27
Fall Harvest Display

Third-Graders Visit Johnson Space Center

by Jenny Matthews

The third-grade classes enjoyed a trip to the Johnson Space Center in Houston last week. They had a busy day. First, they learned about the history of the space program in Texas. Then the students got to see where the astronauts train for their trips into space. After watching a special movie about space, the students returned

Genre: Newsletter

Focus Skill

Locate Information

You can use parts of a book to **locate information**. Study the chart below.

- Where would you look to find the meaning of an important word?
- Where would you look to find the list of chapters?

Knowing how to locate information can help you find what you need quickly and easily.

Part of Book	Description
table of contents	• list of the titles with the page numbers • near the front of the book
heading	• title of a section in a nonfiction book
glossary	• dictionary of terms used in the book • in the back of the book
index	• alphabetical list of topics and page numbers • in the back of the book

Use alphabetical order to scan a glossary page. This will help you quickly find the word you need.

This table of contents is from a book about astronauts. Read the table of contents, and answer the questions below.

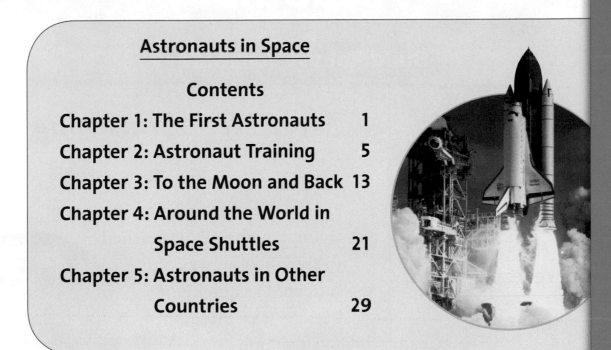

Astronauts in Space

Contents

1. What chapter would you read to learn about exploring the moon?
2. What chapter describes how astronauts train?

Try This!

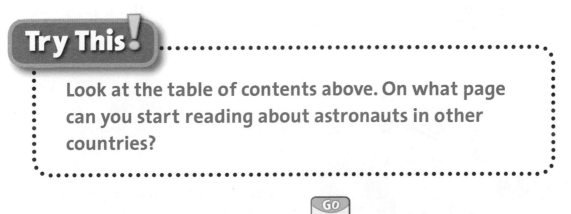

Look at the table of contents above. On what page can you start reading about astronauts in other countries?

www.harcourtschool.com/storytown

Vocabulary

Build Robust Vocabulary

- talented
- apply
- research
- invention
- hinder
- disappointed

Meet Neil Armstrong

As a boy, Neil Armstrong built model airplanes and read magazines about flying machines. He learned to fly when he was only sixteen. He quickly became a **talented** pilot.

After high school, Neil Armstrong decided to **apply** to college. After college, he gained more experience as a **research** pilot. When scientists created an **invention**, he would test it. He tested new gliders, jets, and rockets.

On July 20, 1969, Neil Armstrong took a step that would make him famous forever. He became the first person to set foot on the surface of the moon. He did not let the danger of spaceflight **hinder** his plans.

Neil Armstrong flew to the moon with two other astronauts. They were not **disappointed** that Neil Armstrong took the first step. They were proud to work as a team.

The *Apollo 11* astronauts were Neil Armstrong, Michael Collins, and Buzz Aldrin.

www.harcourtschool.com/storytown

Word Detective

Your mission this week is to look for the Vocabulary Words on websites or in encyclopedia articles about outer space. Each time you read a Vocabulary Word, write it in your vocabulary journal. Don't forget to tell where you found the word.

LOUISIANA GRADE-LEVEL EXPECTATIONS—3ELA-2-E6-27 write for various purposes; 3ELA-5-E1-45(a) use electronic information

3ELA-6-E3-16

Genre Study

A **biography** is the true story of a person's life that is written by another person. Look for

- facts about what the person has done.
- dates and place-names.

Childhood	
School Years	
Adulthood	

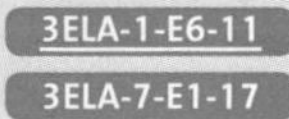

Comprehension Strategy

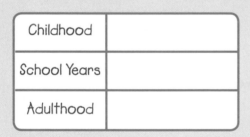

Use Prior Knowledge of a subject to help you understand and remember what you read.

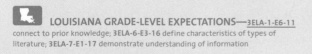

LOUISIANA GRADE-LEVEL EXPECTATIONS—3ELA-1-E6-11 connect to prior knowledge; **3ELA-6-E3-16** define characteristics of types of literature; **3ELA-7-E1-17** demonstrate understanding of information

Ellen Ochoa, Astronaut

by Janet Michaels

When Ellen Ochoa was growing up, her mother told her to "reach for the stars." Ellen had no idea that one day she would explore space. After many years of hard work, she became the first Hispanic woman to travel into space. She is a leader for people of all ages. This is her story.

THE EARLY YEARS

Ellen Ochoa was born in Los Angeles, California, on May 10, 1958. Her mother worked hard to raise Ellen and her sister and brothers. She taught her children how important it was to do well in school. She told them that if they worked hard, they could grow up to be anything they wanted to be.

In 1969, when she was just 11 years old, people first landed on the moon. It was a very exciting time. Many children wanted to be astronauts when they grew up, too. At that time, there were no women astronauts, so Ellen never dreamed of going into space.

The first people on the moon landed there on July 21, 1969.

In school, Ellen was a top student and did well in all her classes. She loved music and learned to play the flute. Ellen spent hours practicing and became a very talented player. In high school, she played with a band for young people.

Ellen would later enjoy music in space, too.

Ellen also loved math. Some people told her that girls were not good math students. She didn't let those people hinder her learning. Ellen always did her best. When she graduated, she had the highest grades in her class.

Ellen decided that she wanted to be an engineer. There were people who did not think that a woman could do such a difficult job. Ellen had to study very hard, but she did well. She felt very proud when she graduated and got a job as an engineer.

INVENTOR AND MUSICIAN

As an engineer, Ellen Ochoa made robots that used special tools to "see" things around them. She and her team found a way for these robots to make computer parts. She wrote and spoke to many people about her invention.

Ellen Ochoa worked as an engineer at the Ames Research Center in California.

Music remained an important part of her life. Playing the flute made her feel happy. She played so well that she won an award.

Ellen Ochoa enjoyed her job and her music, but she wondered what else she could do. Her friends said she should try to become an astronaut. So in 1985, she decided to apply for a job in the space program. She was disappointed when she was not accepted. Then she remembered what her mother had told her. If she worked hard, she could be anything she wanted to be.

Ellen Ochoa enjoyed playing the flute, just as this girl does.

Ellen Ochoa waited for another chance to become an astronaut. While she waited, she joined a space research center. There she helped astronauts learn more about space. She learned to fly a plane and found that she loved to fly.

Ellen Ochoa was now a musician, an inventor, and a pilot. She knew how to work on a team. She knew how to keep trying when things were difficult.

Ellen Ochoa practiced flying and became a pilot.

In 1990, Ellen Ochoa's dream came true. She was chosen for the astronaut program. More than 2,000 people had applied to become astronauts, and she was one of just 22 who were chosen.

Ellen Ochoa and Eileen Collins posed together on their first day of training at NASA.

ASTRONAUT TRAINING

Ellen Ochoa and her husband moved to Texas so that she could begin her astronaut training. Astronauts must learn to do things differently in space. Ellen Ochoa had to learn to use computers and special tools in space. Working inside a heavy space suit is not easy. It takes a lot of practice.

Astronauts wear special suits during much of their training.

Ellen Ochoa made a lot of friends in the astronaut program.

Ellen Ochoa learned to work with a team of other astronauts to get jobs done. Astronauts become good friends because they spend so much time together.

It is important that astronauts exercise to stay in shape. In her training, Ellen Ochoa learned how to use special exercise machines in space. She also had to learn new ways to eat. In space, foods placed on a plate would float away, so astronauts' meals must come in special packages.

Astronaut training was hard, but Ellen Ochoa didn't give up. She knew she would have to keep working to be ready to go into space.

A TRIP INTO SPACE

Finally, in April 1993, Ellen Ochoa became the first Hispanic woman to go into space. She flew on the space shuttle *Discovery*. The *Discovery* astronauts had a special job to do. Their job was to learn about the sun. Ellen Ochoa was able to use what she had learned about robots while she was in space. Her job was to control a robot arm on *Discovery*. She used the arm to catch a satellite that had been studying the sun. The information from the satellite helped the astronauts learn more about the sun's energy.

The crew of the space shuttle *Discovery*.

The space shuttle *Discovery* lifts off from Cape Canaveral, Florida.

Ellen Ochoa was amazed at how beautiful Earth looks from space. She also enjoyed floating from place to place inside the shuttle. The astronauts had to strap themselves down to work and exercise. They slept strapped into sleeping bags on the walls. Ellen Ochoa even strapped herself down when she wanted to play her flute.

Ellen Ochoa made beautiful music in space!

Ellen Ochoa made three more trips into space. On one of those trips, she visited the space station. Her job was to deliver supplies so that other astronauts could live and work there.

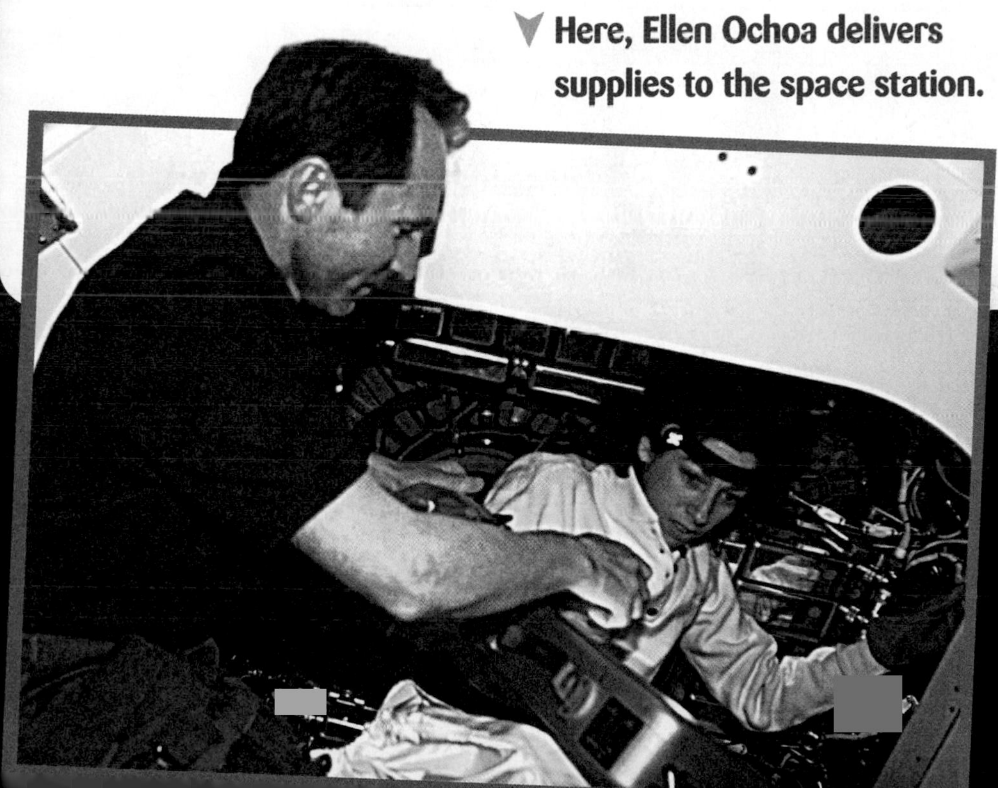

Here, Ellen Ochoa delivers supplies to the space station.

Ellen Ochoa tells her story to children all over the country. They are very interested in what it is like to be an astronaut. The most important thing Ellen Ochoa tells children is what her mother told her. If you work hard, you can make your dreams come true.

This photo was taken aboard space shuttle *Atlantis* in 1994.

Think Critically

1. Which section of this biography would you read if you wanted to find out about Ellen Ochoa's childhood?
 LOCATE INFORMATION

2. What did Ellen Ochoa invent? IMPORTANT DETAILS

3. Do you think Ellen Ochoa is a hero? Explain. EXPRESS PERSONAL OPINIONS

4. How can you tell that the author wants readers to know that music is important to Ellen Ochoa? DRAW CONCLUSIONS

5. **WRITE** Think about the skills you are learning in school. Choose two of these skills, and explain how they might be important for your future. SHORT RESPONSE

LOUISIANA GRADE-LEVEL EXPECTATIONS—3ELA-1-E5-10 summarize main events/ideas/details; **3ELA-7-E1-17(c)** make inferences/draw conclusions; **3ELA-7-E3-20** explain author's viewpoint; **3ELA-7-E4-21** apply basic reasoning skills; **3ELA-2-E6-27** write for various purposes; **3ELA-5-E1-45(b)** use printed resources

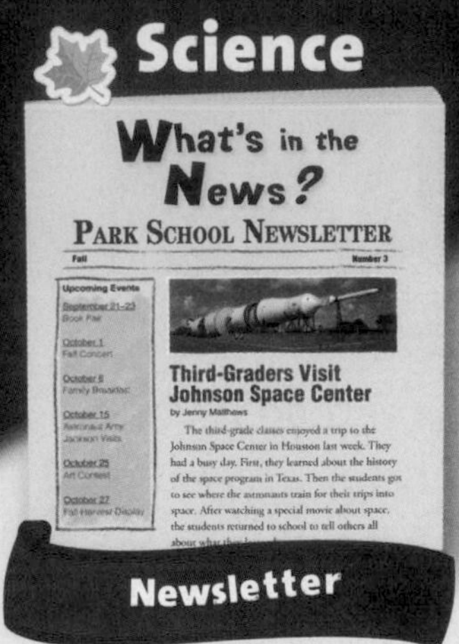

What's in the News?

Park School Newsletter

Fall **Number 3**

Upcoming Events

September 21–23
Book Fair

October 1
Fall Concert

October 6
Family Breakfast

October 15
Astronaut Amy Jackson Visits

October 25
Art Contest

October 27
Fall Harvest Display

Third-Graders Visit Johnson Space Center

by Jenny Matthews

The third-grade classes enjoyed a trip to the Johnson Space Center in Houston last week. They had a busy day. First, they learned about the history of the space program in Texas. Then the students got to see where the astronauts train for their trips into space. After watching a special movie about space, the students returned to school to tell others all about what they learned.

Butterflies Emerge in Room 3B

by Juan Ortiz

On Tuesday, four butterflies spread their wings for the first time. The students in room 3B had raised them. The butterflies were once tiny caterpillars. The students made sure the caterpillars had plenty of milkweed, air, and space to grow. Then each caterpillar made a chrysalis around itself. After almost two weeks, a butterfly came out of each chrysalis. The students saw this and set the butterflies free.

Next Week's Lunch Menu				
Monday: Chicken Sandwich	**Tuesday:** Taco Salad	**Wednesday:** Veggie Pizza	**Thursday:** Spaghetti	**Friday:** Chicken and Rice

Connections

Comparing Texts

3ELA-7-E3-19
3ELA-7-E4-21
3ELA-7-E4-21(e)

1. Think about the author's purpose in writing "Ellen Ochoa, Astronaut" and the author's purpose in writing "What's in the News?" How are they alike?

2. Think about the phrase "reach for the stars." What does that phrase mean to you?

3. What did you learn about being an astronaut that you did not know before?

Vocabulary Review

3ELA-1-E1-06(b)

talented
apply
research
invention
hinder
disappointed

Rate a Situation

Work with a partner. Take turns reading aloud each sentence and pointing to the spot on the word line that shows how disappointed or excited you would feel.

disappointed ———————————— excited

- A teacher said that you were a **talented** artist.
- You get to do **research** about space.
- You **apply** for a library card.

Fluency Practice 3ELA-1-E3-07

Partner Reading

Choose a paragraph from "Ellen Ochoa, Astronaut." Meet with a partner to read your paragraphs aloud. Read nonfiction more slowly than you might read fiction. Give each other tips on how to read more smoothly the next time.

Writing 3ELA-2-E2-23 3ELA-2-E6-27

Write an Invitation

Write an invitation to other classes to hear about Ellen Ochoa. Tell who is invited, what the invitation is for, and when and where the event will take place.

My Writing Checklist

Writing Trait → Organization

- ✔ I use the chart to help plan my invitation.
- ✔ I give details about the event that the invitation is for.

Who	
What	
When	
Where	

CONTENTS

READERS' THEATER

News Script

COMPREHENSION STRATEGIES

Review

Nonfiction

Lesson 5

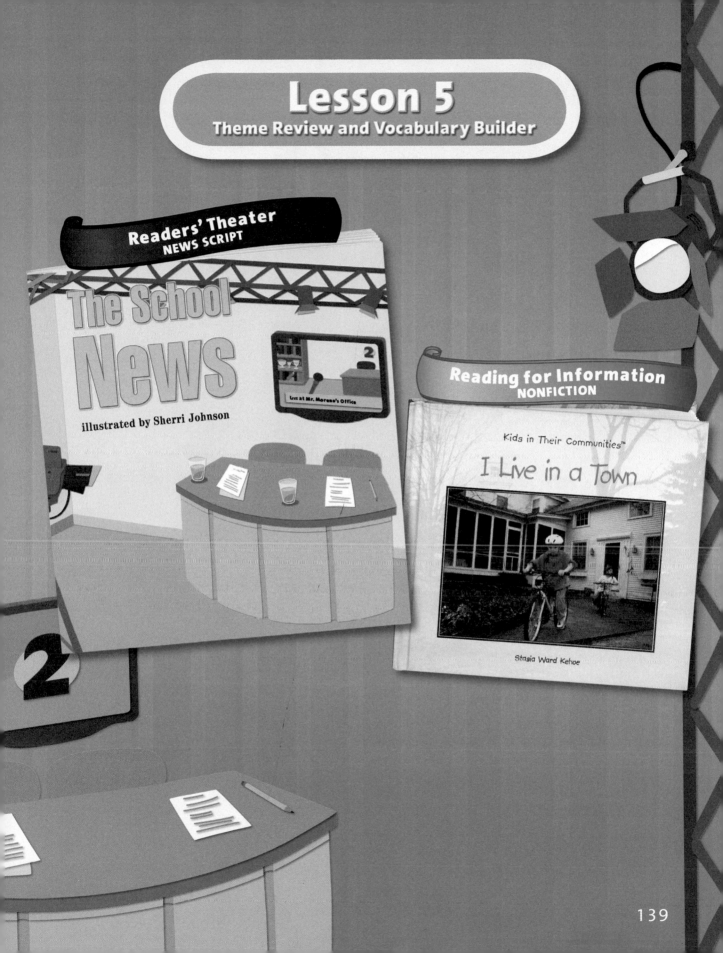

Theme Review and Vocabulary Builder

Readers' Theater
NEWS SCRIPT

The School News

illustrated by Sherri Johnson

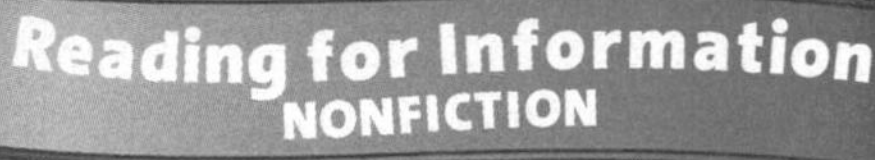

Kids in Their Communities™

I Live in a Town

Stasia Ward Kehoe

READERS' THEATER

viewers

survive

camouflage

concealed

independent

donated

3ELA-1-E3-07

Reading for Fluency

When you read a script aloud,

- say all the words correctly.
- slow down as needed to read accurately.

LOUISIANA GRADE-LEVEL EXPECTATIONS—
3ELA-1-E3-07 adjust reading speed

The School News

illustrated by Sherri Johnson

Roles

Anchor 1
Anchor 2
Roving Reporter
Mr. Moreno
Weather Reporter
Science Reporter
Sports Reporter

Setting: The television studio of a school's morning news network

Anchor 1: Good morning, students! Thank you for watching Kids' News Network. Here's what's happening at our school.

Anchor 2: Mr. Moreno, our principal, has an announcement about the lunch menu.

Anchor 1: We now join our roving reporter, who is talking with him live.

Roving Reporter: I'm here in Mr. Moreno's office. There will be two new choices on the lunch menu. What are these two choices, Mr. Moreno?

Mr. Moreno: Well, starting today, salad and pizza are being added to the menu.

Roving Reporter: So, look for these choices today, viewers. Now back to the studio.

Anchor 1: Thank you. Now it's time for the weather.

Weather Reporter: Today's weather is not pleasant! It's raining cats and dogs!

Anchor 1: When you say it's "raining cats and dogs," you don't mean that pets are falling from the sky, do you?

Weather Reporter: No, just that it's raining very hard! Do you know what you have to do when it rains cats and dogs?

Anchor 2: No. What?

Weather Reporter: You have to be careful not to step in a poodle.

Anchor 1: Ha, ha! Poodle. Puddle. I get it!

Anchor 2: Very funny. Thank you for the weather report and the joke!

Fluency Tip

Think about how Anchor 1 should read these lines to show that the joke is funny.

Anchor 1: Next, we have a science report about our school's favorite pet and mascot, Freddy the Frog. Here's our science reporter.

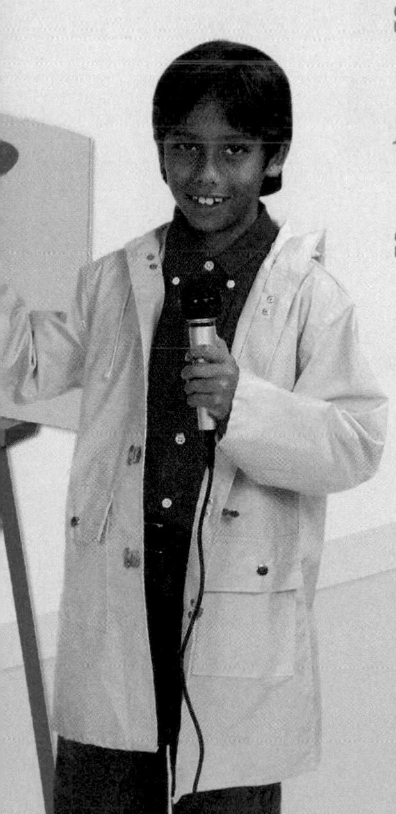

Science Reporter: Thank you. Most of us have seen Freddy in his tank with all his resources around him.

Anchor 2: Freddy's resources are the things he needs to survive.

Science Reporter: That's right. Well, one of my chores is to feed Freddy. A few days ago, I went to give him fresh food, and I couldn't find him!

Anchor 2: Where had Freddy gone?

Science Reporter: Nowhere! He was in his tank the whole time. I just couldn't see him. His skin made him look just like the plants in his tank.

Anchor 2: Very interesting!

Science Reporter: Yes, it is. Suddenly, I had all kinds of questions about frogs. I did research and found the answers to my questions.

Anchor 1: Why did it seem as if Freddy had disappeared?

Science Reporter: His camouflage hid him. Camouflage helps animals blend in with the area around them. This protects them from animals that might want to eat them. Freddy's colors helped him blend in with the plants, so the plants concealed him.

Anchor 2: Fascinating! What else did you learn about Freddy?

Fluency Tip

Anchor 2 is curious. How would you sound curious here?

Science Reporter: Freddy has moist skin because his skin takes in water. He doesn't have to drink water through his mouth. Freddy also has a long, sticky tongue for catching bugs.

Anchor 2: What about his feet? Frogs have funny feet!

Science Reporter: They have webbed back feet that help them swim fast.

Anchor 2: Great reporting, Science Reporter.

Anchor 1: We aren't the only ones who thought that report was great. Back to our roving reporter.

Roving Reporter: Mr. Moreno has a new announcement for us.

Mr. Moreno: The science reporter has shown independent thinking. This student had questions about frogs and did research to find the answers. I am giving our science reporter the Great Thinker award. Well done!

Roving Reporter: So you believe that students who think for themselves can be successful at anything?

Mr. Moreno: That's right!

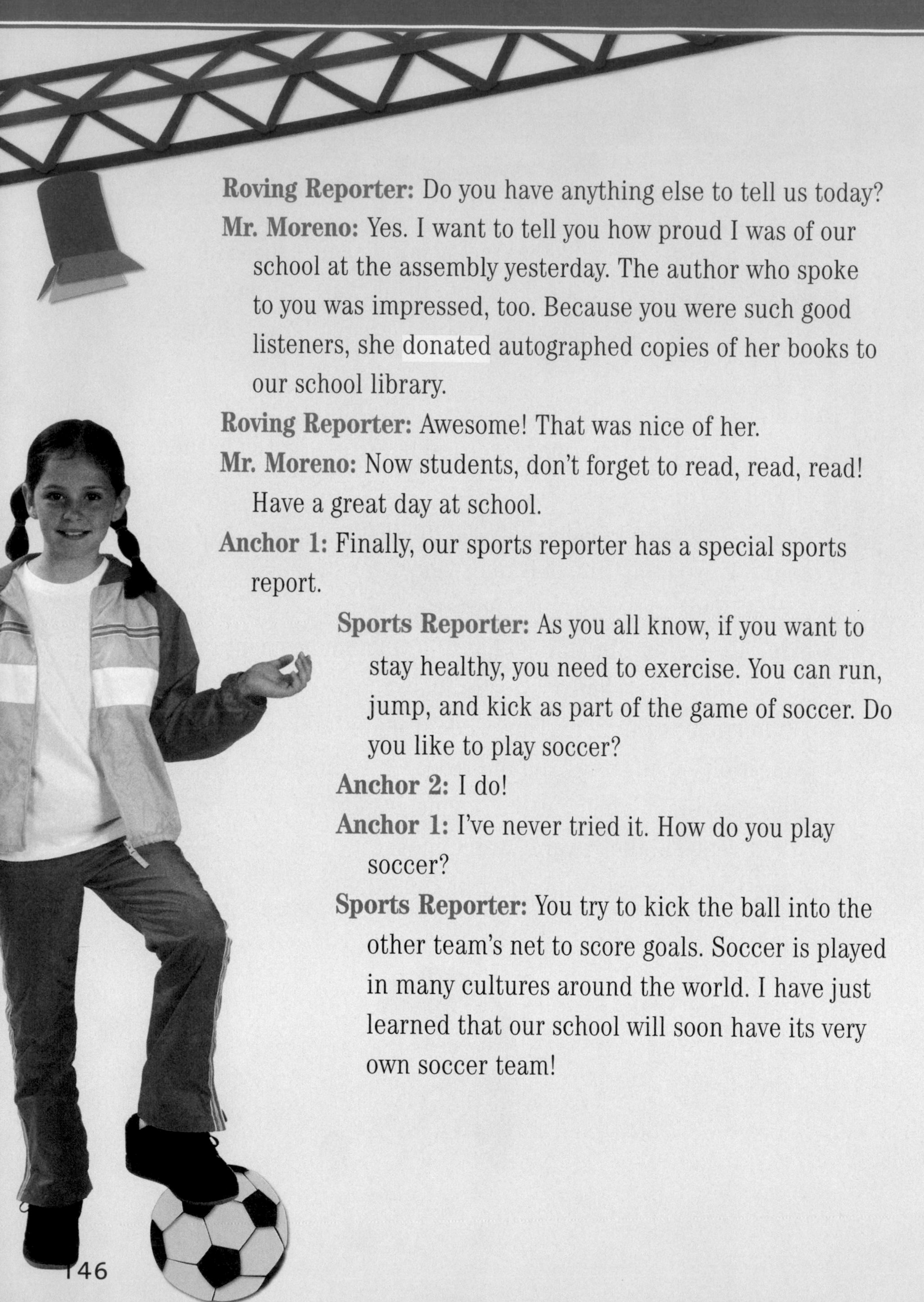

Roving Reporter: Do you have anything else to tell us today?

Mr. Moreno: Yes. I want to tell you how proud I was of our school at the assembly yesterday. The author who spoke to you was impressed, too. Because you were such good listeners, she donated autographed copies of her books to our school library.

Roving Reporter: Awesome! That was nice of her.

Mr. Moreno: Now students, don't forget to read, read, read! Have a great day at school.

Anchor 1: Finally, our sports reporter has a special sports report.

Sports Reporter: As you all know, if you want to stay healthy, you need to exercise. You can run, jump, and kick as part of the game of soccer. Do you like to play soccer?

Anchor 2: I do!

Anchor 1: I've never tried it. How do you play soccer?

Sports Reporter: You try to kick the ball into the other team's net to score goals. Soccer is played in many cultures around the world. I have just learned that our school will soon have its very own soccer team!

Anchor 2: Great! Tell us more.

Sports Reporter: At the end of the day, wait for your teacher to dismiss you. Then go and see Coach Keller in the office. She will tell you about the new team and show you the team's uniforms. Then you can sign up.

Anchor 1: You heard it here first! Thanks for the report, Sports Reporter.

Anchor 2: Well, viewers, that's all the news for today. Good-bye!

Anchor 1: Thank you for watching, and have a great day!

Fluency Tip

How do you think Anchor 2 feels right now?

Reading Nonfiction 3ELA-6-E3-16

Bridge to Reading for Information Nonfiction gives facts or other true information. It is organized using features such as headings, photographs, and captions.

Read the notes above and below the small pages on page 149. How can these features help you read nonfiction?

Review the Focus Strategies

You can also use the strategies you learned in this theme to help you read nonfiction.

Use Graphic Organizers 3ELA-1-E6-11 3ELA-7-E1-17

Use a graphic organizer to help you organize what you already know and what you learn.

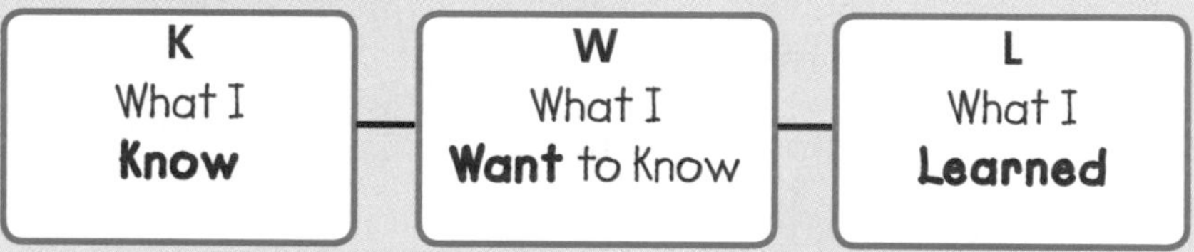

Use Prior Knowledge 3ELA-1-E6-11

Use what you already know to help you understand what you read.

As you read "I Live in a Town" on pages 150–151, think about where and how to use the comprehension strategies.

LOUISIANA GRADE-LEVEL EXPECTATIONS—3ELA-1-E6-11 connect to prior knowledge; 3ELA-6-E3-16 define characteristics of types of literature; 3ELA-7-E1-17 demonstrate understanding of information

TITLE
A nonfiction title will usually tell what the topic of the information is.

I Live in a Town

by Stasia Ward Kehoe

I am eight years old. My family and I live in a town. A town is smaller than a city, but it is still run by its own government.

At my school, there are about 70 students in each grade. The school has kindergarten through third grade.

School

I am in the third grade at school. One of the neat things about going to school in my town is our special ski program. On Wednesdays, students get out of school early to take ski lessons. When I am older and go to high school, I want to be on the ski team.

Town Meeting

Once a year, my parents go to a town meeting. The town meeting is a chance for people to talk about the way they think the town should be run. At the meeting, people talk about how to raise money for schools and road repairs. They vote on laws. Anybody who owns land in our town has the right to go to the town meeting and vote on town issues.

The new library has great books that I can read for school reports or just for fun.

Special Place

One of my favorite places in town is our new library. Many people in my town donated money, time, and ideas to help make the finished library a wonderful place. The library has great books and computers. It also has a fireplace and a community room. I like to sit on one of the couches and read a good book!

SUBHEADINGS
Nonfiction is often divided into sections. Subheadings tell what each section is about.

PHOTOS AND CAPTIONS
Photographs and drawings show images that go with the text. Captions give you more information about the photos and drawings.

Apply the Strategies Read these pages from a nonfiction article. As you read, stop and think about how you are using comprehension strategies.

I Live in a Town

by Stasia Ward Kehoe

I am eight years old. My family and I live in a town. A town is smaller than a city, but it is still run by its own government.

At my school, there are about 70 students in each grade. The school has kindergarten through third grade.

School

I am in the third grade at school. One of the neat things about going to school in my town is our special ski program. On Wednesdays, students get out of school early to take ski lessons. When I am older and go to high school, I want to be on the ski team.

Stop and Think

How does using a graphic organizer help you read? What prior knowledge are you using to understand what you read?

Town Meeting

Once a year, my parents go to a town meeting. The town meeting is a chance for people to talk about the way they think the town should be run. At the meeting, people talk about how to raise money for schools and road repairs. They vote on laws. Anybody who owns land in our town has the right to go to the town meeting and vote on town issues.

Special Place

One of my favorite places in town is our new library. Many people in my town donated money, time, and ideas to help make the finished library a wonderful place. The library has great books and computers. It also has a fireplace and a community room. I like to sit on one of the couches and read a good book!

The new library has great books that I can read for school reports or just for fun.

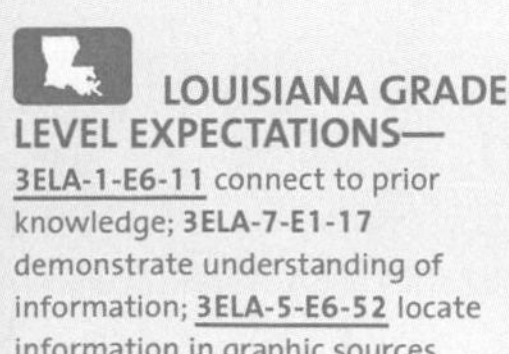

LOUISIANA GRADE-LEVEL EXPECTATIONS— 3ELA-1-E6-11 connect to prior knowledge; 3ELA-7-E1-17 demonstrate understanding of information; 3ELA-5-E6-52 locate information in graphic sources

	Lesson 6	Lesson 7
SELECTION TITLES	**The Babe and I** America's National Pastime	**Aero and Officer Mike** It's About Dogs
Comprehension Strategy	Monitor Comprehension: Reread	Monitor Comprehension: Reread
Focus Skill	Fact and Opinion	Fact and Opinion

Theme 2 Together We Can

Empanadas, Carmen Lomas Garza

Lesson 8	Lesson 9	Lesson 10 Review
How Animals Talk Partners in the Wild	**Stone Soup** The Legend of Johnny Appleseed	**The Case of the Three Bears' Breakfast** How Living Things Survive
Summarize	Summarize	Review Skills and Strategies
Main Idea and Details	Main Idea and Details	

CONTENTS

Lesson 6

Genre: Historical Fiction
The Babe & I
WRITTEN BY
David A. Adler
ILLUSTRATED
Terry Wid
America's
National
Pastime
Genre: Time Line

Focus Skill

Fact and Opinion

A **fact** is something that can be proved. An **opinion** is a person's thoughts or feelings about something. An opinion often has signal words such as *I think* or *I believe.*

To decide if a statement is a fact or an opinion, ask:

- Can this be proved?
- Is this what someone feels but cannot prove?

Identifying facts and opinions can help you understand what is true about the topic.

Fact	Opinion

Tip

Authors of nonfiction often state an opinion and include facts to support the opinion. Authors of fiction often have their characters state opinions in dialogue.

Read the article below. Explain why the sentence shown in the chart is a fact. Then find a sentence in the article that is an opinion.

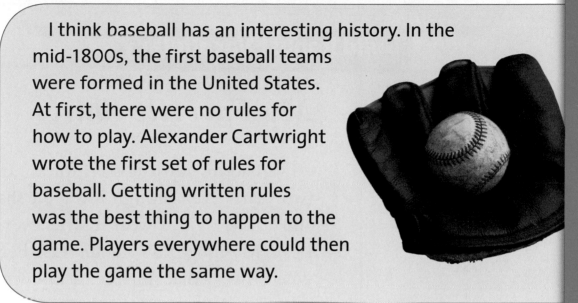

I think baseball has an interesting history. In the mid-1800s, the first baseball teams were formed in the United States. At first, there were no rules for how to play. Alexander Cartwright wrote the first set of rules for baseball. Getting written rules was the best thing to happen to the game. Players everywhere could then play the game the same way.

Fact	Opinion
In the mid-1800s, the first baseball teams were formed.	

Try This!

Look back at the article. Find one other fact and one other opinion that could be added to the chart.

www.harcourtschool.com/storytown

LOUISIANA GRADE-LEVEL EXPECTATIONS—3ELA-7-E4-21(a) identify fact/opinion

Vocabulary

Build Robust Vocabulary

shabby

embarrass

midst

elevated

dazed

collapses

My Favorite Shirt

I've had my favorite shirt for almost two years. Even though it is a bit **shabby** and a little tight, I wear it whenever I can. My mom says I **embarrass** her when I wear that shirt, but I know she is just teasing me.

One day, my mom and I were in the **midst** of shopping for school clothes. On a rack, on an **elevated** platform in a clothing store, I saw my favorite shirt!

Of course, it wasn't really my shirt. The one on the rack was brand-new. I guess I had a **dazed** look on my face, because I didn't notice my mom walking over to me. "Let go," she said, "before the rack **collapses**!"

I had been so excited when I saw the shirt that I had pulled on the clothes rack. Luckily, my mom and I were able to set it back up again. I couldn't stop smiling as we went to the counter to buy my *new* favorite shirt in a bigger size.

www.harcourtschool.com/storytown

Word Champion

Your mission this week is to use the Vocabulary Words in conversation with friends and family. For example, tell a story about something embarrassing that happened to you. Write in your vocabulary journal the sentences you used that had Vocabulary Words.

LOUISIANA GRADE-LEVEL EXPECTATIONS—3ELA-2-E6-27 write for various purposes

Genre Study

3ELA-6-E3-16

Historical fiction is a made-up story that is set in the past and has people, places, and events that are real or could be real. Look for

- a real time and place in the past.
- facts as well as opinions about people in history.

Facts	Opinions

Comprehension Strategy

3ELA-7-E1-17

Monitor comprehension—Reread an earlier part of the selection if something you are reading doesn't make sense.

LOUISIANA GRADE-LEVEL EXPECTATIONS—3ELA-6-E3-16 define characteristics of types of literature; 3ELA-7-E1-17 demonstrate understanding of information

The Babe and I

BY DAVID A. ADLER

ILLUSTRATED BY TERRY WIDENER

For my birthday I was hoping my parents would give me a bicycle. They only gave me a dime. I was disappointed, but not surprised. It was 1932, in the midst of the Great Depression, and millions of people were out of work. We were lucky. My father had a job. But we never seemed to have much money. Where we lived, in the Bronx, New York, everyone was poor.

"Happy birthday," Dad said when I walked him outside. I watched him go off, carrying his briefcase and smiling.

My neighbor Jacob was tossing a ball and catching it. He threw it to me and shouted, "Give me a high one. I'm Babe Ruth, the world's greatest baseball player."

I threw the ball and Jacob reached up. It bounced out of his hands. He was no Babe Ruth!

We played for a while, and then Jacob said, "I have to go to work. Come with me. We can have a catch while we walk."

A few blocks from home we passed a woman selling apples. Her clothes were wrinkled and shabby. I gave her my birthday dime and bought two apples, one for me and one for Jacob. I was glad to be rid of the dime. It reminded me of the present I didn't get.

We turned onto Webster Avenue, and there were more apple sellers. Near the next corner I saw a large briefcase. I looked up and there was Dad, selling apples like the others. Suddenly I couldn't move.

"Come on," Jacob said.

I pointed.

"Oh," he whispered, "I thought your dad had a job."

"So did I. And Mom thinks so, too."

There were tears in my eyes as I watched people walk past my father. I wished so much someone would buy an apple from him. But no one did. I realized how he had earned my birthday dime and was sorry I had spent it.

"I have to get to work," Jacob whispered.

I was too dazed to know where we were going. I just followed Jacob until we came to a small building.

"My dad is out of work, too," Jacob said as he got in line. "That's why I'm a newsie. Sell newspapers with me. It's fun."

I didn't feel like going home, so I stayed with Jacob. We collected our papers, and he said, "Now I'll teach you how to really sell."

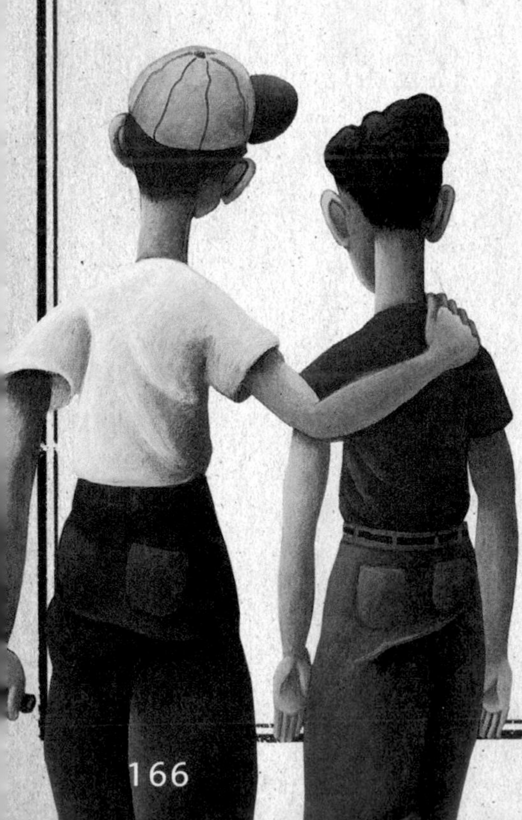

We walked past a newsie on the corner.

"Coney Island fire!" he called out. "One thousand homeless. Read all about it!" There were lots of people around, but I didn't see anyone buy a newspaper.

Jacob and I passed other newsies calling out about the fire. Then we walked beyond the busy streets and apartment buildings.

"Where are we going?" I asked.

"You'll see," Jacob said.

We walked until we came to an elevated train station. People were rushing from it to the large ballpark just ahead.

"We're here," Jacob said. "That's Yankee Stadium."

I held up one of my newspapers and called out the headline. "Coney Island fire! Read all about it!"

"No," Jacob said. "No one here is interested in fires."

He picked up a newspaper and looked through it. "Here it is," he said. "This is what they want."

"Babe Ruth hits home run!" he called out. "Read all about it! The Babe hits number twenty-five! Read all about it!"

"Here, I'll take one," a man said, and gave Jacob two cents.

"Let me see that," another man said.

Jacob was smart. These people were on their way to see a Yankee game. Of course they were interested in Babe Ruth.

"Babe Ruth hits home run," I called out. "Read all about it."

Jacob and I quickly sold all our papers. When we left the stadium the coins in my pocket made a nice jingling sound.

We went back to the small building and paid a penny for each paper we had sold. That left me with twenty-five cents.

When I got home I didn't tell Mom about Dad and the apples, but I told her about my job. She put the coins I earned in our money jar and said, "Don't say anything to your father about the newspapers. It might embarrass him to know you're helping out."

Later Dad came home and put some coins in the jar. He took off his shoes, stretched out on the couch, and said, "I was really busy at the office today. I'm tired."

I wanted to tell him he didn't have to pretend he still had his job, but I couldn't. I just looked at Dad's briefcase and wondered what he had in there.

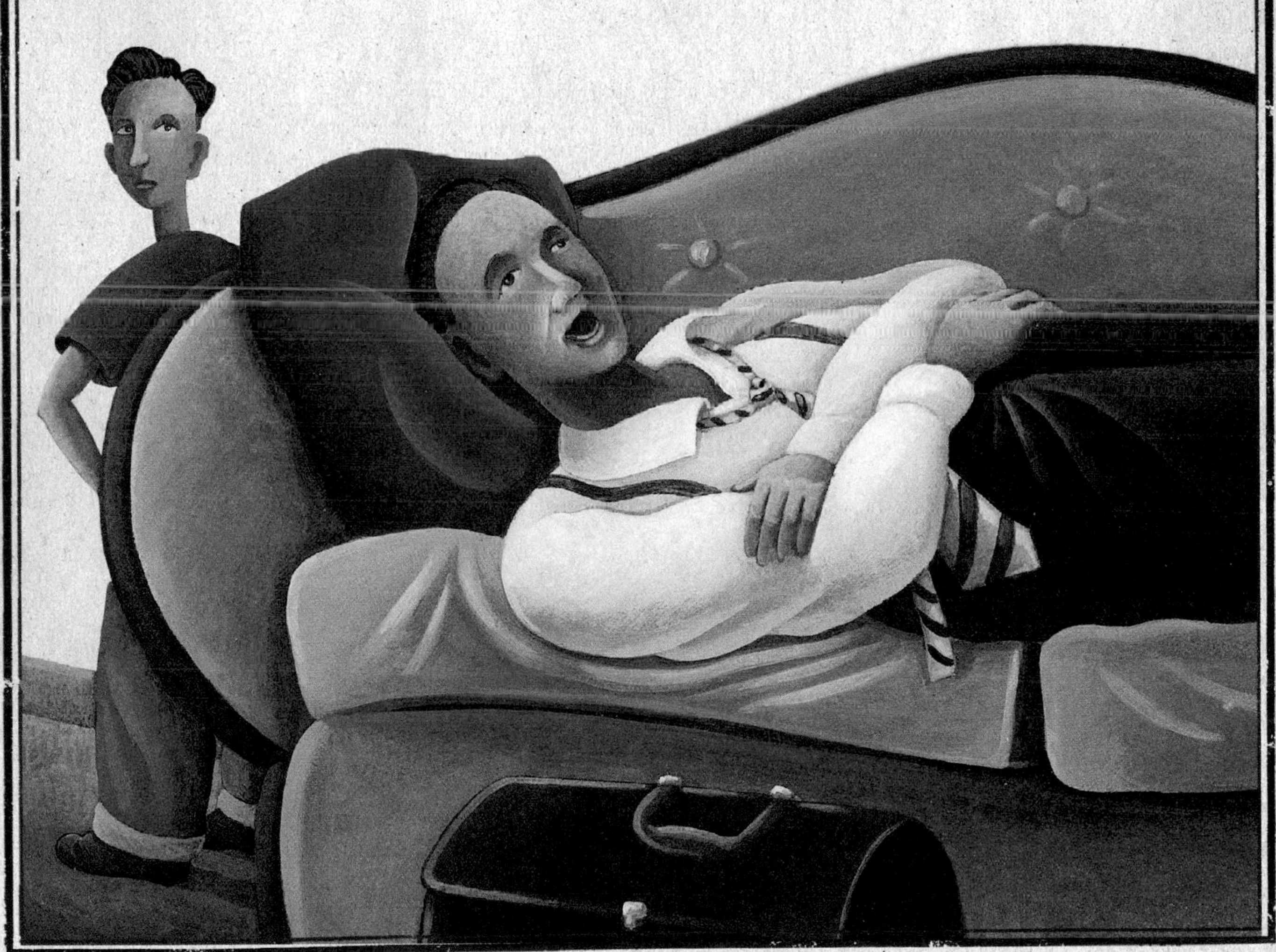

The next day Jacob and I called out about Babe Ruth again. He had hit his twenty-sixth home run! I quickly sold my newspapers. I knew I could have sold more, if only I had some way to get them to the stadium.

When I got home I searched the basement of our building for a wagon, or anything with wheels. All I found were boxes and a torn suitcase. Just before I went back upstairs I saw Mrs. Johnson pushing her baby in a carriage.

"Could I borrow that?" I asked.

"Why?" she asked. "You don't have a baby."

I told her about the newspapers.

"I suppose so," Mrs. Johnson said, thinking. "But this would have to be a business arrangement. With my carriage you'll make extra money, so I should make some, too." She offered to rent the carriage to me for ten cents an afternoon, and I agreed.

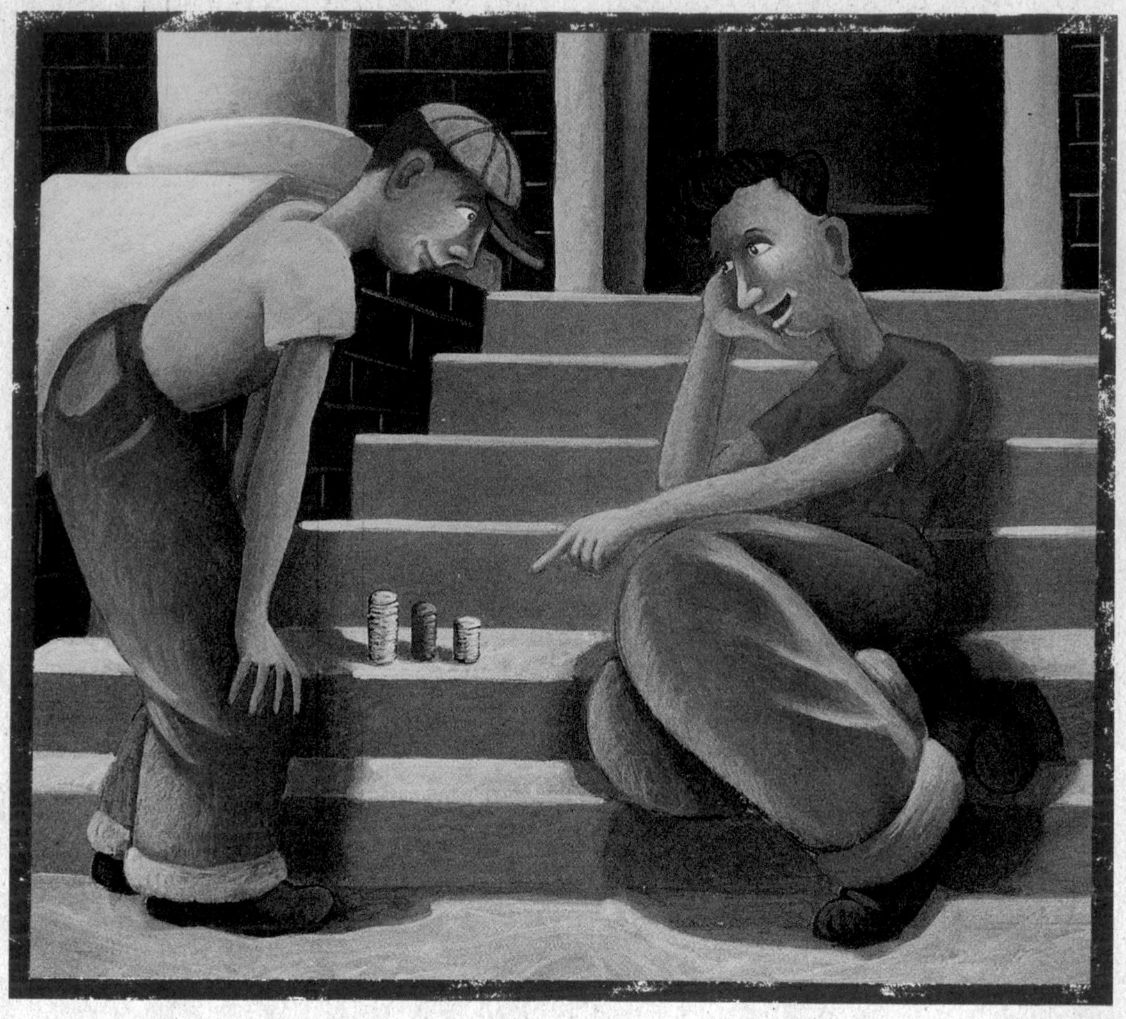

On Monday the front-page story was about a nineteen-year-old boy who had robbed a telegraph office because he wanted to be arrested. He knew he would get something to eat in jail.

Jacob and I didn't call out about the boy. We called out about Babe Ruth. He had won a game for the Yankees with a hit in the twelfth inning.

Thanks to Mrs. Johnson's carriage, I sold lots of papers. I had eighty cents to give Mom for the money jar.

When Dad came home he gave Mom a bottle of milk and a bag of apples, and said, "I bought the apples from an unemployed man I passed on my way home."

"Dad," I said, "that man is not unemployed. Selling apples is a job."

"No it's not," he said sharply. "It's just what you do while you wait and hope for something better."

He looked upset, and I realized how important it was for him to keep his secret.

On Tuesday Jacob and I called out, “Babe Ruth collapses! Read all about it!” And on Wednesday, “Babe Ruth stays home!” He had hurt his leg, and doctors told him he wouldn’t be able to play for three weeks.

That night Dad asked me to walk with him. When we were a few blocks from home he said, “Today I saw you pushing Mrs. Johnson’s baby carriage. I spoke with her, and she told me about the newspapers.”

“I’m just trying to help, Dad.”

He said, “I know.”

Dad held my hand firmly. We walked quietly for a while. Then Dad asked, "Were you ever on Webster Avenue?"

"Once."

He squeezed my hand. Tears were rolling down his cheeks.

"I didn't tell Mom," I said.

Dad didn't say anything after that. I didn't either. We just walked.

The next day Jacob and I called out, "Babe Ruth sits with fans! Read all about it!"

"Here, kid. I'll take one." A tall man gave me a five-dollar bill.

"I'm sorry," I told him. "I can't change that."

"That's okay, kid. Keep the change."

I just looked at the money. I couldn't believe anyone would pay that much for a newspaper.

Jacob ran to me. "Do you know who that was?" he asked. "You sold a paper to Babe Ruth."

In the few pictures I had seen of Babe Ruth, he was wearing his baseball uniform. I didn't recognize him without it.

"Wow!" I said. "I just sold a newspaper to Babe Ruth!"

I kept one hand in my pocket, holding on to my Babe Ruth bill. With my other hand I sold newspapers. And I kept looking across the street, toward where Babe Ruth had gone.

When all our papers were sold, I pointed to Yankee Stadium and told Jacob, "I'm going over there." I needed to see Babe Ruth again.

I checked the prices and realized I could buy two tickets and still have plenty left for the money jar. So that's what I did.

The stadium was noisy. Jacob and I walked through a short tunnel and saw a large baseball field. Babe Ruth was in the Yankee dugout with his teammates. When the game started, he stayed there. I guess his leg still hurt.

SECTION 25

I tried to watch everything: the pitcher, the catcher, the batter, the players on the field, and Babe Ruth. Near the end of the game, with the score tied, the Yankee catcher didn't come up to bat. Out came Babe Ruth.

Everyone shouted and waved. I think I cheered the loudest. "He paid for my tickets," I told the man next to us. "He gave me five dollars so I could see the game."

The man smiled.

I think the Red Sox pitcher was afraid Babe Ruth would hit a home run. He purposely threw wide of the plate four times and walked the Babe. We cheered again as Babe Ruth slowly walked to first base.

We knew he couldn't hit a home run every time, but at least the Babe was back.

Babe Ruth was part of the 1932 Yankees. That year they were the best team in baseball. He and I were a team, too. His home runs helped me sell newspapers. As I left Yankee Stadium, with the coins I had earned making that nice jingling sound in my pocket, I knew Dad and I were also a team. We were both working to get our family through hard times.

1. Read this sentence from the story: <u>Jacob was smart.</u> How can you tell it is an opinion? FACT/OPINION

2. What does the main character in the story do so that he can sell newspapers? IMPORTANT DETAILS

3. Would you feel the same as the boy in the story, if you sold a newspaper to a famous baseball player? Why or why not? EXPRESS PERSONAL OPINIONS

4. How does the author feel about Babe Ruth? Why do you think so? DRAW CONCLUSIONS

5. **WRITE** In what ways are the dad and his son a team? Give examples from the story to support your answer. SHORT RESPONSE

LOUISIANA GRADE-LEVEL EXPECTATIONS—3ELA-1-E5-10 summarize main events/ideas/details; 3ELA-7-E1-17(c) make inferences/draw conclusions; 3ELA-7-E3-20 explain author's viewpoint; 3ELA-7-E4-21(a) identify fact/opinion; 3ELA-7-E4-21(e) connect to real-life situations; 3ELA-2-E4-25 write paragraphs with description/narration

Meet the Author

David A. Adler

David A. Adler was the family artist when he was a child. It wasn't until he was an adult that he decided that he wanted to be an author.

When he writes, David Adler works very quickly. "I don't worry about each word," he says. "I know that I will rewrite the story many times." He likes to write both fiction and nonfiction.

Although "The Babe and I" is fiction, the newspaper stories in it are really from nine days in 1932.

Meet the Illustrator

Terry Widener

Terry Widener likes doing illustrations about people who play sports. Before beginning, he researches the uniforms, stadiums, and equipment. "When I illustrate, my hope is to create a beautiful book," he says.

www.harcourtschool.com/storytown

Social Studies

America's

A professional baseball season lasts about half the year. It starts in April and stretches into the fall. The World Series is played in October.

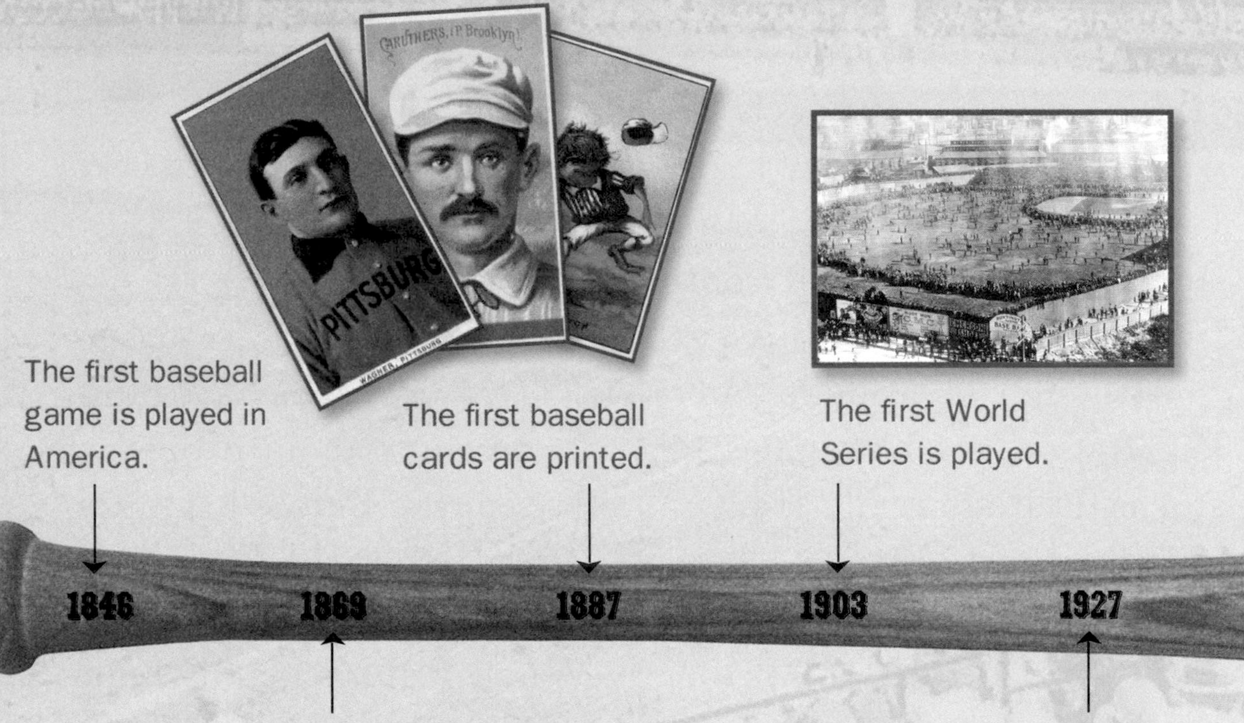

1846 — The first baseball game is played in America.

1869 — Cincinnati gets the first paid baseball team. The team wins 99 games in a row!

1887 — The first baseball cards are printed.

1903 — The first World Series is played.

1927 — Babe Ruth sets a record. He hits 60 home runs in one season. No one breaks his record for 34 years!

National Pastime

The All-American Girls Professional Baseball League gives women a chance to play professional baseball.

Roger Maris breaks the home run record. He hits 61 home runs in one season.

Boys and girls of all ages play baseball. They play in towns and cities all over America. One day, some of them will set new records of their own.

1943 1947 1954 1961 2004 TODAY

Jackie Robinson is the first African American to play in the major leagues.

The Boston Red Sox win the World Series for the first time in 86 years.

Connections

Comparing Texts

3ELA-7-E1-17(d)
3ELA-7-E3-19
3ELA-7-E4-21(e)

1. Compare the author's purpose for "The Babe and I" with the author's purpose for "America's National Pastime." How are they different?

2. Would you like selling newspapers the way the boy in the story did? Explain.

3. How is life in the United States today different from the way it was during the Great Depression?

Vocabulary Review

Word Webs

middle — midst

Work with a partner. Choose two Vocabulary Words. Create a word web for each word. Put the Vocabulary Word in the center of your web. Then write related words in the web. Explain to your partner how each word in your web is related to the Vocabulary Word.

- shabby
- embarrass
- midst
- elevated
- dazed
- collapses

Fluency Practice 3ELA-1-E3-07

Partner Reading

Work with a partner. Read your favorite page from "The Babe and I." Focus on reading smoothly by grouping words that go together. Have your partner listen carefully and provide feedback. Then change roles.

Writing 3ELA-7-E4-21(a) 3ELA-2-E4-25

Write an Opinion Paragraph

Write a paragraph about your favorite sport. Use a variety of sentences to tell about the sport. Include your opinion of the sport and facts that support your opinion.

My Writing Checklist

Writing Trait → Sentence Fluency

- ✔ I use the fact–opinion chart to plan my writing.
- ✔ I use sentences with different lengths.
- ✔ I give my opinion and facts that support it.

Fact	Opinion

LOUISIANA GRADE-LEVEL EXPECTATIONS—3ELA-1-E3-07 adjust reading speed; 3ELA-7-E1-17(d) compare/contrast; 3ELA-7-E3-19 identify author's purpose; 3ELA-7-E4-21(a) identify fact/opinion; 3ELA-7-E4-21(e) connect to real-life situations; 3ELA-2-E4-25 write paragraphs with description/narration

Reading-Writing Connection

Response to Literature

Writing about what you read is called a **response to literature.** Here is my response to "The Babe and I."

Student Writing Model

What a Team!
by Ryan

Do you like to read about teammates? Then read "The Babe and I." It is one of my favorite books. The family in this book works as a team after the father loses his job. I think the father is caring because he sells apples even though he is ashamed. The son is helpful because he earns money by selling newspapers. My favorite part was when Babe Ruth bought a paper from the boy. Babe Ruth paid him enough money to see a baseball game and help his family. The father, son, and the Babe made quite a team!

Writing Trait

SENTENCE FLUENCY
I use a variety of sentences to make my writing interesting to my readers.

Writing Trait

WORD CHOICE
I use exact words to share my ideas and feelings.

Here's how I write a response.

1. **I look back at the story I read. I think about what happened and how the characters acted.**

2. **I use a graphic organizer. I write my ideas about the story.**

"The Babe and I"
Dad loses main job. Has to sell apples.
Boy sees Dad selling apples and wants to help.
Boy sells a newspaper to Babe Ruth.
Boy happy because he and his dad are a team helping the family.
Boy sells newspapers to help make money.

3. **I look at my ideas, and I decide what to write about. I make my plan for writing.**

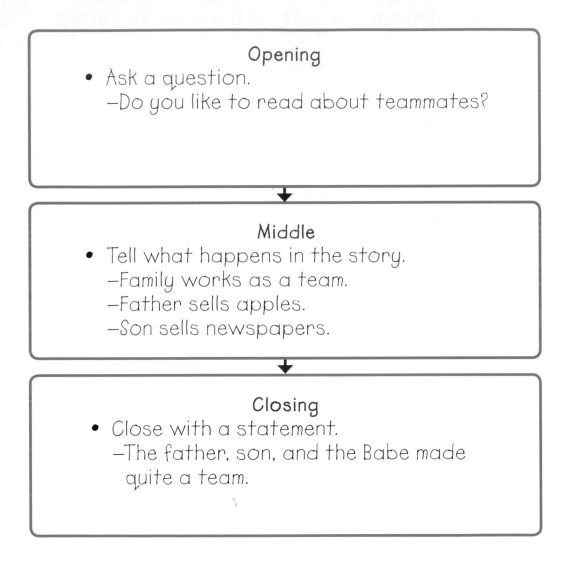

Opening
- Ask a question.
  –Do you like to read about teammates?

↓

Middle
- Tell what happens in the story.
  –Family works as a team.
  –Father sells apples.
  –Son sells newspapers.

↓

Closing
- Close with a statement.
  –The father, son, and the Babe made quite a team.

4. **I write my response.**

Here is a checklist I use when I write a response to literature. You can use it when you write a response.

Checklist for Writing a Response to Literature

- ☐ I look back at the selection to find information.
- ☐ My response gives the story's title.
- ☐ My response tells something about the selection. For a story, it tells what happens or tells about the characters.
- ☐ I use exact words to tell one or more ideas I learned from the story.
- ☐ I include my thoughts and feelings.
- ☐ My sentences are complete. I use a variety of simple and compound sentences. I capitalize proper nouns.

CONTENTS

Lesson 7

Genre: Nonfiction

Aero and Officer Mike
POLICE PARTNERS
by Joan Plummer Russell
Photographs by Kris Turner Sinnenberg

It's About Dogs
by Tony Johnston
illustrated by Stacy Schuett

Genre: Poetry

Focus Skill

Fact and Opinion

Remember that a **fact** is something that can be proved. An **opinion** is a person's feelings about something. You may not share the same opinion as someone else.

To decide if a statement is a fact or an opinion, ask yourself questions such as the following:

- Can this statement be proved?
- Is this what someone thinks or feels but cannot prove?

Identifying facts and opinions can help you know what is true about a topic.

Fact	Opinion

Tip

Sometimes authors include facts in their statements of opinion. If any part of the statement shows a feeling or belief, then the whole statement is an opinion.

Read the article. Tell why one statement in the chart is a fact and the other is an opinion.

Herding dogs are very interesting! Farmers who raise sheep use them to herd and guard their animals. On a signal, the dogs run around the sheep and bark. They can move the sheep along country roads or into a pen. I believe that border collies are the best herding dogs. They are called border collies because they first came from the border area between England and Scotland.

Fact	Opinion
Farmers who raise sheep often use dogs to help them.	Herding dogs are very interesting!

Try This!

Look back at the article. Find one other fact and one other opinion to add to the chart. Explain how you made your choices.

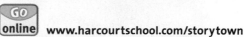

www.harcourtschool.com/storytown

LOUISIANA GRADE-LEVEL EXPECTATIONS—3ELA-7-E4-21(a) identify fact/opinion

Vocabulary

Build Robust Vocabulary

- scent
- wanders
- whined
- obey
- demonstrate
- patrol

Hidden Talents

Sometimes dogs are playmates. Sometimes they are friends who sit quietly with you. Did you know that dogs' senses also allow them to be much more?

A dog can smell a person's **scent** long after the person has walked by. A dog's ears can hear sounds that a person's ears cannot. A dog's eyes can notice something that **wanders** by up to half a mile away.

A dog could hear a child who cried or **whined** by moving its ears in the direction of the sound.

Dogs can be trained to **obey** commands. Some dogs are trained to use their sense of smell to find lost objects, animals, or people. Dogs can be trained to use their keen sense of hearing to help people who cannot hear. Still others are trained to lead people who cannot see.

Once a dog can **demonstrate** that it understands what to do, the dog can go to work. What trained working dogs have you seen?

Police officers who **patrol** with a dog have a helper with special skills.

www.harcourtschool.com/storytown

Word Detective

Your mission this week is to look for the Vocabulary Words on signs and in advertisements. Each time you read a Vocabulary Word, write it in your vocabulary journal. Don't forget to tell where you found the word.

3ELA-6-E3-16 Genre Study

Nonfiction gives information about a topic. Look for

- information about a real person or real events.
- facts about the topic and opinions the author may have.

Fact	Opinion

3ELA-7-E1-17 Comprehension Strategy

Monitor comprehension—Reread a passage if something seems confusing or doesn't make sense. You may have missed an important point.

LOUISIANA GRADE-LEVEL EXPECTATIONS—3ELA-6-E3-16 define characteristics of types of literature; 3ELA-7-E1-17 demonstrate understanding of information

Aero and Officer Mike: Police Partners

by
Joan Plummer Russell

photographs by
Kris Turner Sinnenberg

It is very early in the morning. Everyone in the house is still asleep. A large black-and-tan German shepherd is lying on the floor by Officer Mike's bed. The alarm rings. Officer Mike reaches down to pet his dog, Aero.

Aero is a police dog, also known as a K-9 officer. When Officer Mike puts on his uniform with a silver badge on his chest, Aero jumps up, ready to have his wide black leather collar with a police badge on it slipped over his head. He knows this will be a work day.

WORK AND PLAY

Officer Mike and Aero are partners. They work together. They practice together. They play together.

Aero, with his powerful nose, can do many things Officer Mike cannot. He can sniff and find lost children. He can sniff and find lost things.

Police dogs are very strong and well trained. They have to be ready to go anywhere they are needed. They can be very fierce when they are helping to catch criminals. They can run faster than any human being. But when police dogs are not working, they are gentle pets that like to have their tummies scratched.

Aero's most important jobs are to help and to protect his partner, Officer Mike. Together, Aero and Officer Mike patrol in all kinds of weather. Some weeks they patrol from early morning until dinnertime. Some weeks they sleep in the daytime and work all night.

On Duty

Aero is always eager to jump into the back of the police car. Officer Mike's car is different from other police cars. There is no back seat. The floor is flat and covered with carpet for Aero to lie on. There is a water bowl built into the floor, and a small fan keeps Aero cool in the summer. Screens cover the windows so no one can reach in and pet him.

When Aero is on duty, he's not allowed to play. Officer Mike sits in the driver's seat, but Aero will not let anyone else sit in the front until Officer Mike tells Aero it is OK.

Aero knows that one of his jobs is to protect the police car. When Officer Mike leaves the car, he either opens the front window for Aero to jump through or uses a remote control to open the back door when he needs Aero's help.

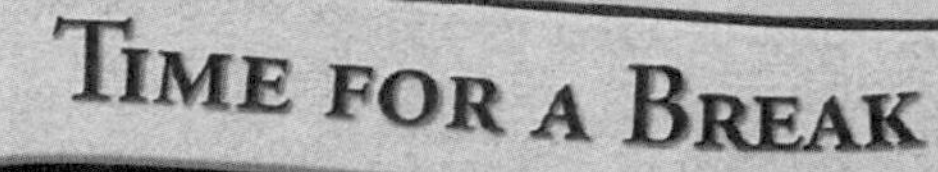

Time for a Break

When Aero and Officer Mike have been in the police car for a few hours, Aero will need to take a break. Aero pushes his head against his partner's head to let him know. Officer Mike parks the cruiser as soon as he can and says to Aero, "Go be a dog!" Aero knows he'll also have time to explore a little and maybe chase a tennis ball while they are stopped.

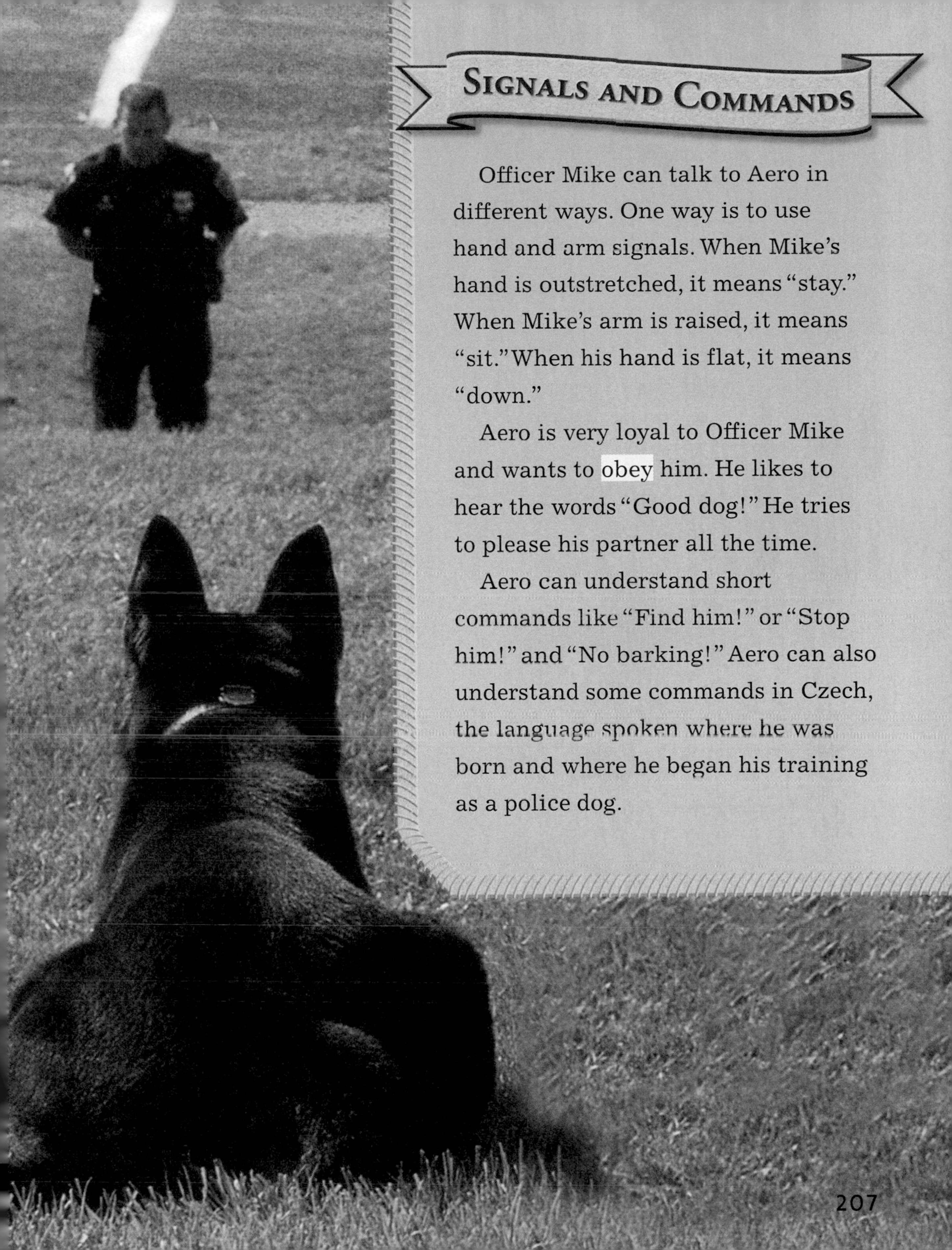

Signals and Commands

Officer Mike can talk to Aero in different ways. One way is to use hand and arm signals. When Mike's hand is outstretched, it means "stay." When Mike's arm is raised, it means "sit." When his hand is flat, it means "down."

Aero is very loyal to Officer Mike and wants to obey him. He likes to hear the words "Good dog!" He tries to please his partner all the time.

Aero can understand short commands like "Find him!" or "Stop him!" and "No barking!" Aero can also understand some commands in Czech, the language spoken where he was born and where he began his training as a police dog.

K-9 Training

Aero's training never ends. Several times a month Aero and Officer Mike train with other officers and their K-9 partners. One exercise the police dogs do is to run through an obstacle course. The dogs practice getting over, under, around, and through difficult spots.

Aero had to learn how to walk up and down very steep, open stairs. He also had to learn to walk over a large, open grating, the kind you often see on city streets. At first he spread his paws to help keep his balance. His legs began to quiver, and he whined a frightened cry. He had to practice over and over. Officer Mike kept saying, "Good boy, you can do it." Aero was brave and trusted his partner, but he still does not like open gratings or steep stairs.

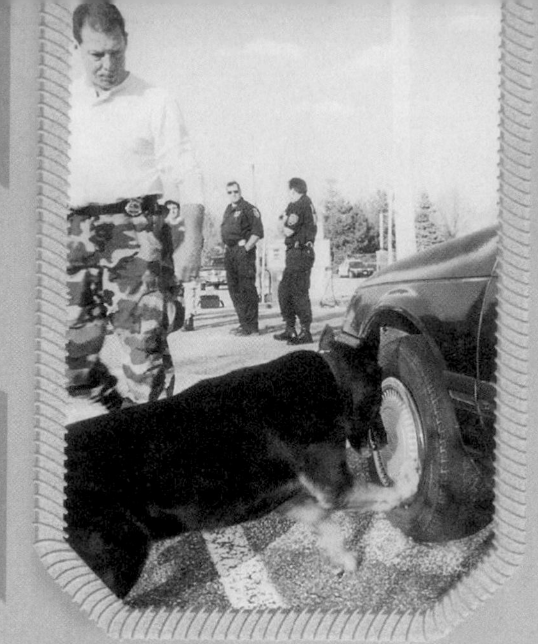

Aero's Sense of Smell

K-9s have very powerful noses—hundreds of times more powerful than human noses. That's why one of Aero's most helpful talents on the police force is his ability to find things by smell.

When children play hide-and-seek, they may think they are well hidden. Their dog can find them right away. The same is true when a child is lost or wanders away from home. Aero can find the child by using his sense of smell. Each person has a scent that is different from everyone else's scent. Even twins do not smell the same. A person's unique smell comes from the food he or she eats, the soap and shampoo he or she uses, the clothes he or she wears, and the place he or she lives.

At the Vet's

Aero goes to Dr. Morse, a veterinarian, for regular checkups. Aero must lie still on a table while the doctor examines him. Once Aero had a small infection on his neck. Dr. Morse gave him some medicine so he would get better. Because a police dog works so hard and has such an important job, he needs to be healthy. At the end of the checkup, Dr. Morse lifts Aero to the floor, pets him, and says, "Good dog."

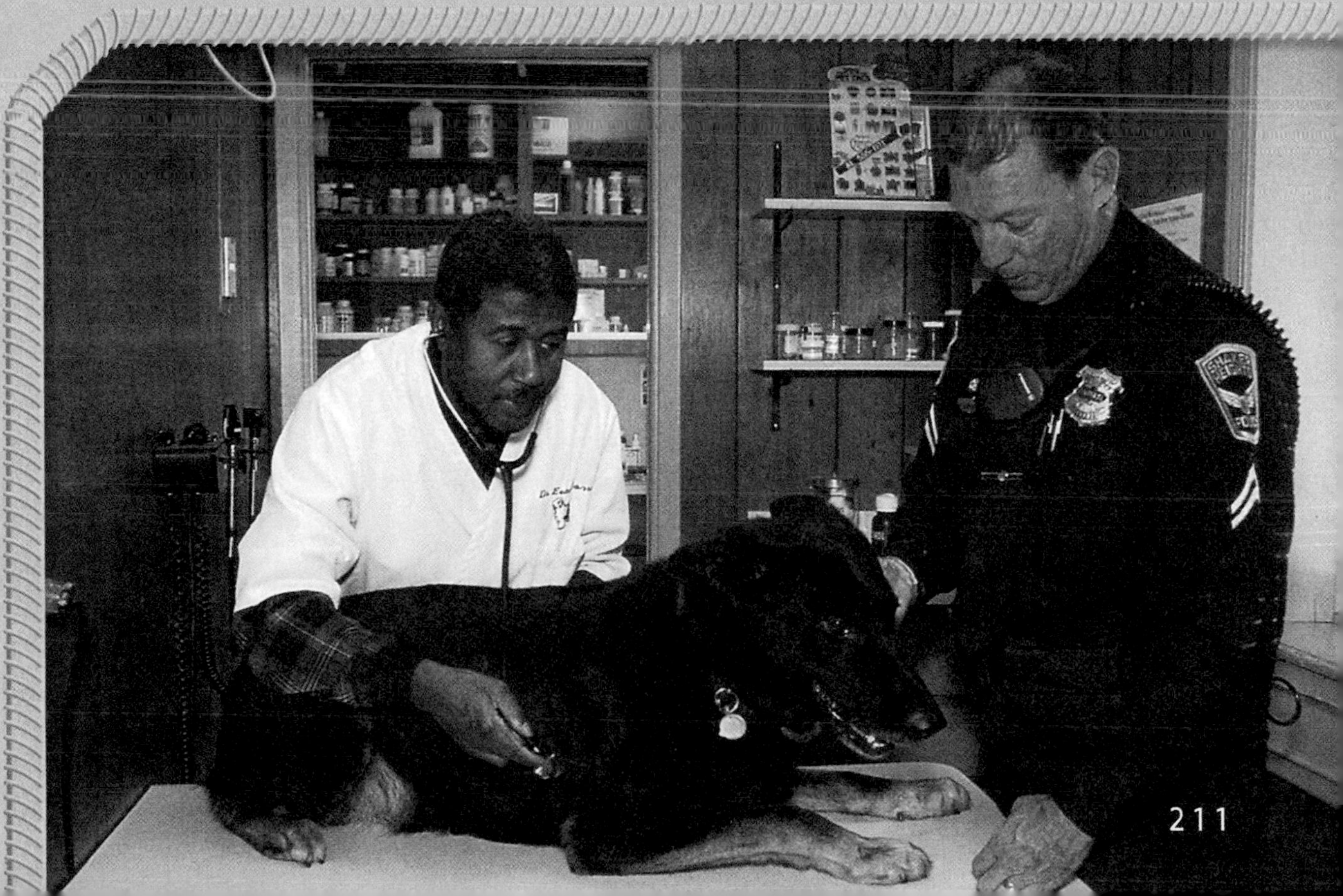

Visiting in the Community

Nurses and teachers often write to the chief of police to ask if Aero can visit children in their hospital or school. Aero likes children and is always gentle with them. He is even gentler when visiting a sick child. He lies down, staying very still and quiet so the child won't be afraid of him.

When Officer Mike and Aero visit schools, Aero rests on the floor beside Officer Mike. Together they demonstrate the different commands Aero will obey. The children ask many questions. Why is there a police badge on Aero's collar? How high can Aero jump? How fast can Aero run?

Officer Mike carefully answers the questions. Aero's badge shows everyone that he is a working police dog. He can jump over an eight-foot wall when he is chasing a criminal. He can run very fast, about forty miles an hour. Even the fastest person can only run about twenty-four miles an hour.

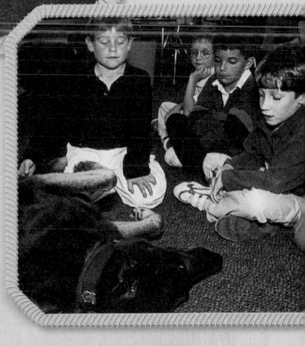

Petting Aero

Children often want to pet Aero. Officer Mike tells them the rules. Never try to pet a strange dog until you ask permission from the owner. Never come up behind Aero. He might get frightened and snap at you. Never ever hug a K-9 around the neck. Walk up to a police dog slowly from the front so he can see you. Let him sniff your hand. Pet his head and ears gently. Talk to him softly.

Back at the Station

At the end of a twelve-hour work shift, there is always a final job to be done at the police station. After talking with his friends on the force, Officer Mike sits down and writes a report for the police chief about the whole day or night. Aero lies down by Officer Mike's chair.

Fellow Officers

After the report is written, Officer Mike and Aero go home together. When Officcr Mike goes to bed, Aero will plop down on the floor near the bed. He lays his head on his paws, and with a sigh goes to sleep near his best friend. Neither of them knows what surprises tomorrow's patrol will bring, but they are well prepared. They both love being police officers.

Think Critically

1. Read this sentence from the selection: "Together, Aero and Officer Mike patrol in all kinds of weather." How can you tell that this is a fact? FACT/OPINION

2. Why is Aero's sense of smell important to the police? IMPORTANT DETAILS

3. Do you think Aero is smarter than most other dogs? Why or why not? EXPRESS PERSONAL OPINIONS

4. How can you tell that the author thinks K-9s help people? DRAW CONCLUSIONS

5. **WRITE** How do K-9s help the police do their jobs? Give examples from the selection to support your answer. EXTENDED RESPONSE

LOUISIANA GRADE-LEVEL EXPECTATIONS—3ELA-1-E6-11 connect to prior knowledge; 3ELA-7-E1-17 demonstrate understanding of information; 3ELA-7-E1-17(c) make inferences/draw conclusions; 3ELA-7-E3-20 explain author's viewpoint; 3ELA-7-E4-21(a) identify fact/opinion; 3ELA-2-E1-22 write organized paragraphs

MEET THE AUTHOR

Joan Plummer Russell says that she was always encouraged to write. Even so, she was never interested enough in any topic to write a book about it. That changed when she met Officer Mike and Aero.

To prepare to write her first book, the author rode along with Officer Mike and Aero twice a month for two years. She took notes, took photographs, and tape-recorded many conversations. Some of her tapes are filled with Aero's barking!

Joan Plummer Russell was fascinated with what Aero could do. She found great joy in watching a well trained K-9 team.

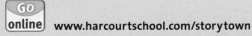

GO online www.harcourtschool.com/storytown

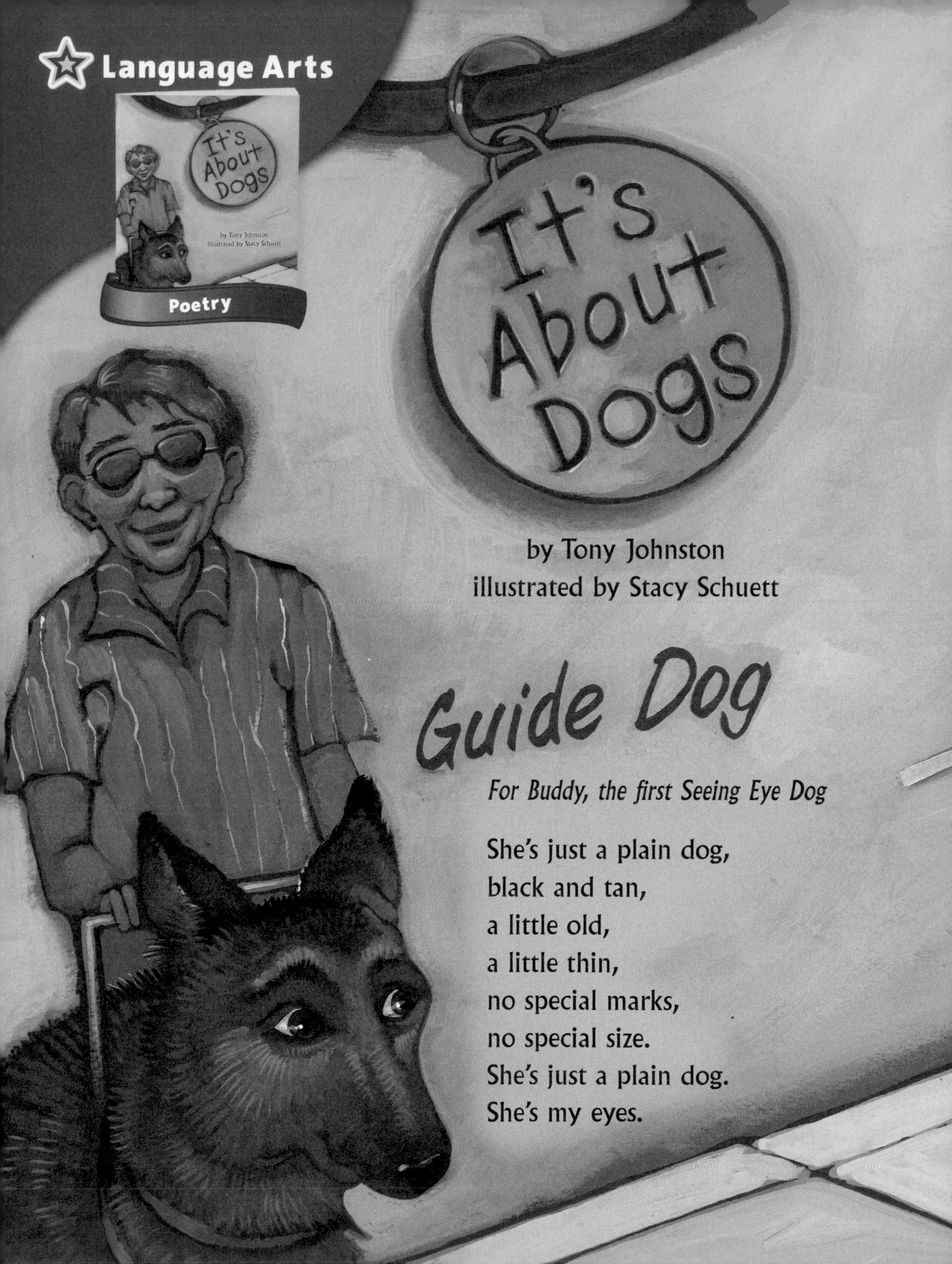

It's About Dogs

by Tony Johnston
illustrated by Stacy Schuett

Guide Dog

For Buddy, the first Seeing Eye Dog

She's just a plain dog,
black and tan,
a little old,
a little thin,
no special marks,
no special size.
She's just a plain dog.
She's my eyes.

A Beagle Speaks of Noses

I should be good.
I wish I could
but
I sniff and sniff.
I catch a whiff
of something new
or old to chew.
What can it be?
My nose drags me
so I drag you.
What can I do
but twine through trees,
check at each pole,
inspect each hole?
Please don't be cross
My nose is boss.

Connections

Comparing Texts

3ELA-1-E6-11
3ELA-7-E1-17
3ELA-7-E4-21(e)

1. In what ways is Aero like the dog described in the poem "Guide Dog"?

2. What would you like about having a dog like Aero live with you? What might be difficult about it?

3. How do K-9s help make the world a better place?

Vocabulary Review

3ELA-2-E6-27

Buddy whined at the scent of bacon.

Word Sort

Work with a partner. Sort the Vocabulary Words into two categories. Decide whether each word fits better with *Aero* or with *Officer Mike.* Compare your sorted words with your partner. Take turns explaining why you put each word where you did. Then choose one word from each category and write a sentence that uses both words.

- **scent**
- **wanders**
- **whined**
- **obey**
- **demonstrate**
- **patrol**

Fluency Practice 3ELA-1-E3-07

Partner Reading

Work with a partner. Read pages from "Aero and Officer Mike." Focus on reading smoothly by grouping words that go together. Ask your partner for feedback about how you read. Then switch roles.

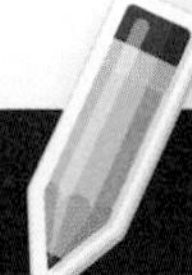

Writing 3ELA-2-E4-25

Write a Paragraph of Information

Write a paragraph that gives facts about the use of K-9s by police departments or about another animal that helps people. Remember to use only facts in your writing. Try to keep opinions out of this paragraph.

My Writing Checklist

Writing Trait → Sentence Fluency

- ✔ I plan my writing.
- ✔ I give only facts.
- ✔ My sentences vary in length.

Fact	Opinion

LOUISIANA GRADE-LEVEL EXPECTATIONS—3ELA-1-E3-07 adjust reading speed; 3ELA-1-E6-11 connect to prior knowledge; 3ELA-7-E1-17 demonstrate understanding of information; 3ELA-7-E4-21(e) connect to real-life situations; 3ELA-2-E4-25 write paragraphs with description/narration; 3ELA-2-E6-27 write for various purposes

CONTENTS

Lesson 8

Genre: Photo Essay

How Animals Talk

BOOKS FOR YO
NATIONAL GEO

PARTNERS IN THE WILD

by Pete Liu

Genre: Expository Nonfiction

Phonics Skill

Words with *ou, ow; oi, oy*

The letters *ou* and *ow* can stand for the vowel sound you hear in *cow*. The letters *oi* and *oy* can stand for the vowel sound you hear in *boy*. Read the words in each column and listen for the vowel sounds.

Words with the Vowel Sound in *Cow*	Words with the Vowel Sound in *Boy*
plowing sound	toy spoiled

Read each sentence. Look at the chart below. Tell in which column of the chart each underlined word goes.

1. Grace <u>enjoys</u> her new puppy.
2. Can animals tell if it is going to rain <u>now</u> or later?
3. The frightened rabbits raced to a hole in the <u>ground</u>.
4. What scents might a wolf find in the <u>soil</u>?
5. A wolf might <u>growl</u> at a bear.
6. One moose <u>annoyed</u> the other as they ate.

Words with the Vowel Sound in *Cow*	Words with the Vowel Sound in *Boy*

Try This!

Look back at other stories in Theme 2. Find two words with the vowel sound in *boy*. Find two words with the vowel sound in *cow*. Tell where they go in the chart.

www.harcourtschool.com/storytown

Vocabulary

Build Robust Vocabulary

- signal
- flick
- alert
- communicate
- chatter
- grooms

Dry Tortugas National Park

When you visit Dry Tortugas National Park near Key West, Florida, take a camera and binoculars. Take a swimsuit, too, because most of the park is water. The dry parts are seven islands. They do not have any fresh water.

When you swim, give a **signal** to your friends if you see a sea turtle. Sea turtles are fun to watch. The females go on land to lay their eggs. They **flick** sand over the eggs to protect them.

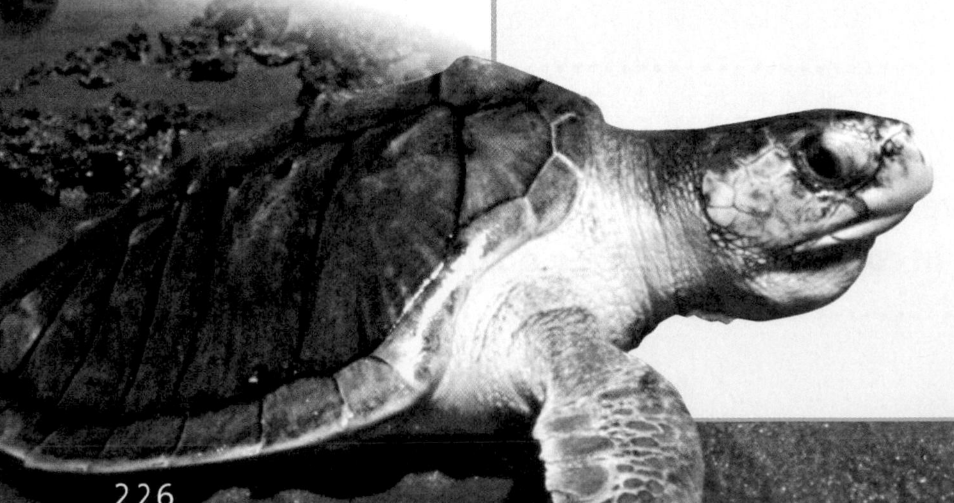

Rangers **alert** people when it is time for sea turtles to lay their eggs.

In April and May, you can go on bird-watching tours in the park. You may see birds called terns and noddies fly down to the water to catch fish and squid. They make loud calls to **communicate** with one another.

After your tour, you can visit an old fort. You will hear tales of pirates and of gold on sunken ships. Visitors may **chatter** to one another. Could the stories be true?

A heron **grooms** its feathers.

www.harcourtschool.com/storytown

Word Scribe

Your mission this week is to use the Vocabulary Words in your writing. For example, write about a time when you saw animals communicate with each other. Read what you write to a classmate.

Genre Study

3ELA-6-E3-16

A **photo essay** presents information with photographs and text. Look for

- photographs that are supported by the text.
- paragraphs of information with details that support the main idea.

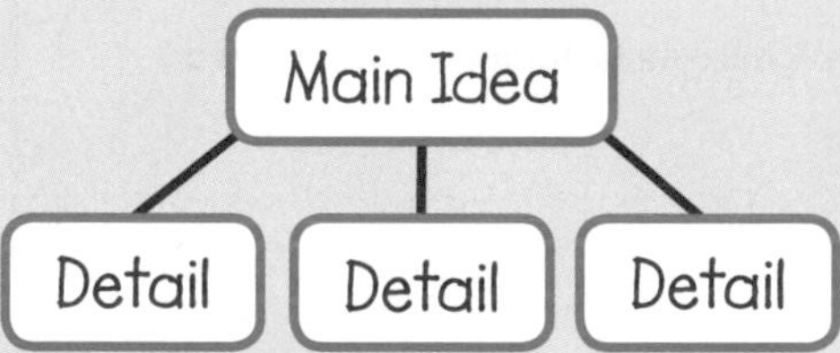

Comprehension Strategy

3ELA-7-E1-17

Summarize or review the main points of the selection, to help you understand and remember what you read.

LOUISIANA GRADE-LEVEL EXPECTATIONS—3ELA-6-E3-16 define characteristics of types of literature; 3ELA-7-E1-17 demonstrate understanding of information

HOW ANIMALS TALK

BY SUSAN McGRATH

Wolves howl and yap and growl. A coyote lifts its head and howls. Wolves and coyotes don't use words. But they do send messages with sounds and smells and in other ways. All animals tell each other things. They communicate.

An angry wolf raises its back and walks with its legs stiff. With its body, the wolf shows other wolves what it is feeling.

A wolf sniffs the snow for smells left by other wolves. A male deer rubs against a tree, leaving his smell there. The smell tells other deer, "Stay away from here."

Animals don't talk as we do. But they have many different ways of communicating with each other.

Three white-tailed deer flick their tails up as they race across a stream. The snowy white tails alert other deer to danger. The signal means, “Run! Follow me!”

A little pika communicates danger, too. It calls out a loud warning, “Eeek!” Other pikas run to safety.

Crack! Two bull elk crash horns. "Which one of us is the boss?" they communicate to each other. "Let's see which one is stronger."

Two arctic hares send the same message. The large, woolly hares jump up and hit at each other with their paws.

Insects also communicate. A praying mantis makes itself look as big as it can. This is a warning that says, "Better leave me alone."

Even a caterpillar has things to say. This swallowtail caterpillar can give off a bad smell that helps keep enemies away.

The light of the male firefly says, "Here I am." To a female passing by, his signal says, "Come over here."

The male spider, the smaller of these two, walks carefully on the female spider's web. "I am your kind of spider—not your food," his steps say. Then she lets him come in. The red shape on her belly tells us that she is a poisonous black widow spider.

Three baby robins open their mouths wide for a meal of worms. "Feed me," the open mouths signal. "Feed me! Feed me!"

Barn swallows chatter on a branch. Chinstrap penguins seem to have a lot to say. But no one knows just what the birds are saying. We can only guess. What do you think they are talking about?

Big birds called albatrosses are getting to know each other. They clap their bills and move around. These birds are also called gooney birds.

A male gooney bird dances for his mate. He twists his wings and bows his head. "Will you be my mate?" his dance says.

"Yes, I'll be your mate," she lets him know. After a while, he hugs her with his neck.

Two male elephant seals rise up in a crowd of females. The males, called bulls, snort and roar through their big noses.

"This group is mine!" one bull roars.

"No, no. It is mine!" the other roars.

The females don't seem to notice all the noise.

Even under the sea, animals communicate with each other. Three humpback whales—a baby, a female, and a male—are swimming along together. The male sings a loud song. "Here I am," says his song.

A beluga whale chirps and clicks. Its sounds made sailors think of a songbird. They used to call the beluga "the canary of the sea."

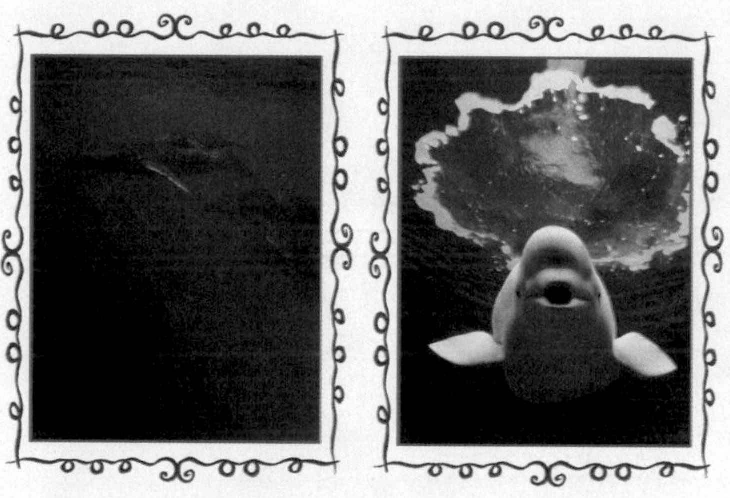

Two sea mammals called manatees meet and touch whiskers underwater. Manatees often kiss like this when they greet each other. They also chirp and squeal.

Who ever would have thought that animals could have so much to say! On the ground, in the air, and under the water, they are sending signals.

An older female grooms the hair of a young chimpanzee. She picks out pieces of dry skin with her fingers. Chimpanzees often comfort each other by grooming. "I like you," their touch says.

A young owl pecks an adult, begging to be fed. All animals communicate, using sight, sound, touch, and smell. Next time you see birds, or squirrels, or cats, or dogs, watch them closely. What do they have to say?

THINK CRITICALLY

1. What is the main idea of "How Animals Talk"?
   Focus Skill MAIN IDEA

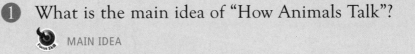

2. What are some ways that wolves communicate with each other? IMPORTANT DETAILS

3. Think about how some animals communicate with each other. How is it similar to the way that humans communicate? MAKE COMPARISONS

4. How can you tell that the author wants the reader to study nature? DRAW CONCLUSIONS

5. **WRITE** What is similar about the way that two bull elk and two arctic hares communicate? Give examples to explain your answer.
   SHORT RESPONSE

LOUISIANA GRADE-LEVEL EXPECTATIONS—3ELA-7-E1-17 demonstrate understanding of information; 3ELA-7-E1-17(c) make inferences/draw conclusions; 3ELA-7-E1-17(d) compare/contrast; 3ELA-7-E1-17(f) identify main ideas; 3ELA-7-E3-20 explain author's viewpoint; 3ELA-2-E4-25 write paragraphs with description/narration

Science

PARTNERS IN THE WILD

by Pete Liu

Bald Eagle Pairs Work Together

Did you know that bald eagles live in pairs? Before an eagle builds a nest, it chooses a partner. Then the pair finds an area with open space for hunting. Since eagles eat a lot of fish, they build their nests near rivers or lakes. Eagles usually build their nests in tall trees that provide a great lookout for food. Building nests high off the ground also protects the nests and the babies that will live there.

Bald Eagle Pairs in the Lower 48 States

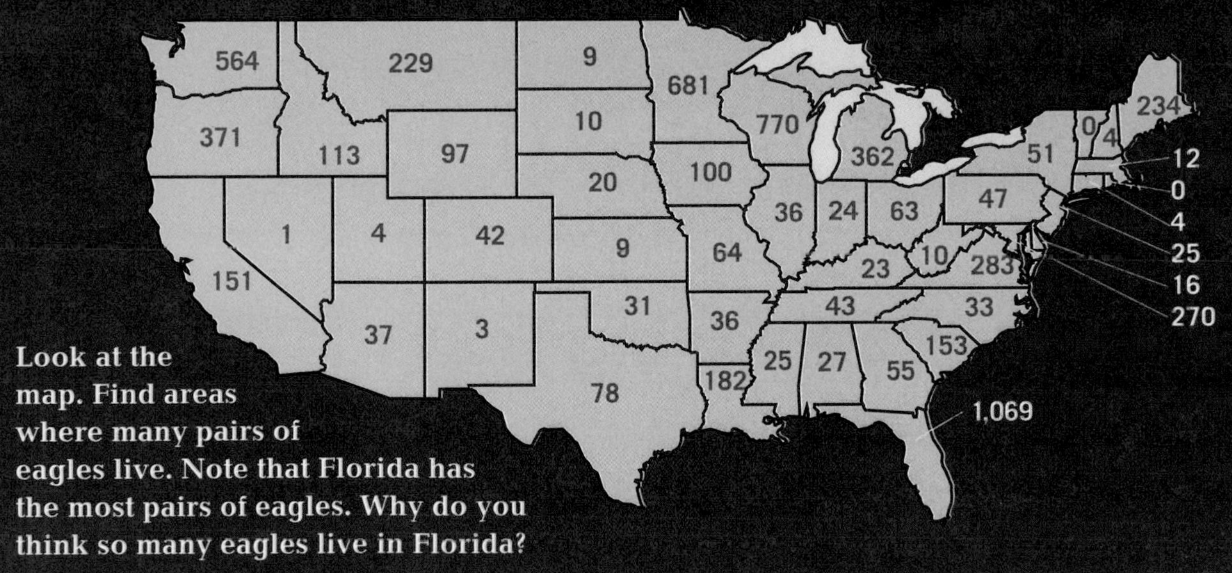

Look at the map. Find areas where many pairs of eagles live. Note that Florida has the most pairs of eagles. Why do you think so many eagles live in Florida?

Eagle Communication

Bald eagle parents care for their chicks by feeding them and keeping them warm. Eagles also protect their young by communicating with them. Adult eagles make a loud warning sound when danger is near. Eagles make softer sounds to greet each other in the nest.

Young eagles use body language to show their parents that they are hungry. After four months, an eagle is ready to leave the nest. The young eagle remembers how to communicate when it starts a family of its own.

Connections

Comparing Texts

3ELA-7-E1-17
3ELA-7-E4-21(e)

1. Think about what you read about bird communication in "How Animals Talk." What body language would young eagles use to show their parents they are hungry?

2. Would you tell a friend to read "How Animals Talk"? Explain.

3. How did reading "How Animals Talk" help you understand the natural world?

Vocabulary Review

3ELA-2-E6-27

The deer gave a signal with a flick of its tail.

Word Pairs

Work with a partner. Write each Vocabulary Word on a card. Place the cards face down. Take turns flipping over two cards and writing a sentence that uses both words. Read your sentences to your partner and decide whether the Vocabulary Words are used correctly.

- signal
- flick
- alert
- communicate
- chatter
- grooms

Fluency Practice 3ELA-1-E3-07

Repeated Reading

Choose a section of "How Animals Talk." Read it aloud, pausing at commas and end marks. Next, use a stopwatch to time your reading. Set a goal for a better time. Repeat the reading until you meet your goal.

Writing 3ELA-2-E4-25 3ELA-3-E2-29

Write a Description

Write a paragraph to describe the way one animal from "How Animals Talk" communicates. State the main idea in the first sentence. Then write descriptive details. Use a main idea and details chart to help you plan.

My Writing Checklist

Writing Trait → Word Choice

- ✔ I use exact language to describe the animal's actions.
- ✔ My paragraph has a main idea and descriptive details.
- ✔ I use correct punctuation in my paragraph.

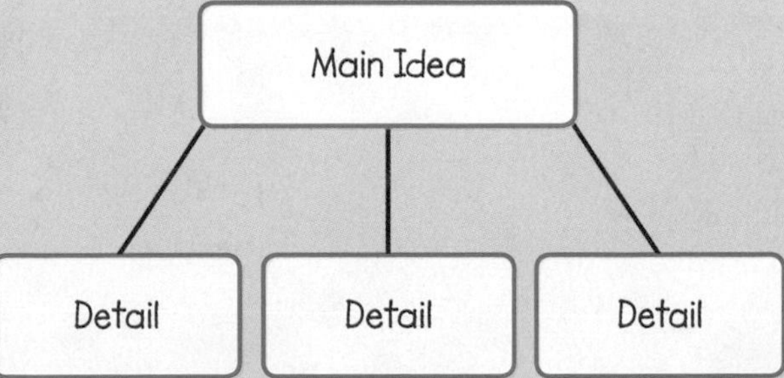

LOUISIANA GRADE-LEVEL EXPECTATIONS—3ELA-1-E3-07 adjust reading speed; 3ELA-7-E1-17 demonstrate understanding of information; 3ELA-7-E4-21(e) connect to real-life situations; 3ELA-2-E6-27 write for various purposes; 3ELA-2-E4-25 write paragraphs with description/narration; 3ELA-3-E2-29 use standard punctuation

CONTENTS

Lesson 9

Genre: Folktale

Genre: Legend

Focus Skill

Main Idea and Details

The **main idea** tells what a paragraph is mostly about. **Details** support the main idea with more information.

- Sometimes an author gives the main idea of a paragraph in the first sentence. The rest of the sentences are details that tell more about the main idea.
- Sometimes, the author does not tell you the main idea and you have to figure out what it is.

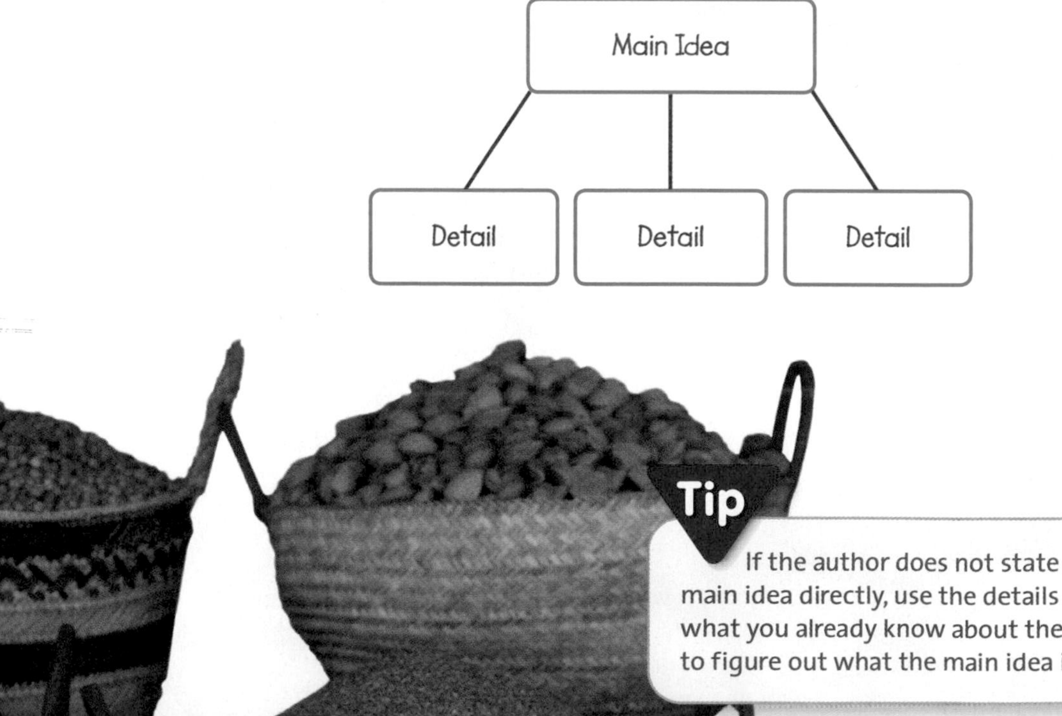

Tip

If the author does not state the main idea directly, use the details and what you already know about the topic to figure out what the main idea is.

Read the paragraph. Think about what main idea the details support.

Traders and other travelers in ancient China moved across deserts and through mountain passes. Sometimes the traders used horses or camels to carry goods they wanted to trade. Traders took goods such as tea, silk, sugar, and salt from China to faraway places. They traded, or exchanged, those goods for other goods they wanted. Many traders carried medicines, gold, and silver back to China.

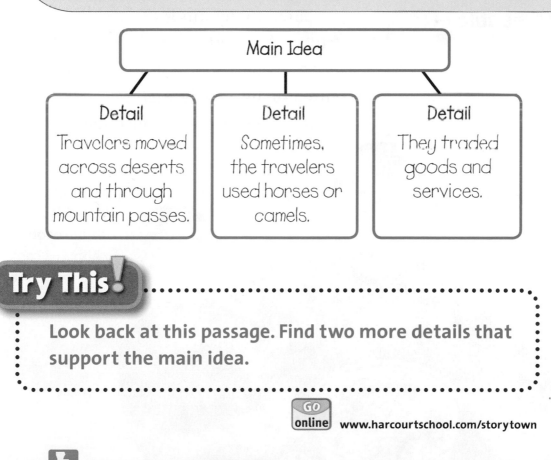

Main Idea

Detail	Detail	Detail
Travelers moved across deserts and through mountain passes.	Sometimes, the travelers used horses or camels.	They traded goods and services.

Try This!

Look back at this passage. Find two more details that support the main idea.

www.harcourtschool.com/storytown

Vocabulary

Build Robust Vocabulary

- generous
- banquet
- gaze
- agreeable
- curiosity
- famine

Foods of China

Long ago, emperors ruled China. An emperor lived in a palace. Every day more than two thousand workers prepared **generous** meals for the emperor. For each **banquet**, the cooks prepared many kinds of cereals, meats, fruit and desserts. The cooks could only **gaze** at the wonderful foods. Only the emperor, his family, members of the court, and special visitors could eat them.

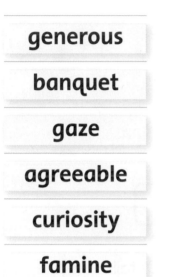

The emperor wanted food that was **agreeable** to him. His cooks chose and tasted his food.

For hundreds of years, the people of China grew or hunted for all the food they needed. In time, some Chinese people traveled to other countries. They found new foods that were a **curiosity** to them. They carried these interesting new foods back to China. Corn, hot peppers, and potatoes soon became important to Chinese cooking.

Today, many Chinese people live in other countries. They share their delicious cooking with others.

People knew which wild plants to eat during a **famine**.

GO online www.harcourtschool.com/storytown

Word Detective

Your mission this week is to look for the Vocabulary Words in folktales from China or other countries. Each time you read a Vocabulary Word, write it in your vocabulary journal. Don't forget to tell where you found the word.

3ELA-6-E3-16

Genre Study

A **folktale** is a story passed down through time by word of mouth. Look for

- events that repeat.
- story details that come together to teach a lesson.

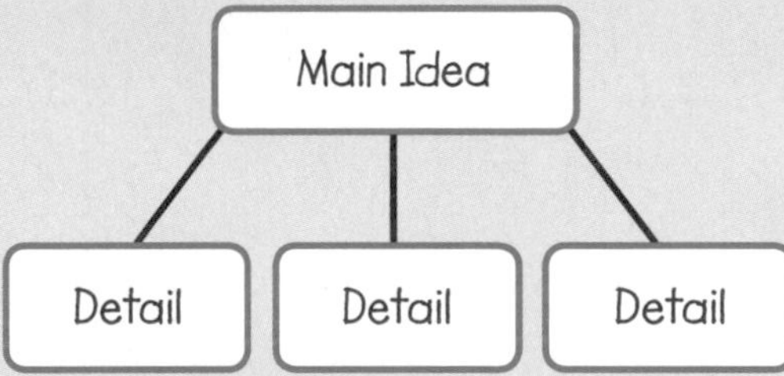

3ELA-1-E5-10
3ELA-7-E1-17

Comprehension Strategy

Focus Strategy

Summarize, or review, the main events in a story to help you think about the important parts of the story.

LOUISIANA GRADE-LEVEL EXPECTATIONS—3ELA-1-E5-10 summarize main events/ideas/details; **3ELA-6-E3-16** define characteristics of types of literature; **3ELA-7-E1-17** demonstrate understanding of information

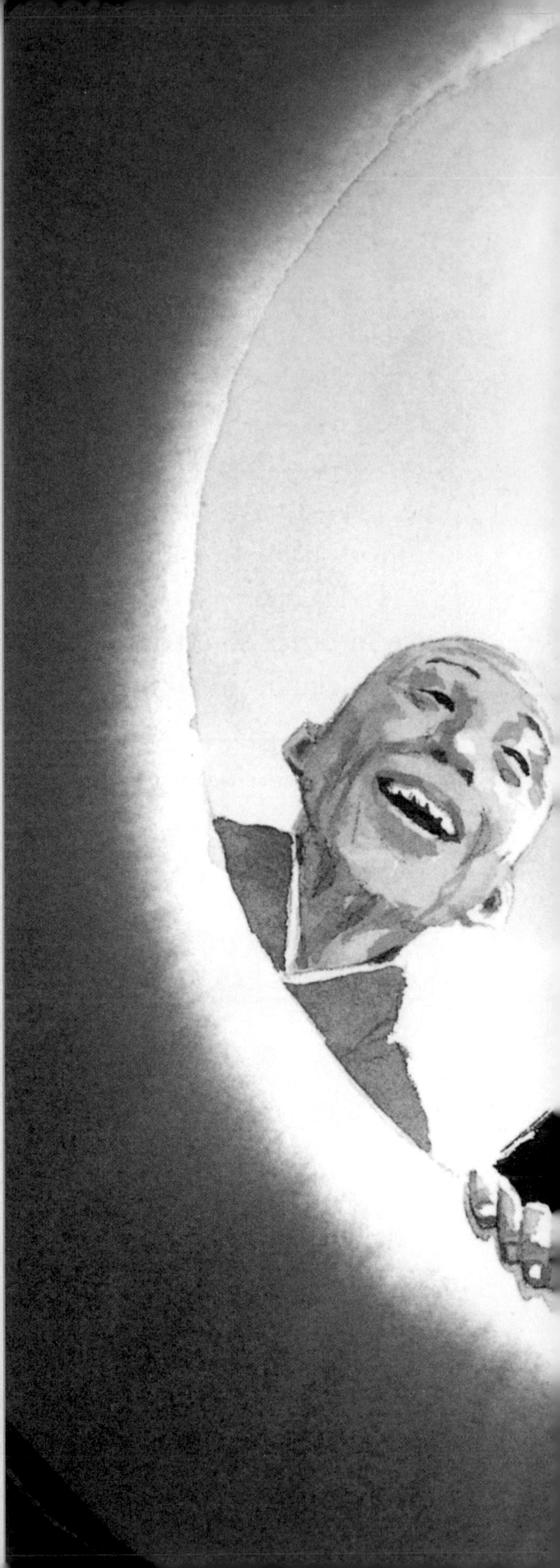

Stone Soup

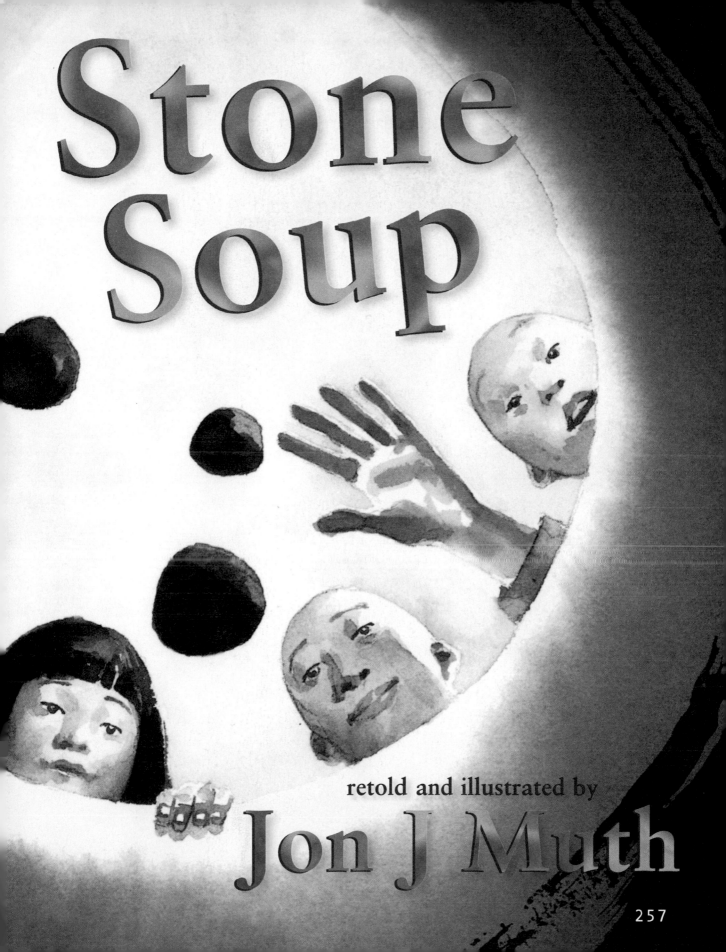

retold and illustrated by

Jon J Muth

Three monks, Hok, Lok, and Siew, traveled along a mountain road. They talked about cat whiskers, the color of the sun, and giving.

"What makes one happy, Siew?" asked Hok, the youngest monk.

Old Siew, who was the wisest, said, "Let's find out."

The sound of a bell brought their gaze to the rooftops of a village below. They could not see from so high above that the village had been through many hard times. Famine, floods, and war had made the villagers weary and untrusting of strangers. They had even become suspicious of their neighbors.

The villagers worked hard, but only for themselves.

There was a farmer.

A tea merchant.

A scholar.

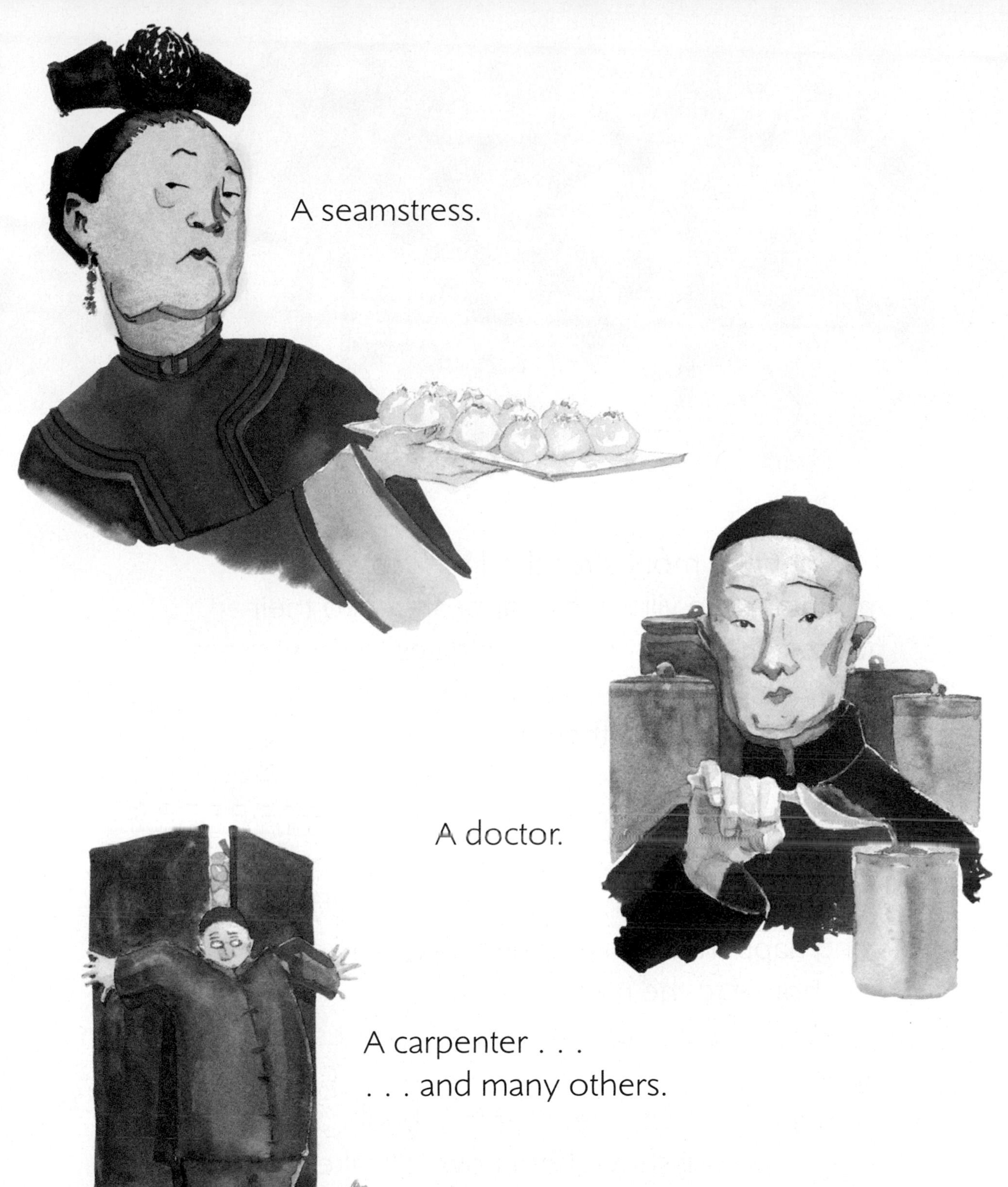

A seamstress.

A doctor.

A carpenter . . .
. . . and many others.

But they had little to do with one another.

When the monks reached the foot of the mountain, the villagers disappeared into their houses. No one came to the gates to greet them.

And when the people saw them enter the village, they closed their windows tight.

The monks knocked on the door of the first house. There was no answer. Then the house went dark.

They knocked on a second door and the same thing happened. It happened again and again, from one house to the next.

"These people do not know happiness," they all agreed.

"But today," said Siew, his face bright as the moon, "we will show them how to make stone soup."

They gathered twigs and branches and made a fire.

They placed a small tin pot on top and filled it with water from the village well.

A brave little girl who had been watching came to them. "What are you doing?" she asked.

"We are gathering twigs," said Lok.

"We are making a fire," said Hok.

"We are making stone soup and we need three round, smooth stones," said Siew.

The little girl helped the monks look around the courtyard until they found just the right ones. Then they put them in the water to cook.

"These stones will make excellent soup," said Siew. "But this very small pot won't make much, I'm afraid."

"My mother has a bigger pot," said the girl.

The little girl ran home. As she started to take a pot, her mother asked what she was doing.

"The three strangers are making soup from stones," she said. "They need our biggest pot."

"Hmm," said the girl's mother. "Stones are easy to come by. I'd like to learn how to do that!"

The monks poked the coals. As smoke drifted up, the neighbors peered out from their windows. The fire and the large pot in the middle of the village were a true curiosity!

One by one, the people of the village came out to see just what this stone soup was.

"Of course, old-style stone soup should be well seasoned with salt and pepper," said Hok.

"That is true," said Lok as he stirred the giant pot filled with water and stones. "But we have none. . ."

"I have some salt and pepper!" said the scholar, his eyes big with curiosity. He disappeared and came back with salt and pepper and even a few other spices.

Siew took a taste. "The last time we had soup stones of this size and color, carrots made the broth very sweet."

"Carrots?" said a woman from the back. "I may have a few carrots! But just a few." And off she ran. She returned with as many carrots as she could carry and dropped them into the pot.

"Do you think it would be better with onions?" asked Hok.

"Oh, yes, maybe an onion would taste good," said a farmer, and he hurried off. He returned in a moment with five big onions, and he dropped them into the bubbling soup.

"Now, that's a fine soup!" he said.

The villagers all nodded their heads, as the smell was very agreeable.

"But if only we had some mushrooms," said Siew, rubbing his chin.

Several villagers licked their lips. A few dashed away and returned with fresh mushrooms, noodles, pea pods, and cabbages.

Something magical began to happen among the villagers. As each person opened his or her heart to give, the next person gave even more. And as this happened, the soup grew richer and smelled more delicious.

"I imagine the Emperor would suggest we add dumplings!" said one villager.

"And bean curd!" said another.

"What about cloud ear and mung beans and yams?" cried some others.

"And taro root and winter melon and baby corn!" cried other villagers.

"Garlic!" "Ginger root!" "Soy sauce!" "Lily buds!"

"I have some! I have some!" people cried out. And off they ran, returning with all they could carry.

The monks stirred and the pot bubbled. How good it smelled! How good it would taste! How giving the villagers had become!

At last, the soup was ready. The villagers gathered together. They brought rice and steamed buns. They brought lychee nuts and sweet cakes. They brought tea to drink, and they lit lanterns. Everyone sat down to eat. They had not been together for a feast like this for as long as anyone could remember.

After the banquet, they told stories, sang songs, and celebrated long into the night.

Then they unlocked their doors and took the monks into their homes and gave them very comfortable places to sleep.

In the gentle spring morning, everyone gathered together near the willows to say farewell.

"Thank you for having us as your guests," said the monks. "You have been most generous."

"Thank you," said the villagers. "With the gifts you have given, we will always have plenty. You have shown us that sharing makes us all richer."

"And to think," said the monks, "to be happy is as simple as making stone soup."

Think Critically

❶ What is the main idea of the story "Stone Soup"? MAIN IDEA

❷ What happens to the villagers at the feast?
IMPORTANT DETAILS

❸ Do you think that the change in the way the villagers act will continue? Explain.
EXPRESS PERSONAL OPINIONS

❹ How can you tell that the author believes the monks brought a good change to the village?
DRAW CONCLUSIONS

❺ **WRITE** Why do the monks show the villagers how to make stone soup? Explain what happens as a result. SHORT RESPONSE

LOUISIANA GRADE-LEVEL EXPECTATIONS—**3ELA-1-E5-10** summarize main events/ideas/details; **3ELA-1-E6-11** connect to prior knowledge; **3ELA-7-E1-17(b)** make predictions; **3ELA-7-E1-17(c)** make inferences/draw conclusions; **3ELA-7-E1-17(f)** identify main ideas; **3ELA-7-E3-20** explain author's viewpoint; **3ELA-2-E6-27** write for various purposes

Meet the Author and Illustrator

Jon J Muth

Jon J Muth illustrated comic books for many years. After his son was born, he began to write and illustrate books for children.

Jon J Muth likes creating books based on fables and folktales. *Stone Soup* is based on a story from Europe. He rewrote it and illustrated it so that it takes place in China. Monks, like those in *Stone Soup*, are often characters in Chinese folktales.

Sometimes Jon J Muth uses his children as models for illustrations of characters in his books. By the way, the "J" in his name doesn't stand for Jamal, or Jake, or Jason, or any name at all.

www.harcourtschool.com/storytown

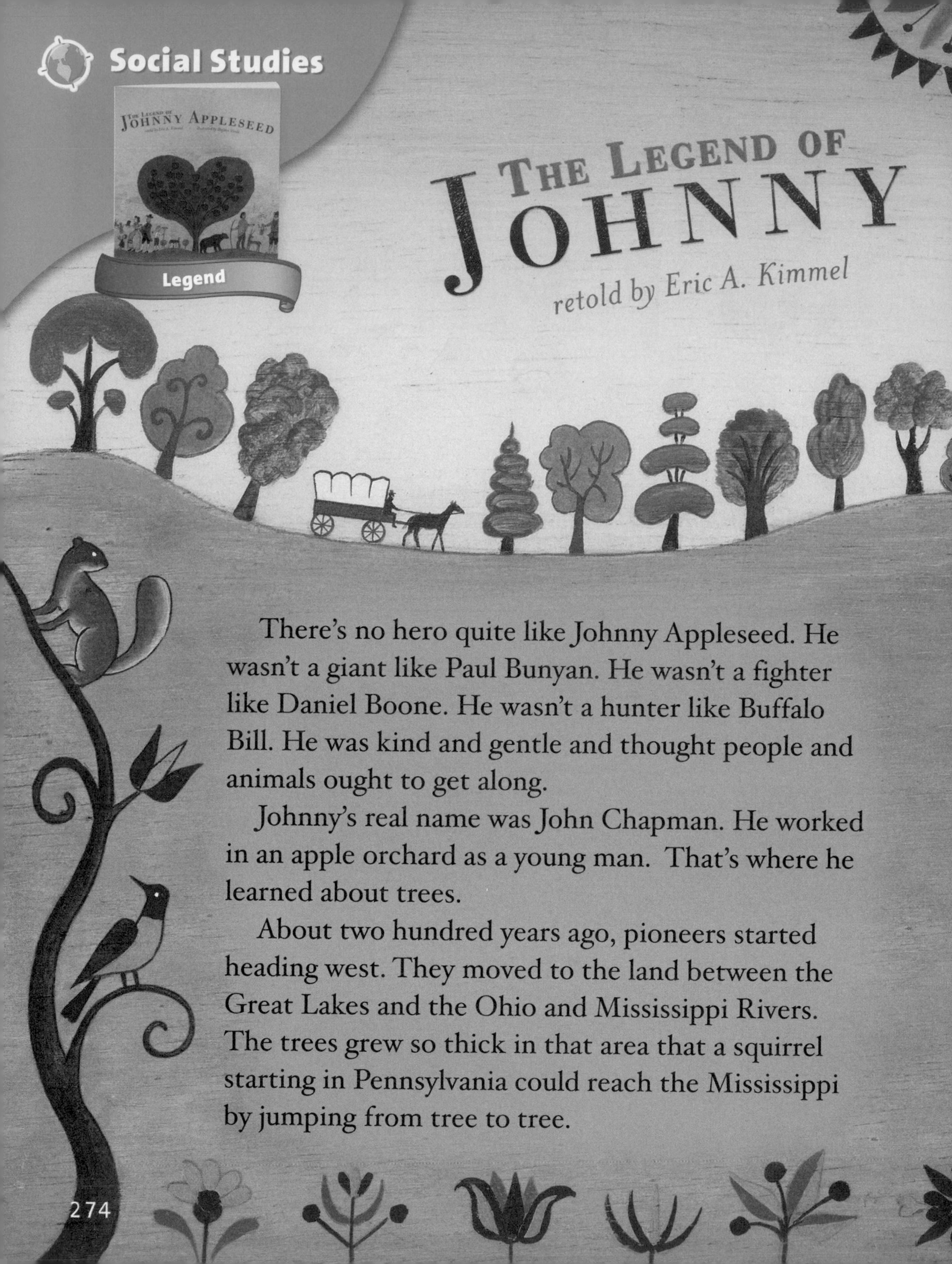

THE LEGEND OF JOHNNY

retold by Eric A. Kimmel

There's no hero quite like Johnny Appleseed. He wasn't a giant like Paul Bunyan. He wasn't a fighter like Daniel Boone. He wasn't a hunter like Buffalo Bill. He was kind and gentle and thought people and animals ought to get along.

Johnny's real name was John Chapman. He worked in an apple orchard as a young man. That's where he learned about trees.

About two hundred years ago, pioneers started heading west. They moved to the land between the Great Lakes and the Ohio and Mississippi Rivers. The trees grew so thick in that area that a squirrel starting in Pennsylvania could reach the Mississippi by jumping from tree to tree.

APPLESEED

illustrated by Stefano Vitale

Johnny was one of the first pioneers to arrive in that area. While some people thought about getting rich, Johnny thought about the families who would soon be coming. They would need apples. Apples were good to eat. They could be pressed to make apple juice and cider. They could be stored over the winter. But although there were plenty of trees in the new territory, not one grew apples.

Johnny decided to change that. He went back to the big cider presses in Pennsylvania. There, he found plenty of leftover seeds from cider apples. Johnny picked out the best seeds and carried them west. He planted them in forest clearings. He watered the seedlings to help them grow.

The settlers wanted to buy Johnny's young trees. Johnny sold his saplings for whatever people could pay. An old hat, a shirt, or a pair of moccasins would do. If people had nothing to trade, he gave them saplings anyway. He wanted them to have apples.

Sometimes Johnny would take a sack of apple seeds and visit faraway cabins. He showed people how to plant the seeds and grow apple trees. Folks started calling him Johnny Appleseed.

Johnny was a strange sight. He walked barefoot, wearing an old shirt or even a sack, with a tin pot on his head for a hat. Everybody seemed to love him anyway.

Johnny often stayed with different families as he traveled. In the evening he told the families stories about his travels. Johnny Appleseed was welcome everywhere.

The Native Americans welcomed Johnny, too. They knew that this strange man was their friend. So did the animals. One winter night, as the story goes, Johnny got caught in a snowstorm. He stayed in a hollow tree with a mother bear and her cub. The bears kept Johnny warm through the long, cold night.

Johnny Appleseed was more than 70 years old when he died. He had planted thousands of apple trees. Seeds from Johnny's trees were carried farther west over the Oregon Trail. An apple you eat today may come from a tree descended from one that Johnny planted.

John Chapman, or Johnny Appleseed, left his mark on our country. Whenever we show kindness or give freely to others, we are walking in his footsteps.

Connections

Comparing Texts

3ELA-7-E1-17
3ELA-7-E1-17(d)
3ELA-7-E4-21(e)

1. How are Johnny Appleseed and the monks in "Stone Soup" alike? How are they different?

2. Would you like to go to a banquet similar to the one in "Stone Soup"? Why or why not?

3. What did you learn about living in a community from "Stone Soup"?

Vocabulary Review

3ELA-1-E1-06(b)

Rate a Situation

Work with a partner. Read aloud each sentence and point to the spot on the word line that shows how you would feel. Discuss your answers.

happy ———————————— sad

- Your friend was **generous** with his snack.
- You are invited to a **banquet**.
- You received a gift that was a **curiosity** to you.

generous
banquet
gaze
agreeable
curiosity
famine

Fluency Practice 3ELA-1-E3-07

Readers' Theater

Meet with a group to prepare a Readers' Theater. Choose a section of "Stone Soup" to read. Each student should read the part of a character or the narrator. Speak clearly, pausing at commas and end marks.

Writing 3ELA-2-E4-25

Write a How-To Paragraph

Write a paragraph that tells how to make stone soup. Tell the main idea first. Then add details that tell more about the main idea. Use a main idea and details chart to help you plan.

My Writing Checklist

Writing Trait → Word Choice

- ✔ **I give details that support the main idea.**
- ✔ **I choose words that clearly describe the details.**

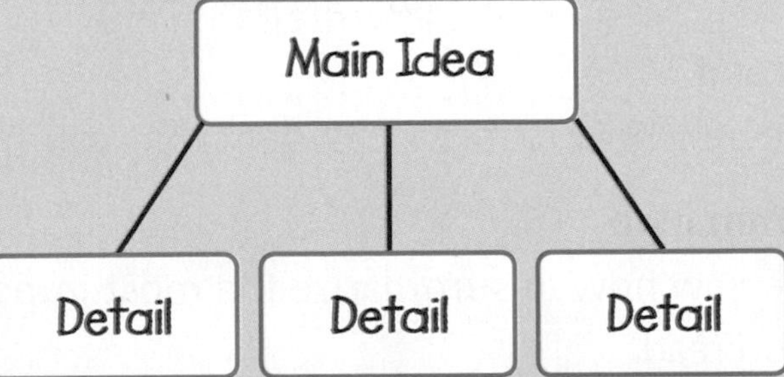

LOUISIANA GRADE-LEVEL EXPECTATIONS—3ELA-1-E1-06(b) use context clues; 3ELA-1-E3-07 adjust reading speed; 3ELA-7-E1-17 demonstrate understanding of information; 3ELA-7-E1-17(d) compare/contrast; 3ELA-7-E4-21(e) connect to real-life situations; 3ELA-2-E4-25 write paragraphs with description/narration

CONTENTS

READERS' THEATER

COMPREHENSION STRATEGIES
Review

Lesson 10

Theme Review and Vocabulary Builder

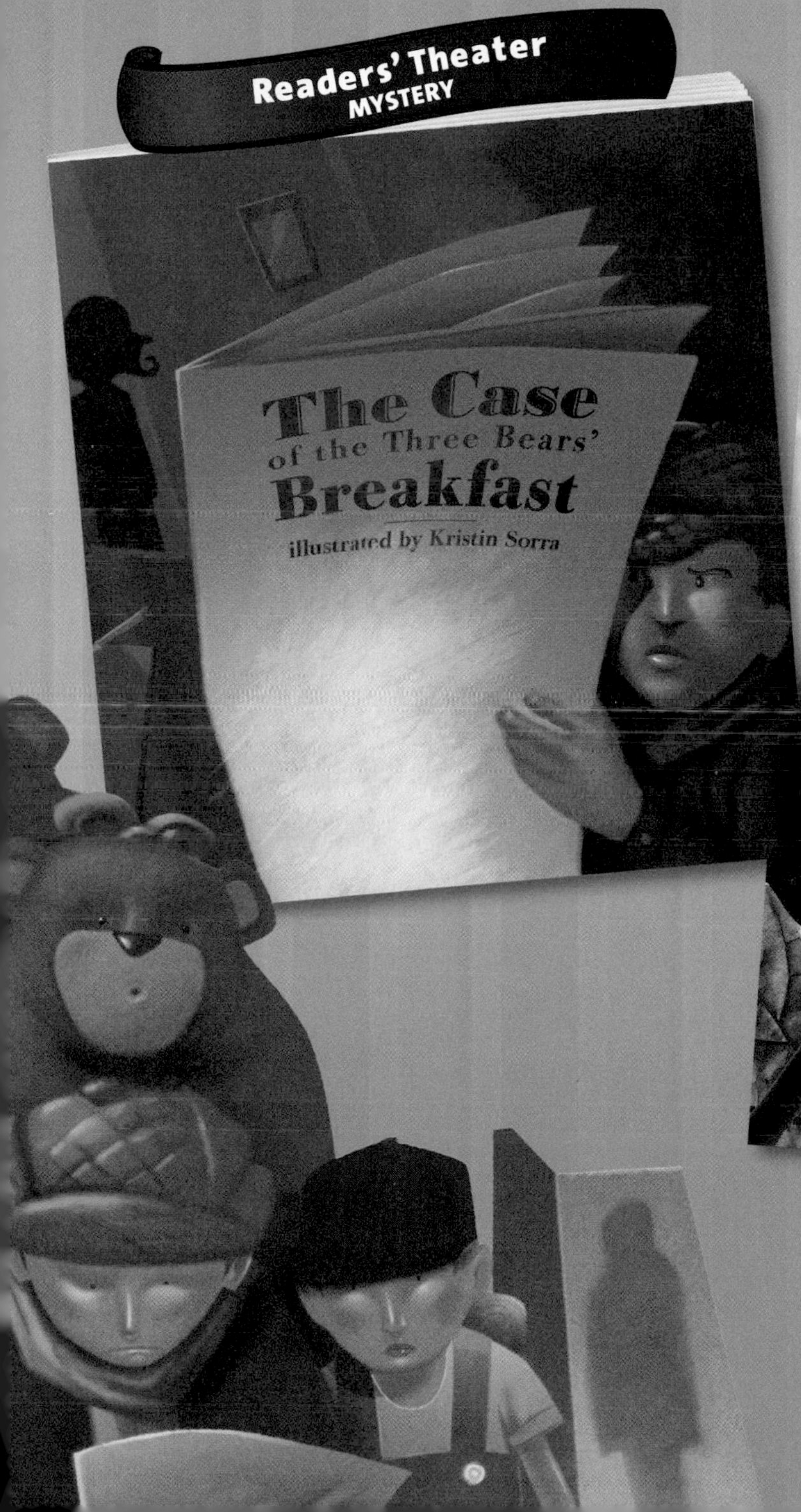

Readers' Theater
MYSTERY

The Case of the Three Bears' Breakfast
illustrated by Kristin Sorra

Content-Area Reading
SCIENCE TEXTBOOK

YOUR Science TEXTBOOK

READERS' THEATER

investigate

expert

laboratory

various

suspect

confess

3ELA-1-E3-07 Reading for Fluency

When you read a script aloud,

- group words that go together to read naturally.
- use punctuation to help you read your character's lines with expression.

Characters
Cam
Sam
Mama Bear
Papa Bear
Junior Bear
Professor
Bananas Bennett

LOUISIANA GRADE-LEVEL EXPECTATIONS—3ELA-1-E3-07
adjust reading speed

The Case of the Three Bears' Breakfast

SCENE 1

SETTING: The Cam and Sam Detective Agency

Cam: This certainly is a lazy day. We haven't solved one mystery.

Sam: Who's that knocking so loudly on our door? We'd better investigate.

Cam: Sam! There are three bears at the door. They don't look happy.

Sam: I think this day just got a bit more interesting.

Cam: May I help you?

Mama Bear: We have a mystery that needs to be solved!

Junior Bear: Someone has been sitting in our chairs! Someone has been eating our food!

Cam: Hold on there. Start from the beginning. Tell us everything.

Papa Bear: Earlier today, Mama Bear made her famous banana pancakes. We went out for a morning walk while our breakfast cooled.

Mama Bear: When we got home, the house was a mess!

Junior Bear: Someone had been sitting in our chairs! Someone had been watching a movie on our DVD player!

Sam: It sounds as if you had an intruder. We'd better go to your house and look for clues.

All the Bears: Let's go.

Scene 2

SETTING: The Bears' House

Sam: I see what you mean, Bears. Can you help us look for clues?

Junior Bear: Look at my chair. Someone was sitting in it. It has banana pancake crumbs all over it.

Papa Bear: I'm so embarrassed. Our house isn't usually this messy.

Cam: We're used to this sort of thing. You have a nice house. You can blame the mess on the intruder.

Sam: I found these yellow hairs in the kitchen.

Sam: Strange. This sounds as if we need some help. I'll call Professor Evvie Dense. The professor is an expert at studying clues.

Papa Bear: We'll take all the help we can get.

Cam: What is that delicious scent?

Sam: It smells like bananas and maple syrup.

All the Bears: Mama Bear's famous banana pancakes!

Mama Bear: You can still smell them, but whoever was here ate every last one!

Cam: Oh, look! Here comes the professor now.

Professor: Hello, Cam and Sam. What smells so good in here?

Sam: Some missing pancakes, Professor. These nice folks had an intruder this morning. Thanks for coming.

All the Bears: Hello, Professor.

Fluency Tip

Mama Bear seems upset. How does the exclamation point here help you read the line?

Sam: Professor, here is what seems to have happened. The intruder sat in the Bears' chairs.

Cam: The intruder ate the Bears' food.

Junior Bear: The intruder even watched one of our movies!

Professor: What movie was it?

Junior Bear: *The Banana That Ate Belmont.* It's about a banana that grows so big it falls on top of a whole town!

Mama Bear: The intruder didn't watch the whole movie.

Papa Bear: The movie was stopped just before the end.

Professor: Interesting. Are there other clues?

Cam: We found crumbs and yellow hairs.

Papa Bear: The intruder ate the rest of our bananas, too! No more banana pancakes for us. What are we supposed to eat for breakfast?

Fluency Tip

Pay attention to the different types of punctuation in Papa Bear's speech.

Sam: Don't worry. We'll solve this mystery. The professor will take the yellow hairs to the laboratory.

Mama Bear: Thanks for your help, Professor.

Professor: You're welcome. Good-bye, Cam. Good-bye, Sam. I'll call you when I know more about these hairs.

Sam: So, Cam, let's put together the various clues.

Cam: We have yellow hairs, banana pancake crumbs, and missing bananas.

Junior Bear: Don't forget the movie, *The Banana That Ate Belmont.*

Sam: Right. I see a pattern here. I think we need to talk to Bananas Bennett.

All the Bears: Who is Bananas Bennett?

Sam: The biggest banana fan in the world. He lives in a banana-shaped house. I'm sure you've seen it. It's down the street. It's quite a curiosity. I suspect he may know something about this mystery. Let's go!

SCENE 3

SETTING: Bananas Bennett's House

Cam: Ring the doorbell, Sam.

Sam: He's coming now. Wait! I just saw him flick a crumb off of his sweater. He looks nervous.

Bananas: Who is it? Ahhhh! Bears! Help! Alert the park rangers!

Cam: Relax, Bananas. These bears are your neighbors. We're Detectives Cam and Sam.

Sam: The Bears came to us to help them solve a mystery. They had an intruder at their house this morning. Did you notice anything strange this morning?

Bananas: I was busy all morning. I was watching a movie called *The Banana That Ate Belmont.*

Sam: How does the movie end, Bananas?

Bananas: I don't know. You see, just when the banana in the movie got really big, I had to stop the movie.

Junior Bear: That's where the intruder stopped the movie at our house!

Cam: What happened, Bananas?

Bananas: I had to get some more syrup for my banana pancakes. Oops!

Sam: Hold on. My cell phone is ringing. It's the professor. Hello, Professor.

Professor: Sam, I'm in the lab. The yellow hairs aren't hairs at all. They're pieces of yellow yarn!

Sam: So the intruder was probably wearing a yellow sweater. Thanks, Professor. Good-bye. Well, Bananas, it's time for you to tell the truth. We know the intruder wore a yellow sweater, just like the one you're wearing!

Fluency Tip

Bananas is going to tell the truth here. Group words in phrases to help you read the lines smoothly.

Bananas: Okay, I confess! It was me, but I planned to pay the Bears back. I smelled a delicious banana scent this morning. I followed my nose and it led me to the Bears' house. The door was open. Then I saw that movie I had always wanted to see, and I sat down to watch it. I tried all three chairs. The little one was just right.

Junior Bear: That's my chair!

Bananas: I'm very sorry. Look, I'm making fresh banana pancakes right now. They're for you.

All the Bears: Is that what smells so good?

Papa Bear: We forgive you, Bananas. Just ask us for permission the next time you need something.

Mama Bear: Thanks for your help, Cam and Sam! Would you like to join us for a banquet of banana pancakes?

Cam: That's very generous of you, but I've heard enough about bananas for one day.

Sam: Besides, we have another mystery to solve. I just got a call from Little Red Riding Hood. It seems someone took her basket of blueberry muffins.

Cam: Here we go again!

Reading a Science Textbook 3ELA-5-E6-52

Bridge to Content-Area Reading Science textbooks have special features that help you understand the text you are reading. These features include headings, photos and captions, science vocabulary, and graphic aids such as diagrams. Scan the pages for this information each time you read.

Read the notes above and below the small pages on page 295. How can the features help you read a science lesson?

Review the Focus Strategies

You can also use the strategies you learned in this theme to help you read your science textbook.

Monitor comprehension—Reread 3ELA-7-E1-17

Reread to monitor comprehension and better understand what you have read.

Summarize 3ELA-1-E5-10

Summarize after reading a paragraph, a section of text, or the complete lesson. Do this to help you remember the most important ideas.

As you read "How Living Things Survive" on pages 296–297, think about where and how to use the comprehension strategies.

LOUISIANA GRADE-LEVEL EXPECTATIONS—3ELA-1-E5-10 summarize main events/ideas/details; 3ELA-7-E1-17 demonstrate understanding of information; 3ELA-5-E6-52 locate information in graphic sources

VOCABULARY

Science **vocabulary** words are usually boldfaced. The meaning of each word is given in the sentence. You can also find vocabulary words and definitions in the glossary of your science book.

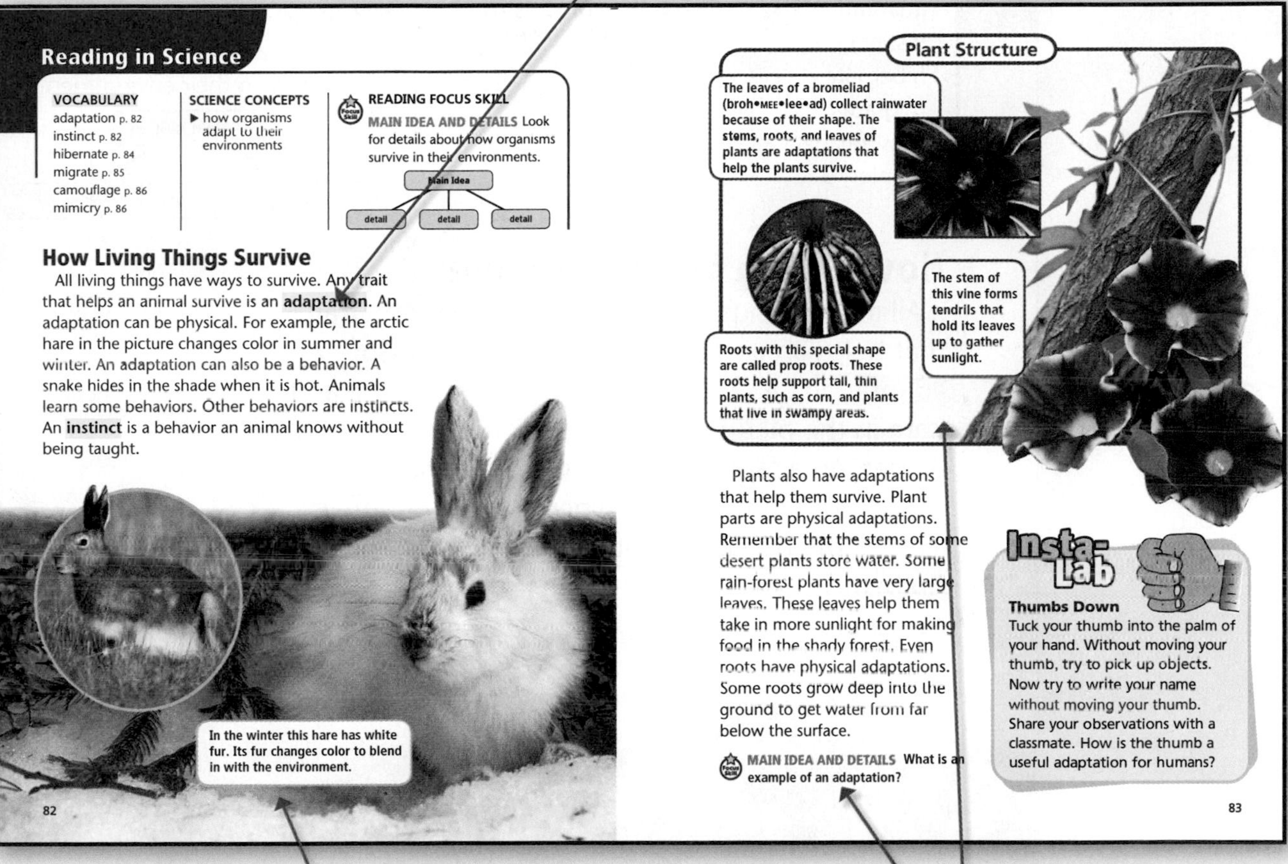

Reading in Science

VOCABULARY
adaptation p. 82
instinct p. 82
hibernate p. 84
migrate p. 85
camouflage p. 86
mimicry p. 86

SCIENCE CONCEPTS
▶ how organisms adapt to their environments

READING FOCUS SKILL
MAIN IDEA AND DETAILS Look for details about how organisms survive in their environments.

Main Idea
detail detail detail

How Living Things Survive

All living things have ways to survive. Any trait that helps an animal survive is an **adaptation**. An adaptation can be physical. For example, the arctic hare in the picture changes color in summer and winter. An adaptation can also be a behavior. A snake hides in the shade when it is hot. Animals learn some behaviors. Other behaviors are instincts. An **instinct** is a behavior an animal knows without being taught.

In the winter this hare has white fur. Its fur changes color to blend in with the environment.

82

Plant Structure

The leaves of a bromeliad (broh•MEE•lee•ad) collect rainwater because of their shape. The stems, roots, and leaves of plants are adaptations that help the plants survive.

Roots with this special shape are called prop roots. These roots help support tall, thin plants, such as corn, and plants that live in swampy areas.

The stem of this vine forms tendrils that hold its leaves up to gather sunlight.

Plants also have adaptations that help them survive. Plant parts are physical adaptations. Remember that the stems of some desert plants store water. Some rain-forest plants have very large leaves. These leaves help them take in more sunlight for making food in the shady forest. Even roots have physical adaptations. Some roots grow deep into the ground to get water from far below the surface.

MAIN IDEA AND DETAILS What is an example of an adaptation?

Insta-Lab

Thumbs Down

Tuck your thumb into the palm of your hand. Without moving your thumb, try to pick up objects. Now try to write your name without moving your thumb. Share your observations with a classmate. How is the thumb a useful adaptation for humans?

83

CAPTIONS

Captions give more information about what is shown in photographs.

GRAPHIC AIDS AND QUESTIONS

Special features may include **graphic aids,** such as diagrams—and questions at the ends of sections to help you summarize.

Apply the Strategies Read these pages from a science textbook. As you read, stop and think about how you are using comprehension strategies.

Reading in Science

VOCABULARY
adaptation p. 82
instinct p. 82
hibernate p. 84
migrate p. 85
camouflage p. 86
mimicry p. 86

SCIENCE CONCEPTS
▶ how organisms adapt to their environments

READING FOCUS SKILL
MAIN IDEA AND DETAILS Look for details about how organisms survive in their environments.

How Living Things Survive

All living things have ways to survive. Any trait that helps an animal survive is an **adaptation**. An adaptation can be physical. For example, the arctic hare in the picture changes color in summer and winter. An adaptation can also be a behavior. A snake hides in the shade when it is hot. Animals learn some behaviors. Other behaviors are instincts. An **instinct** is a behavior an animal knows without being taught.

In the winter this hare has white fur. Its fur changes color to blend in with the environment.

82

Stop and Think

How does rereading help you understand something? Why is it helpful to summarize?

Plant Structure

The leaves of a bromeliad (broh•MEE•lee•ad) collect rainwater because of their shape. The stems, roots, and leaves of plants are adaptations that help the plants survive.

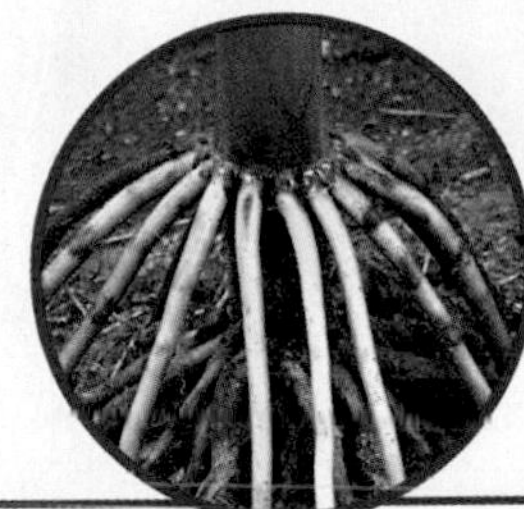

Roots with this special shape are called prop roots. These roots help support tall, thin plants, such as corn, and plants that live in swampy areas.

The stem of this vine forms tendrils that hold its leaves up to gather sunlight.

Plants also have adaptations that help them survive. Plant parts are physical adaptations. Remember that the stems of some desert plants store water. Some rain-forest plants have very large leaves. These leaves help them take in more sunlight for making food in the shady forest. Even roots have physical adaptations. Some roots grow deep into the ground to get water from far below the surface.

MAIN IDEA AND DETAILS **What is an example of an adaptation?**

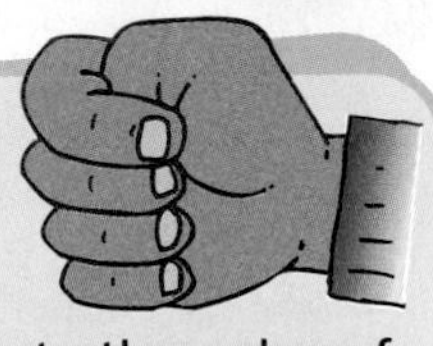

Thumbs Down

Tuck your thumb into the palm of your hand. Without moving your thumb, try to pick up objects. Now try to write your name without moving your thumb. Share your observations with a classmate. How is the thumb a useful adaptation for humans?

LOUISIANA GRADE-LEVEL EXPECTATIONS—
3ELA-1-E5-10 summarize main events/ideas/details; 3ELA-7-E1-17 demonstrate understanding of information

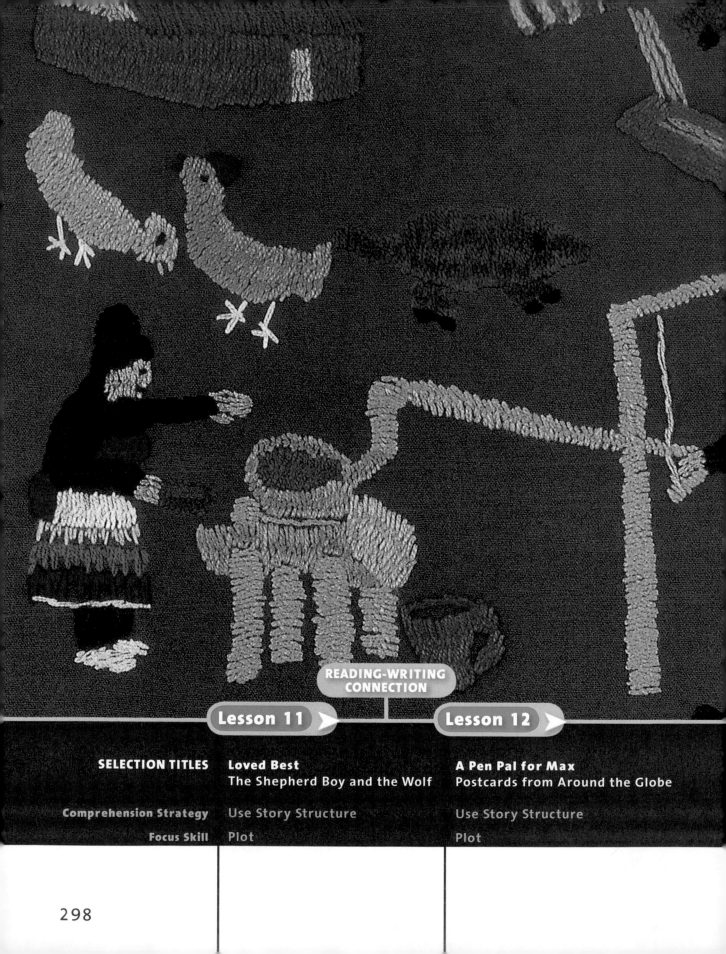

READING-WRITING CONNECTION

	Lesson 11	Lesson 12
SELECTION TITLES	**Loved Best** The Shepherd Boy and the Wolf	**A Pen Pal for Max** Postcards from Around the Globe
Comprehension Strategy	Use Story Structure	Use Story Structure
Focus Skill	Plot	Plot

Theme 3 As We Grow

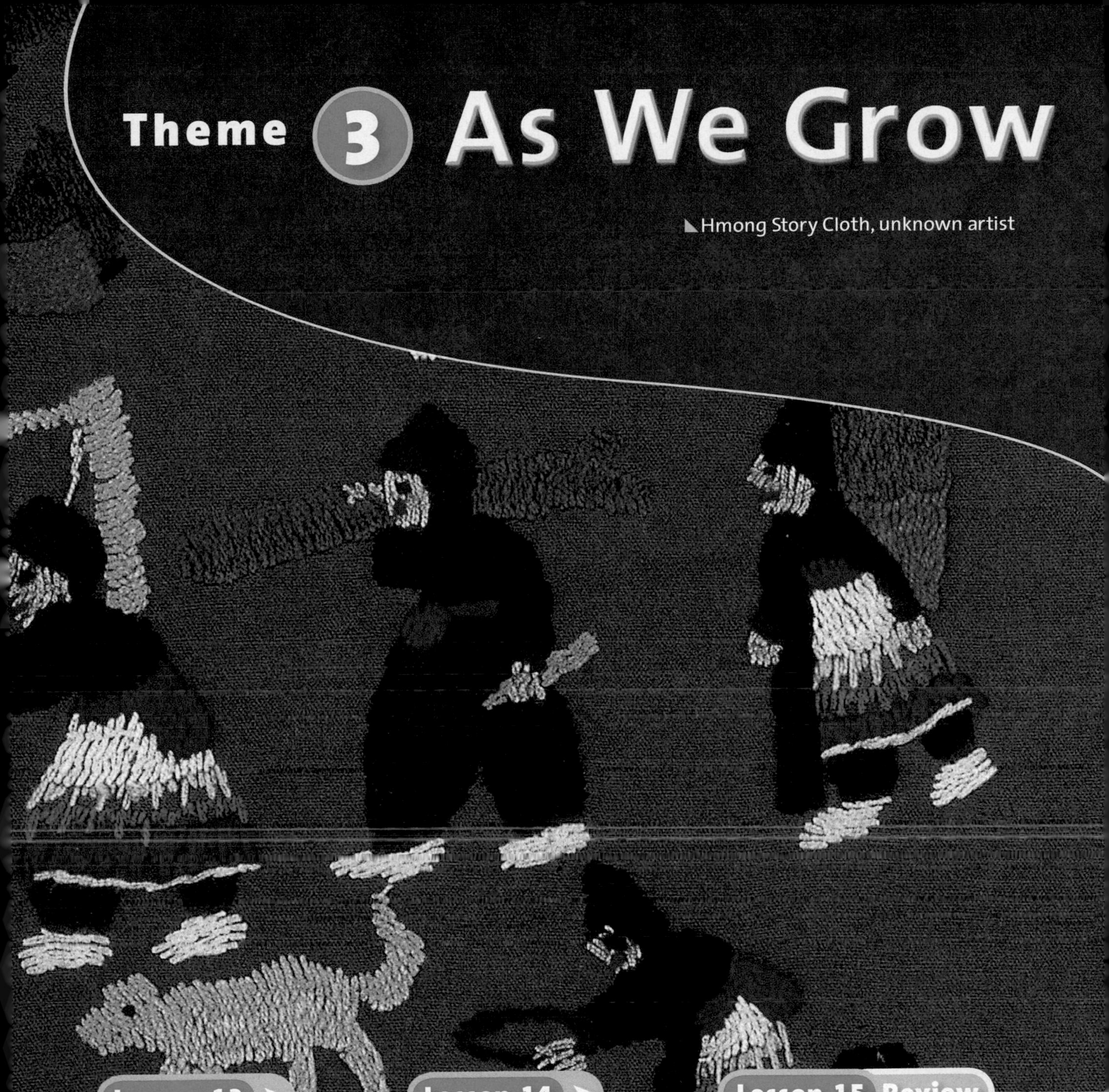

Hmong Story Cloth, unknown artist

Lesson 13

A Tree Is Growing
Ancient Trees Survive in California's Mountains

Ask Questions

Author's Purpose

Lesson 14

One Small Place in a Tree
Be a Birdwatcher

Ask Questions

Author's Purpose

Lesson 15 Review

Ask the Experts
Iris and Walter, True Friends

Review Skills and Strategies

CONTENTS

Lesson 11

Genre: Realistic Fiction
Loved Best
By Patricia C. McKissack illustrated by Yvonne Buchanan
The Shepherd Boy and the Wolf
RETOLD BY DORIS ORGEL AND
ILLUSTRATED BY DAVID SCOTT MEIER
Genre: Fable

Focus Skill

Plot

Remember that every story has characters, a setting, and a **plot.** The plot is what happens in a story.

The plot presents a problem and tells how the characters solve it.

Identifying the characters, setting, and plot in a story will help you better understand what is happening.

Tip

You can understand the plot by thinking about the order of events. What was the first important thing that happened? What happened next?

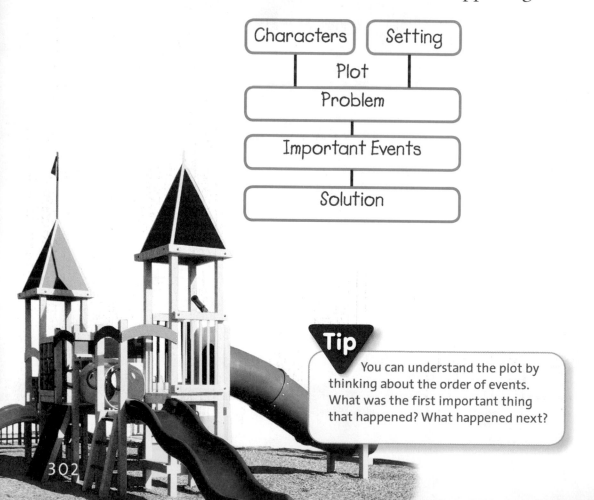

Read the story. Tell how to complete a story map like the one shown.

Lea and Britney wanted to put on a circus. On the playground, they asked Tamika and Nell to be in it. Nell said she would be a clown. Tamika said she would be a juggler. Lea said she would be the ringleader.

"No, I think I'd do a better job," Britney said. They flipped a coin and Britney won.

"You're really good at tumbling, Lea," Britney said. "You can be an acrobat."

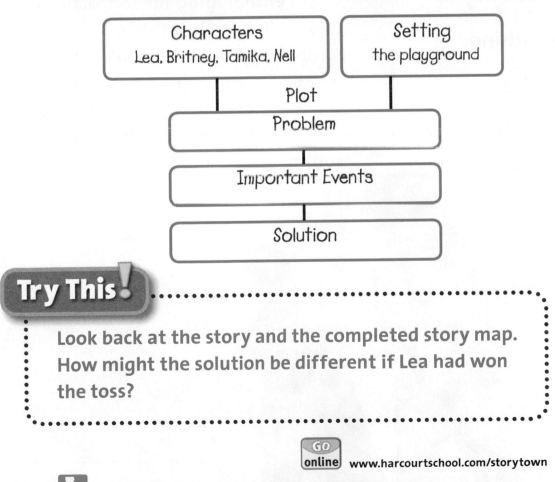

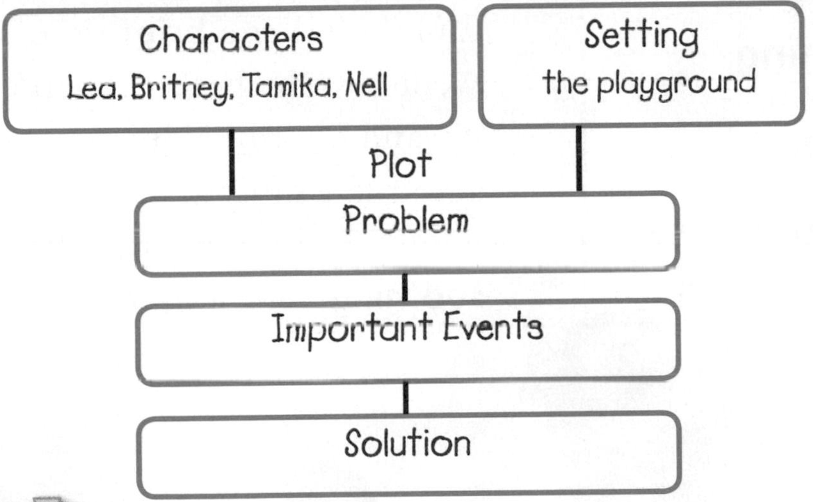

Try This!

Look back at the story and the completed story map. How might the solution be different if Lea had won the toss?

www.harcourtschool.com/storytown

Vocabulary

Build Robust Vocabulary

- encouraging
- brief
- chuckling
- soothing
- sobbed
- praised

Jacob's Journal

Monday, November 3

In the afternoon, I went to the playground with Gary, my big brother. We raced to the basketball court. Gary began **encouraging** me to practice my foul shots. For a **brief** time, all my shots went into the basket. Then Vince showed up, and I got nervous. He saw me miss about five shots in a row. I got upset when I heard him **chuckling**, but Gary's **soothing** voice told me to ignore him.

Friday, November 7

Today I entered the big foul-shot contest at the playground. All the kids stood in line on the basketball court. Vince took his shot before me. It went in! The crowd cheered. I was next. I shot the ball. It went up in an arc, but it bounced off the rim. I almost **sobbed**. I saw my brother, Gary, in the crowd. He **praised** me anyway. "Great try!" he called. That made me feel better.

www.harcourtschool.com/storytown

Word Champion

Your mission this week is to use Vocabulary Words in conversation with your friends and family. You may want to tell your friends about a time when you were praised for doing a good job. Each day write in your vocabulary journal the sentences you spoke that had the Vocabulary Words.

LOUISIANA GRADE-LEVEL EXPECTATIONS—3ELA-2-E6-27 write for various purposes

3ELA-6-E3-16

Genre Study

Realistic fiction has characters and events that are like people and events in real life. Look for

- characters who behave as real people might.
- problems that are similar to problems in real life.

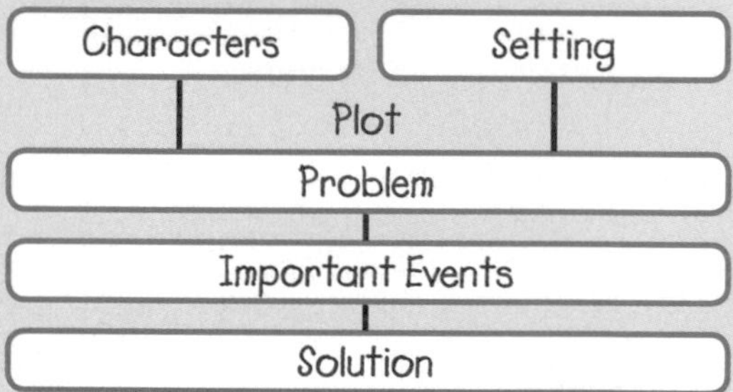

3ELA-7-E1-17

Comprehension Strategy

Use Story Structure to help you understand the problem and the solution of the problem.

LOUISIANA GRADE-LEVEL EXPECTATIONS—3ELA-6-E3-16 define characteristics of types of literature; 3ELA-7-E1-17 demonstrate understanding of information

Loved Best

BY PATRICIA C. McKISSACK
ILLUSTRATED BY YVONNE BUCHANAN

Carolyn thinks that her parents should love her the best of all their children. After all, she has been around longer than her younger brother and sister, Josh and Dana! Recently, she has not been so sure that they do.

All three children have parts in a community play. Carolyn will recite a poem about a river. Mrs. Lasiter, the play director, has praised *Carolyn for reciting her poem perfectly. Carolyn is sure that her performance will be better than Josh's bird or Dana's sunflower. When her parents see how wonderful she is, they will once more love her best.*

On the evening of the program, everybody began arriving at the community center. The room was fully decorated like a bright spring day. Bees were buzzing, birds were chirping, and rabbits were hopping about. Then it was show time. "Break a leg, everybody," whispered Mrs. Lasiter nervously.

The audience sang the "Star-Spangled Banner" way off-key. Somebody else gave a welcome. And the play began.

The first scene up was performed by Dana's age group. The sunflower garden.

Dana and all ten of the little three- through five-year-old sunflowers followed the six-year-old sun across the sky. White fluffy clouds hung from the ceiling, and a carpet of green grass covered the floor.

Carolyn looked from behind the big sheet that served as a curtain. Mama was smiling as she watched little Dana lean toward the sun just as a real flower does.

Daddy was busy taking video, never missing a minute of it. Granddaddy was enjoying himself too. He was snapping pictures, one after the other. *She is cute,* thought Carolyn. *But wait until it's my turn. I'm going to blow them all away.*

When it was Josh's turn Carolyn could see Mama holding her breath, especially when it was time for Josh to sing. He was so good. Not one mistake. Daddy got so involved with listening, he almost forgot to start the camera. In fact Grandmama took over the video so Daddy could concentrate on Josh's performance.

At the end Josh stepped forward and took a bow. Everybody cheered and applauded. Carolyn applauded and yelled out a big, "Yo, bro!" Josh heard her and grinned. He'd never looked happier.

Wait till I do my thing, though, thought Carolyn.

There was a brief intermission while the set was changed. Then it was time for the older children. Carolyn lined up behind Greg Steward, who was the mountain. Debra Miller, who was the valley, and Janet Parson, who was the sky, were behind Carolyn.

Greg finished his poem. Then Carolyn heard her name announced. She stepped onstage like she had at practice many times. But this time, she didn't see the microphone cord and she tripped. People laughed, and that made her nervous.

She looked at the audience. There were so many people in the room. And they were all looking at her. It wasn't like practice, when kids were running around making noise and nobody was paying attention. Now every eye was on her, including Mama's, Daddy's, Granddaddy's, and Grandmama's.

Carolyn searched for the first words of the poem, but she couldn't remember them.

"I am the river," Mrs. Lasiter whispered from offstage. Everybody heard her and they laughed again.

"I . . . am . . . the river," said Carolyn. The microphone squeaked and she jumped. More laughter.

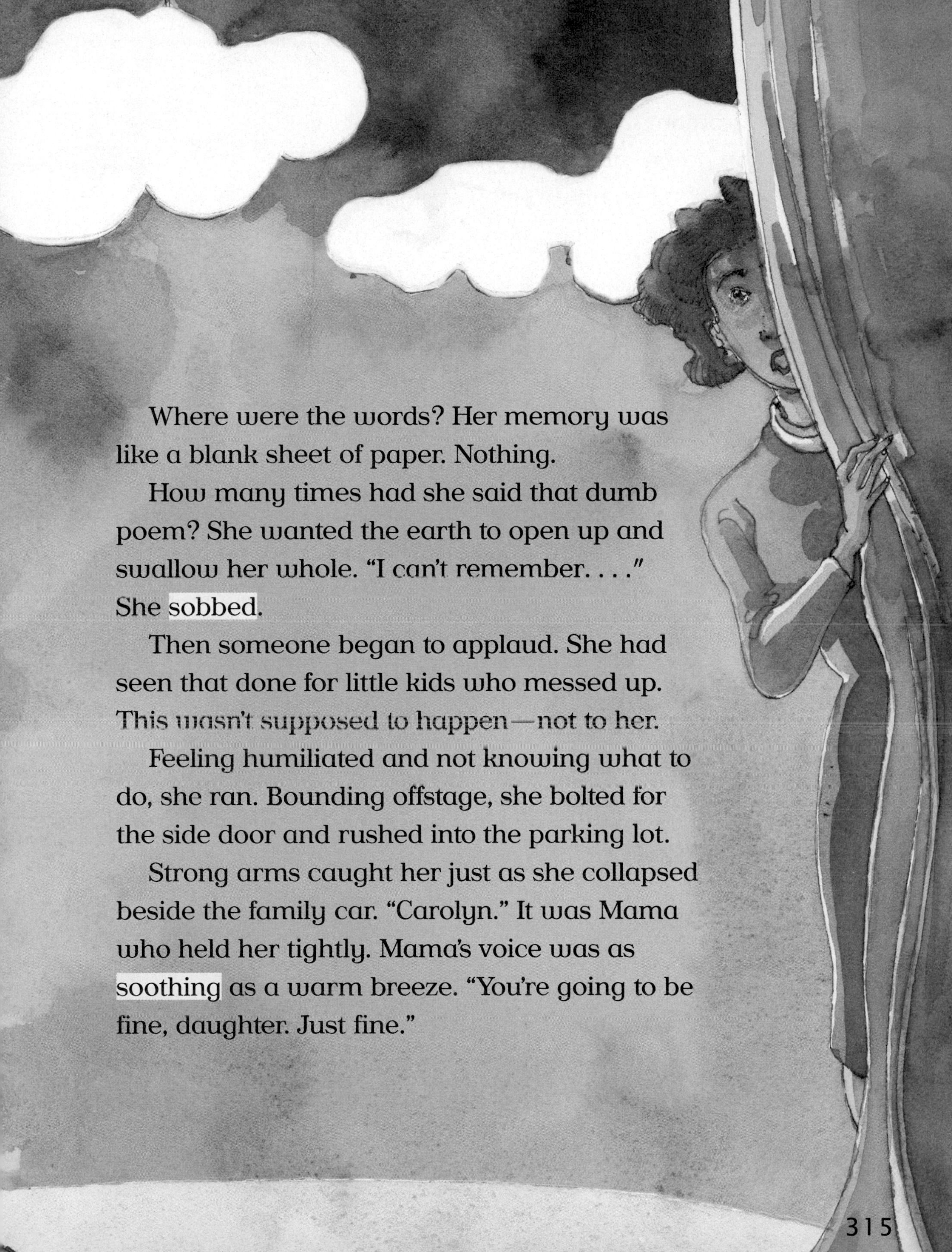

Where were the words? Her memory was like a blank sheet of paper. Nothing.

How many times had she said that dumb poem? She wanted the earth to open up and swallow her whole. "I can't remember. . . ." She sobbed.

Then someone began to applaud. She had seen that done for little kids who messed up. This wasn't supposed to happen—not to her.

Feeling humiliated and not knowing what to do, she ran. Bounding offstage, she bolted for the side door and rushed into the parking lot.

Strong arms caught her just as she collapsed beside the family car. "Carolyn." It was Mama who held her tightly. Mama's voice was as soothing as a warm breeze. "You're going to be fine, daughter. Just fine."

At that moment Carolyn's world seemed over. How do you go on when you've made such a mess of things? She couldn't stop crying. "I know I'm not loved most. But can you still love me at all after messing up?"

Mama sighed. "Where do you get such ideas? You are my daughter, and I love you very much."

Carolyn sniffed. "Just one very."

Mama didn't get it. "Carolyn, why are you so concerned about being loved the most and being the favorite?"

"Well, Janet Parson said she was her mama's favorite."

"For goodness sake, Carolyn! Janet is an only child."

Carolyn shrugged. "Well, I was the only child for four years. So I decided I was your favorite because you'd loved me longest. But then . . ." Carolyn's voice trailed off.

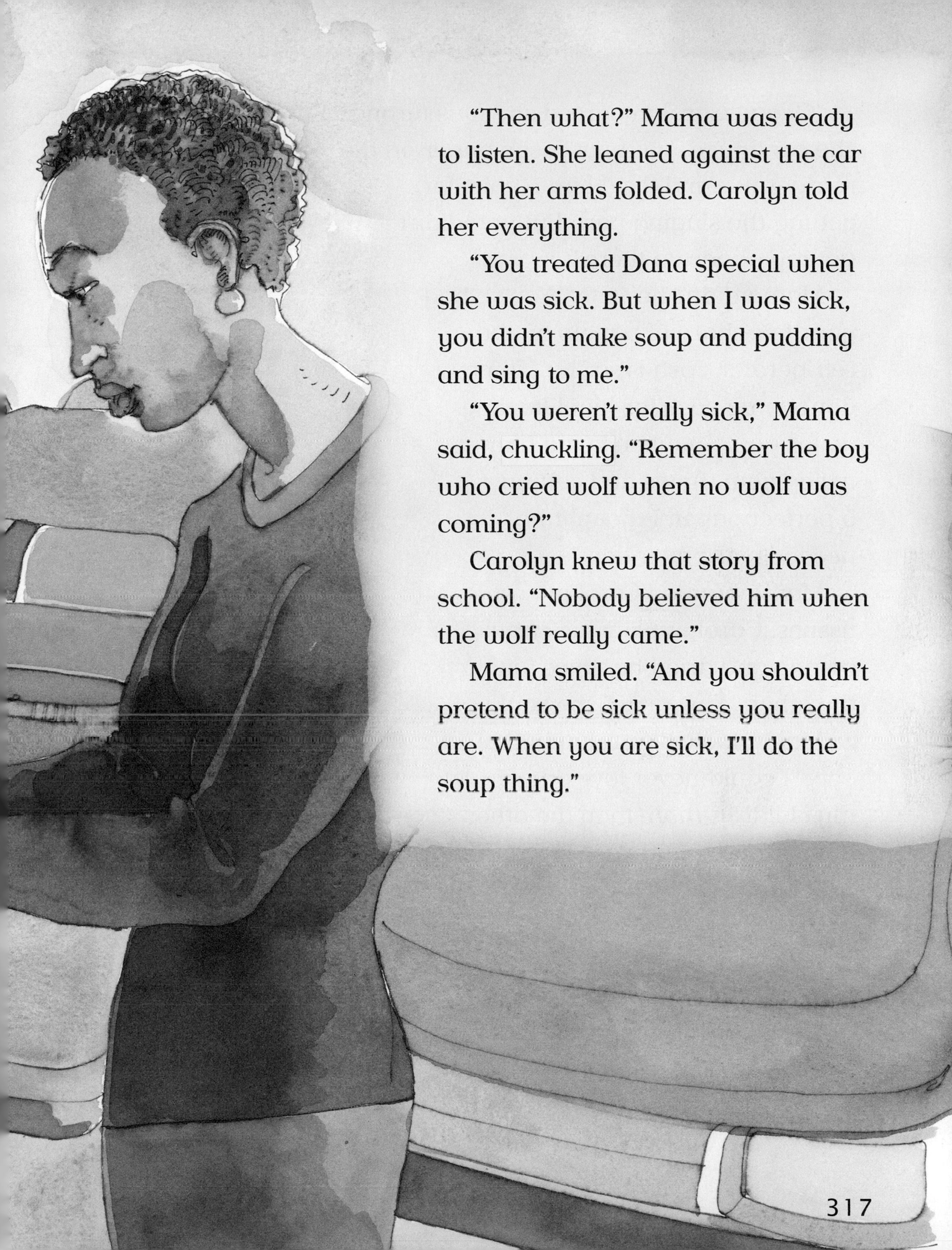

"Then what?" Mama was ready to listen. She leaned against the car with her arms folded. Carolyn told her everything.

"You treated Dana special when she was sick. But when I was sick, you didn't make soup and pudding and sing to me."

"You weren't really sick," Mama said, chuckling. "Remember the boy who cried wolf when no wolf was coming?"

Carolyn knew that story from school. "Nobody believed him when the wolf really came."

Mama smiled. "And you shouldn't pretend to be sick unless you really are. When you are sick, I'll do the soup thing."

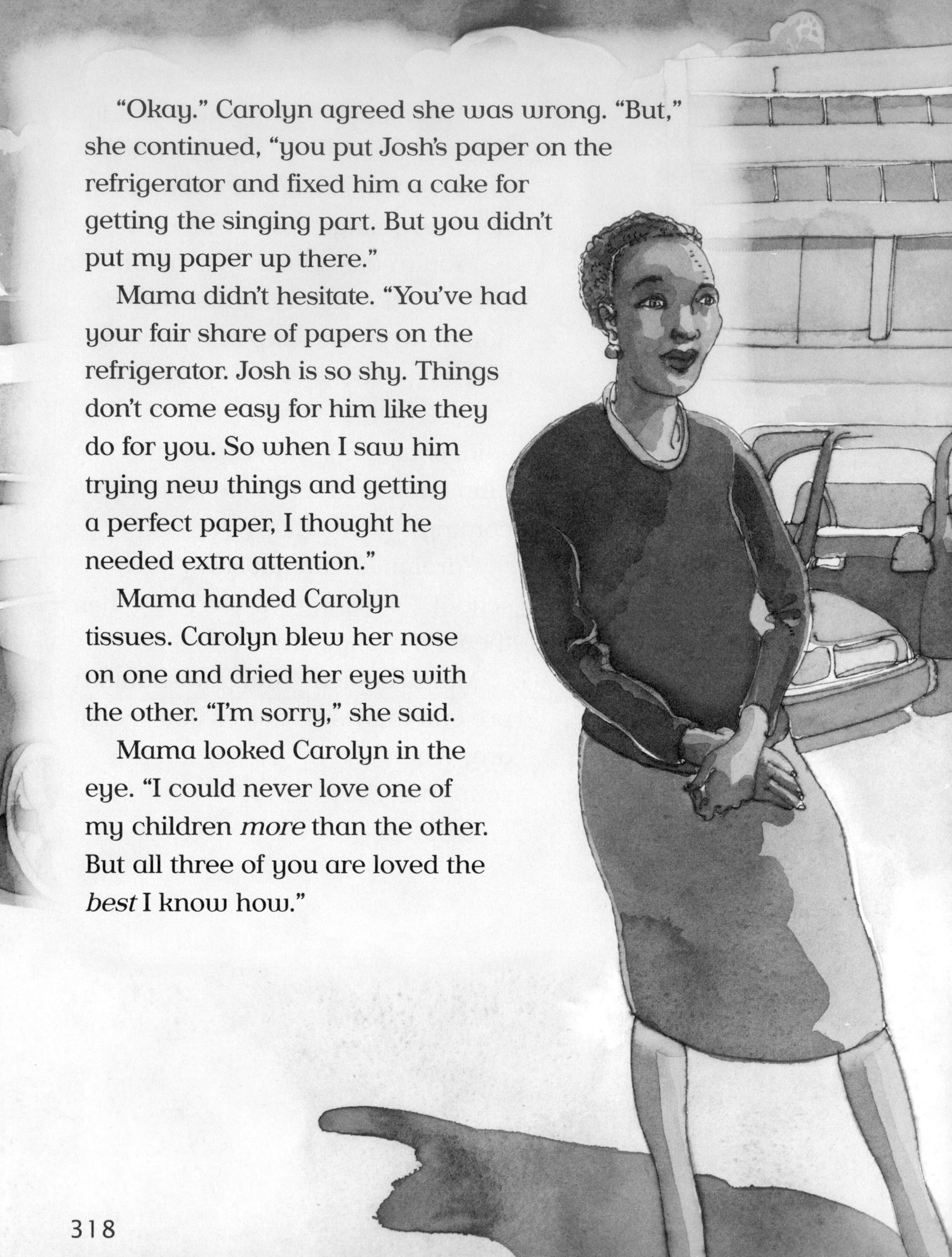

"Okay." Carolyn agreed she was wrong. "But," she continued, "you put Josh's paper on the refrigerator and fixed him a cake for getting the singing part. But you didn't put my paper up there."

Mama didn't hesitate. "You've had your fair share of papers on the refrigerator. Josh is so shy. Things don't come easy for him like they do for you. So when I saw him trying new things and getting a perfect paper, I thought he needed extra attention."

Mama handed Carolyn tissues. Carolyn blew her nose on one and dried her eyes with the other. "I'm sorry," she said.

Mama looked Carolyn in the eye. "I could never love one of my children *more* than the other. But all three of you are loved the *best* I know how."

Suddenly a sunflower and a bird appeared around the side of the car.

"Don't cry, Carolyn," said Dana. "It will be okay."

"Come on Carolyn. Don't give up. You wouldn't let me give up," said Josh. "You're our big sister, the only one we have."

Just then Dad found them. And behind him were Grandmama and Granddaddy.

"Carolyn," Daddy said, "do you think, maybe, you might want to try doing your poem again? Mrs. Lasiter said you could go on after the sky."

Carolyn thought about it. Mama gave her an encouraging nod. "You know who's loved best?" Carolyn said.

"No. Who?" the family asked.

"You are all loved best," said Carolyn, winking at Mama. Then she went back inside with her scarves flowing like a river.

Think Critically

1. What is the problem in "Loved Best," and how is it solved? PLOT

2. How does Carolyn feel after she sobs onstage? CHARACTERS' EMOTIONS

3. If you were Carolyn, would you have tried to say the poem again? Explain. EXPRESS PERSONAL OPINIONS

4. How can you tell that the author thinks Carolyn is wrong to pretend she is sick? DRAW CONCLUSIONS

5. **WRITE** Write about a time when you did something brave. SHORT RESPONSE

LOUISIANA GRADE-LEVEL EXPECTATIONS—3ELA-1-E4-08 identify story elements; **3ELA-1-E4-08(c)** identify character traits/feelings/motivation; **3ELA-7-E1-17(c)** make inferences/draw conclusions; **3ELA-7-E2-18** explain chosen solutions to problems; **3ELA-7-E3-20** explain author's viewpoint; **3ELA-7-E4-21(e)** connect to real-life situations; **3ELA-2-E6-27** write for various purposes

Meet the Author

Patricia C. McKissack

Before Patricia McKissack became a writer, she was a listener. On hot summer evenings her family would sit on the porch and recite poems and tell stories. When she was older she realized that those stories helped her become a writer.

When Patricia McKissack grew up, she became a teacher. It was then that she realized there were not many books about African Americans. So she decided to write one. She thought that she would then go back to teaching or do something else. More than twenty years later, Patricia McKissack is still writing!

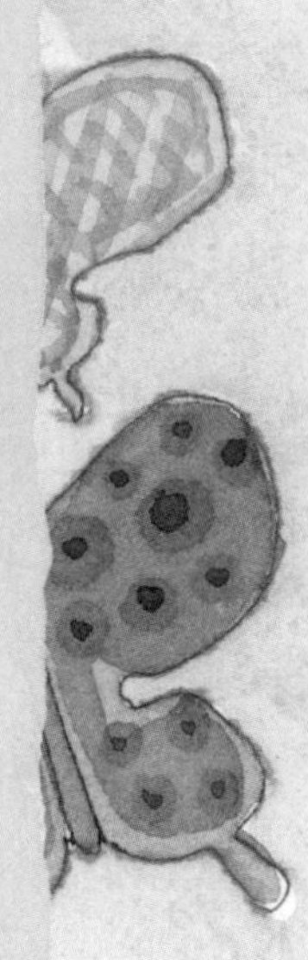

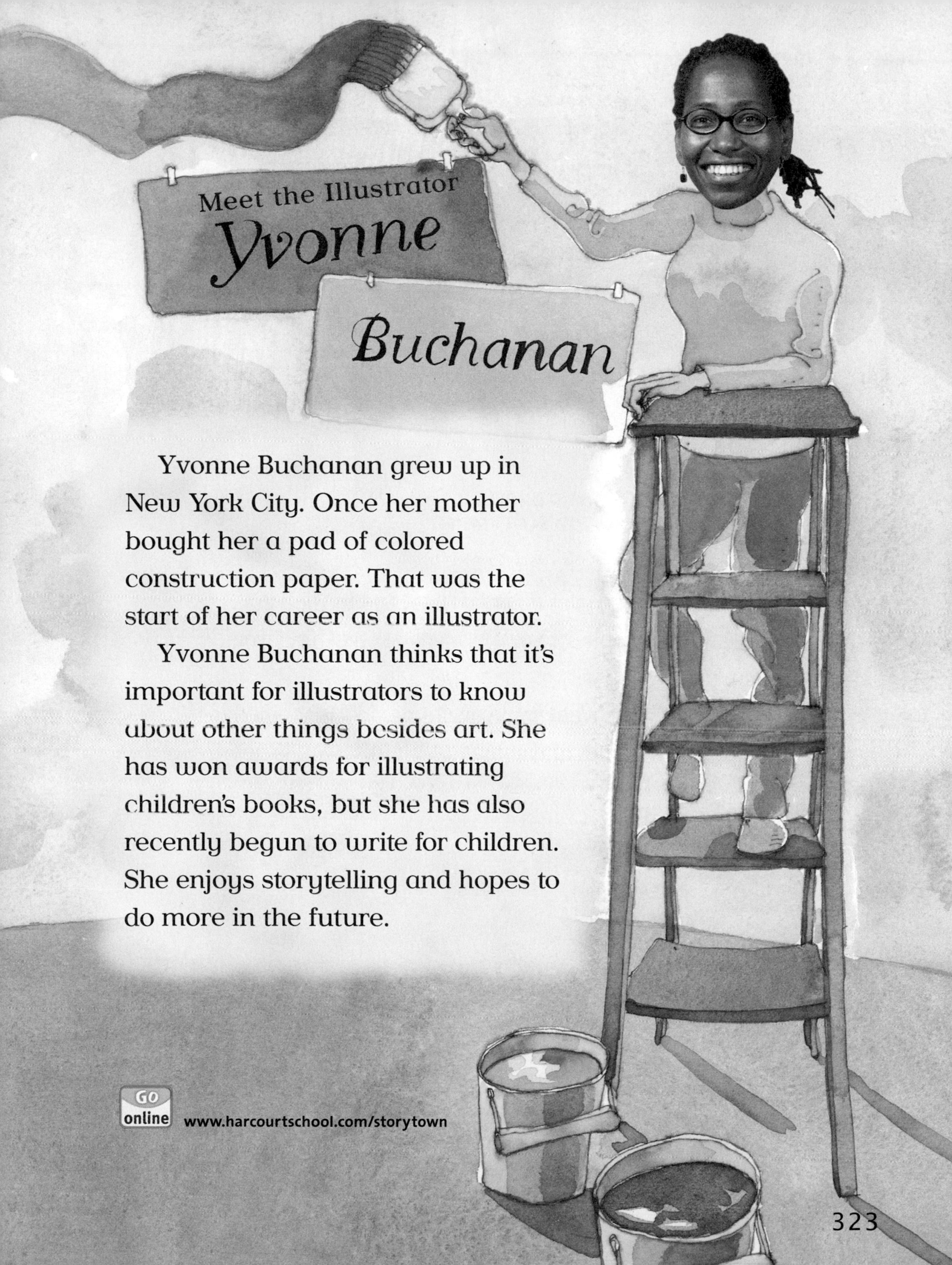

Meet the Illustrator Yvonne Buchanan

Yvonne Buchanan grew up in New York City. Once her mother bought her a pad of colored construction paper. That was the start of her career as an illustrator.

Yvonne Buchanan thinks that it's important for illustrators to know about other things besides art. She has won awards for illustrating children's books, but she has also recently begun to write for children. She enjoys storytelling and hopes to do more in the future.

GO online www.harcourtschool.com/storytown

The Shepherd Boy and the Wolf

RETOLD BY DORIS ORGEL
ILLUSTRATED BY DAVID SCOTT MEIER

"All the sheep ever do is say 'baa' and munch grass," thought the shepherd boy. He wished something would happen.

"I know: I'll invent some excitement." He cupped his hands to his mouth and shouted: "Help, a wolf is near!"

The villagers came running. "Where's the wolf?" they asked.

The shepherd boy laughed and said, "Fooled you!"

Another day, for fun, he cried, "Wolf! Wolf!" again. The villagers came running — and were fooled again.

One day a wolf really did appear, hungrily eyeing the sheep. "Help! WOLF!" the shepherd boy yelled, terrified. "This time it's really true!"

But nobody believed him.

Well, *you* know what happened: The wolf killed many sheep that day and had himself a mutton feast. The shepherd boy was sorry and never cried "wolf" again.

Connections

Comparing Texts

3ELA-7-E1-17(d) 3ELA-7-E4-21(e)

1. How is Carolyn's behavior in "Loved Best" similar to the behavior of the shepherd boy in "The Shepherd Boy and the Wolf"?

2. What did you like about Carolyn's parents?

3. In what ways does the setting in "Loved Best" seem like a place you could visit in real life?

Vocabulary Review

3ELA-2-E6-27

Danny sobbed for a brief moment.

Word Pairs

Work with a partner. Write each Vocabulary Word on a card. Place the cards face down. Take turns flipping over two cards and writing a sentence that uses both words. Read your sentences to your partner and decide whether the Vocabulary Words are used correctly.

- **encouraging**
- **brief**
- **chuckling**
- **soothing**
- **sobbed**
- **praised**

Fluency Practice 3ELA-1-E3-07

Partner Reading

Choose your favorite section from "Loved Best." Take turns with a partner reading your sections aloud. Read each character's words as if a real person were speaking. Give feedback after each reading.

Writing 3ELA-7-E1-17(b) 3ELA-2-E4-25

Write a New Scene

Write what you think happens next in "Loved Best." Use the same characters and setting, but think of new events to help you plan the next scene.

My Writing Checklist

Writing Trait — Voice

✔ I use words that tell how Carolyn feels.

✔ I use a story map to plan my scene.

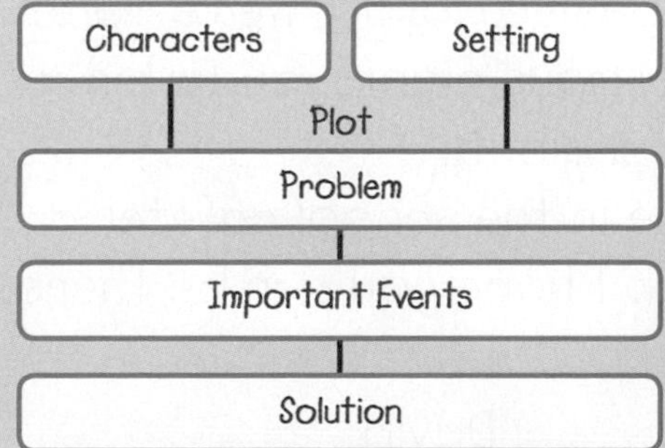

LOUISIANA GRADE-LEVEL EXPECTATIONS—3ELA-1-E3-07 adjust reading speed; 3ELA-7-E1-17(b) make predictions; 3ELA-7-E1-17(d) compare/contrast; 3ELA-7-E4-21(e) connect to real-life situations; 3ELA-2-E4-25 write paragraphs with description/narration; 3ELA-2-E6-27 write for various purposes

Reading-Writing Connection

Friendly Letter

In a **friendly letter,** a person writes to someone he or she knows. A friendly letter has five parts, like those in the letters in "A Pen Pal for Max." I wrote this letter to tell my grandmother about my school's play.

Student Writing Model

14 Daisy Dot Dr.
Sebring, FL 32811
November 9, 20--

Dear Grandma,

I got the lead part in our school play! I will be Jack in "The New Jack and the Beanstalk." I have so many lines! My classmates and I are making costumes and building sets. Everything for the giant's house needs to be very large. We've made huge dishes, enormous plants, and even a giant picture of a giant!

The play will be in the school cafeteria next Friday night. I hope you can be there!

Love,
David

Writing Trait

SENTENCE FLUENCY
Use long and short sentences. Make some sentences longer by adding important details.

Writing Trait

VOICE
Sentences should sound natural. Let your feelings show through.

Here's how I write a letter.

1. I think of all the parts that I need to include in the letter.

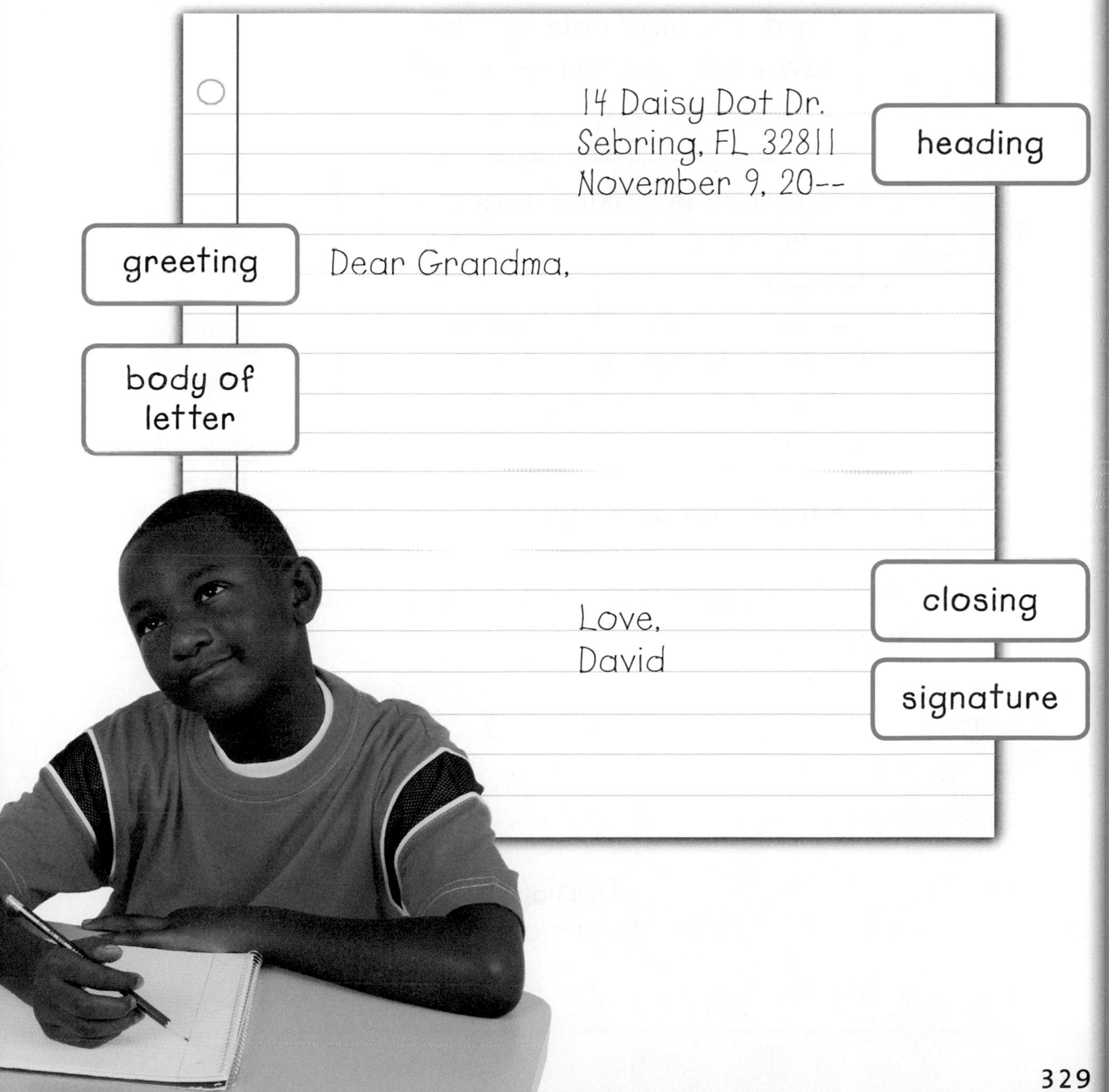

14 Daisy Dot Dr.
Sebring, FL 32811
November 9, 20--
heading
greeting
Dear Grandma,
body of letter
Love,
David
closing
signature

2. **I think about the person who will read the letter. I think about what I want to tell him or her. I use a graphic organizer to help me get started.**

I got the lead role in "The New Jack and the Beanstalk."

↓

My class is making sets and costumes.

↓

I need to tell when and where the play will take place.

3. **I write my letter and sign it.**

4. **I address an envelope, add a stamp, and mail my letter.**

David Longas
245 Park Green St.
Chicago, IL 64811

Mrs. Carmen Longas
14 Daisy Dot Dr.
Sebring, FL 32811

Here is a checklist I use when I write a friendly letter. You can use it, too.

Checklist for Writing a Friendly Letter

- ☐ My letter has five parts—a heading, greeting, body, closing, and signature.
- ☐ I use an order that makes sense.
- ☐ I use my own voice and write naturally to share my thoughts and feelings.
- ☐ I use correct grammar and punctuation.
- ☐ I use a variety of sentence lengths. I make some sentences longer by adding important details.
- ☐ I use my best handwriting, or I type my letter and sign it by hand.

CONTENTS

Lesson 12

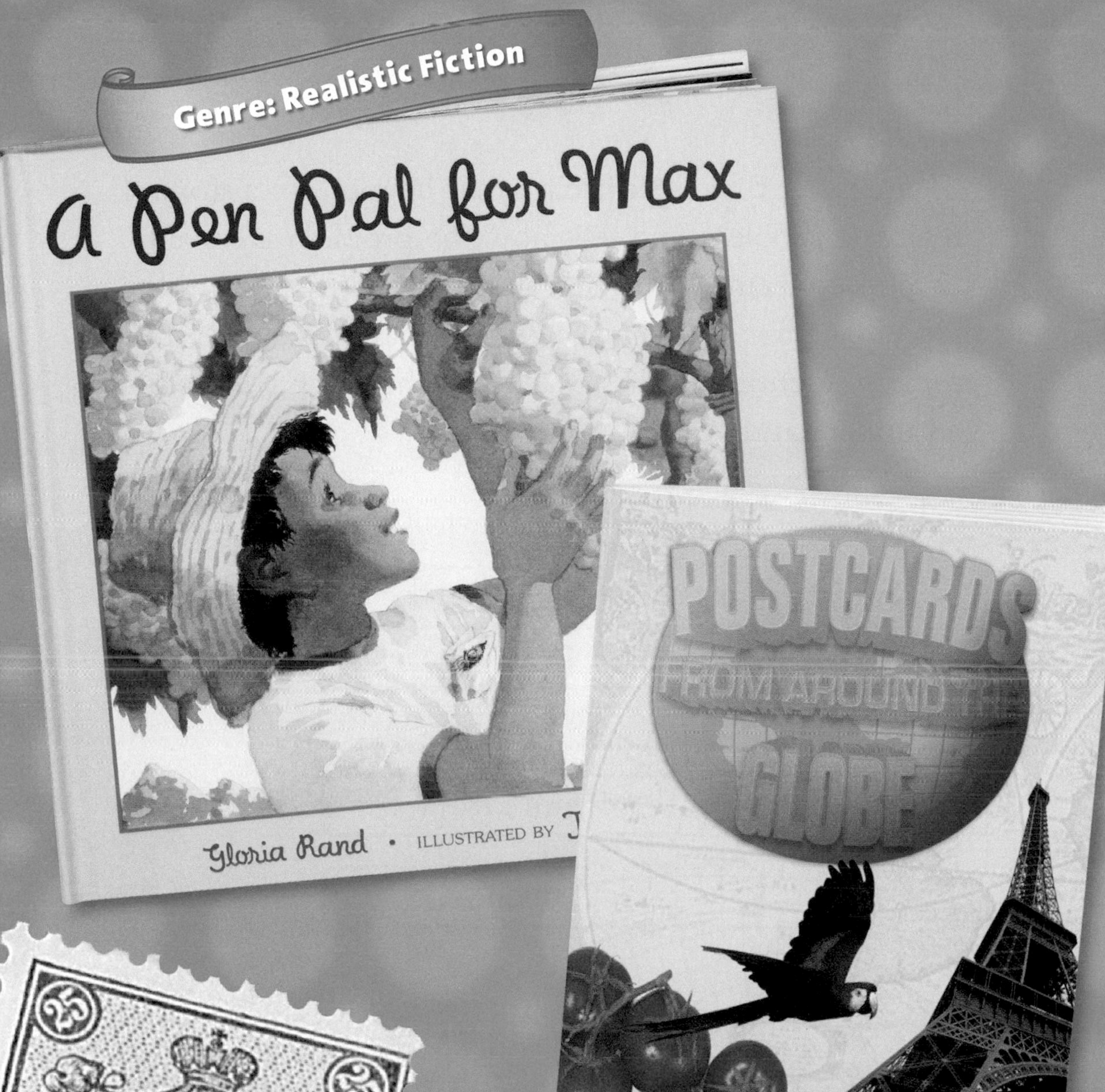
Genre: Realistic Fiction
A Pen Pal for Max
Gloria Rand • ILLUSTRATED BY
POSTCARDS
FROM AROUND THE
GLOBE
Genre: Postcards

Focus Skill

Plot

Remember that a **plot** tells what happens in a story. It presents a problem and tells how the problem is solved.

A plot contains information and events that set up the problem. Other events tell how the characters solve the problem. Identifying these events in the story will help you understand what you read.

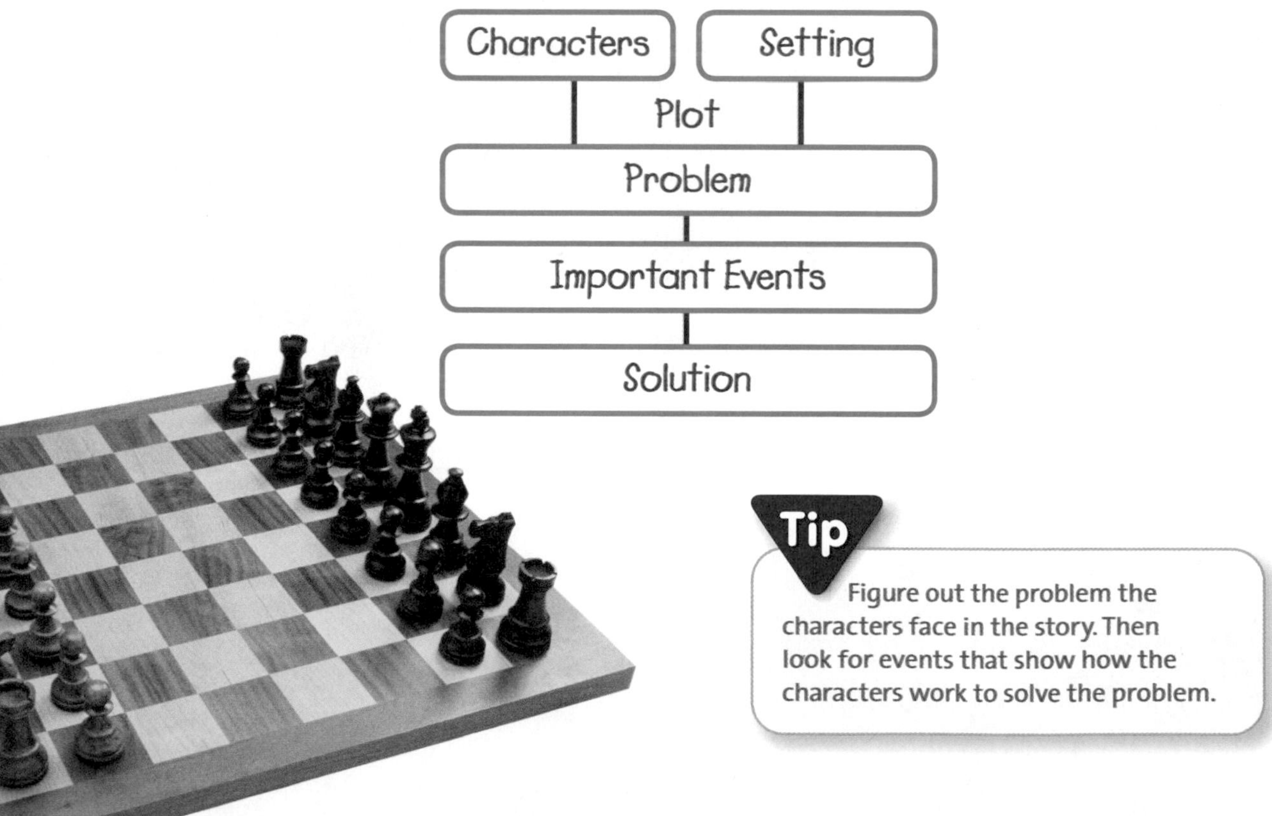

Tip

Figure out the problem the characters face in the story. Then look for events that show how the characters work to solve the problem.

Read the story, and complete a story map like the one below.

Emma liked to play chess at her school in Orlando, Florida. She wished she could have a chessboard to practice at home.

"Let's make one," her father said. He cut a square piece of wood. Emma painted the chessboard on the wood.

Then they used modeling clay to make the chess pieces.

"Now, teach me how to play!" her father said.

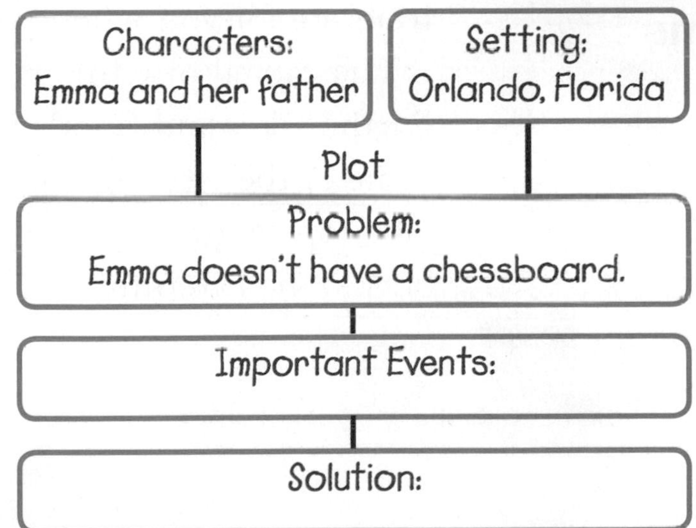

Characters:
Emma and her father
Setting:
Orlando, Florida
Plot
Problem:
Emma doesn't have a chessboard.
Important Events:
Solution:

Try This!

Look back at the problem. Who helps Emma solve it?

www.harcourtschool.com/storytown

LOUISIANA GRADE-LEVEL EXPECTATIONS—3ELA-7-E2-18 explain chosen solutions to problems

Vocabulary

Build Robust Vocabulary

- translate
- repairs
- heaving
- bothersome
- din
- dodging

Visiting Chile

Chile is a narrow country between the Andes Mountains and the Pacific Ocean. Chile looks like a long finger, so it is easily found on a map! If you don't speak Spanish, you can hire a guide to **translate** for you when you visit.

The capital of Chile is Santiago. Earthquakes and floods have damaged some of the city's historic buildings. The **repairs** to these buildings have been done carefully.

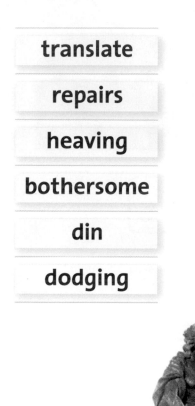

If you like adventures, you can climb mountains in Chile. Some mountains in Chile are active volcanoes, still **heaving** rocks and lava when they erupt!

Chile has earthquakes, too. Most are too small to be **bothersome**, but a large one can create quite a **din**. In 1980, the largest earthquake in history was recorded off the coast of Chile. Most of the time, however, Chile is a safe place to visit.

Rock climbers share tales of **dodging** rocks during rockslides.

www.harcourtschool.com/storytown

Word Scribe

Your mission this week is to use the Vocabulary Words in your writing. For example, write about something you find bothersome. Read what you write to a classmate.

LOUISIANA GRADE-LEVEL EXPECTATIONS—3ELA-2-E6-27 write for various purposes

Genre Study

3ELA-6-E3-16

Realistic fiction has characters and events that are like people and events in real life. Look for

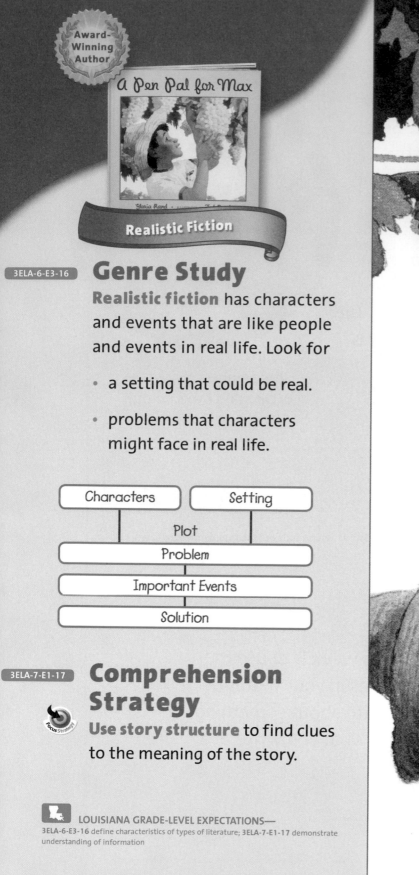

- a setting that could be real.
- problems that characters might face in real life.

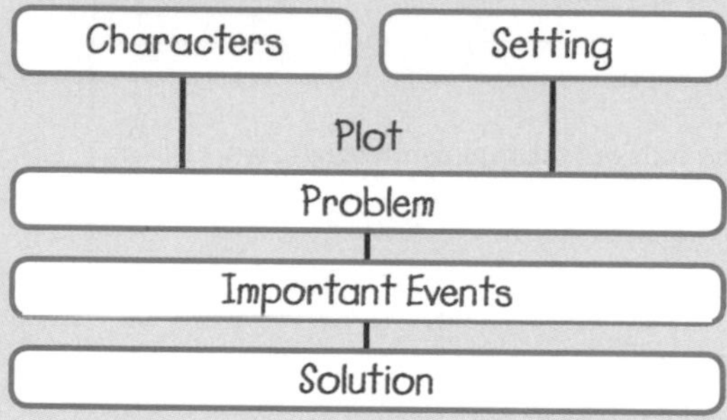

Comprehension Strategy

3ELA-7-E1-17

Use story structure to find clues to the meaning of the story.

LOUISIANA GRADE-LEVEL EXPECTATIONS—
3ELA-6-E3-16 define characteristics of types of literature; 3ELA-7-E1-17 demonstrate understanding of information

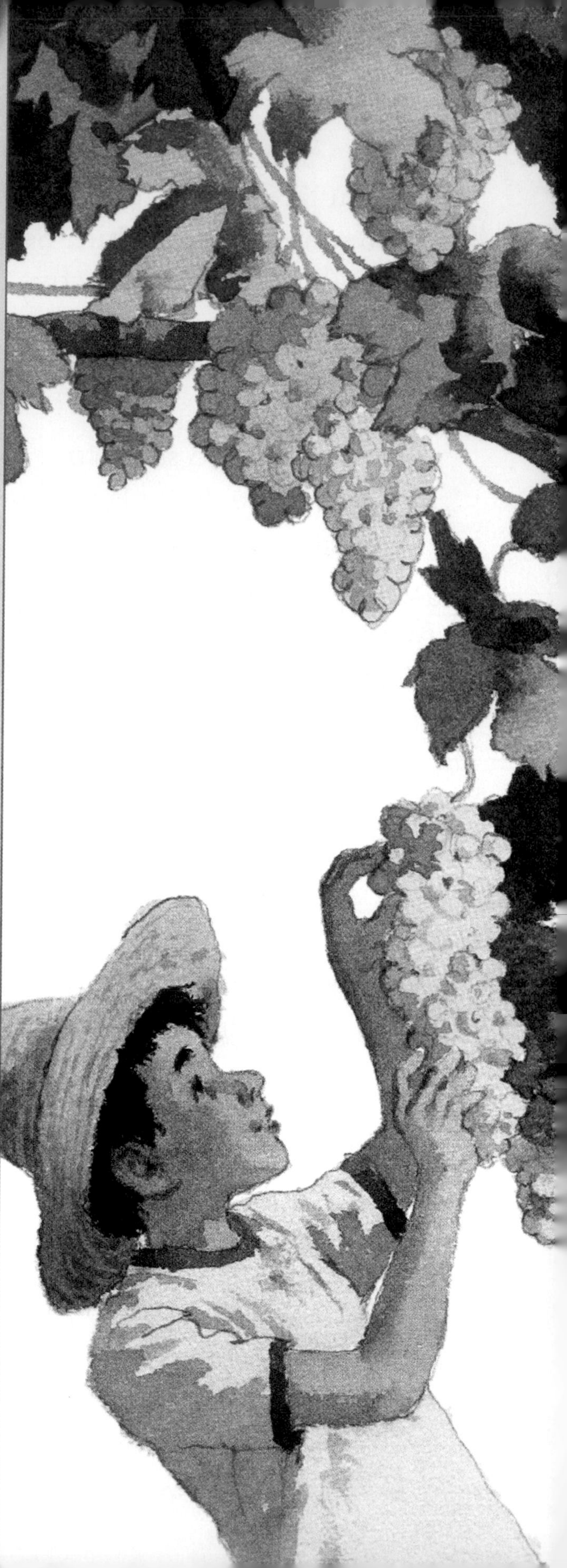

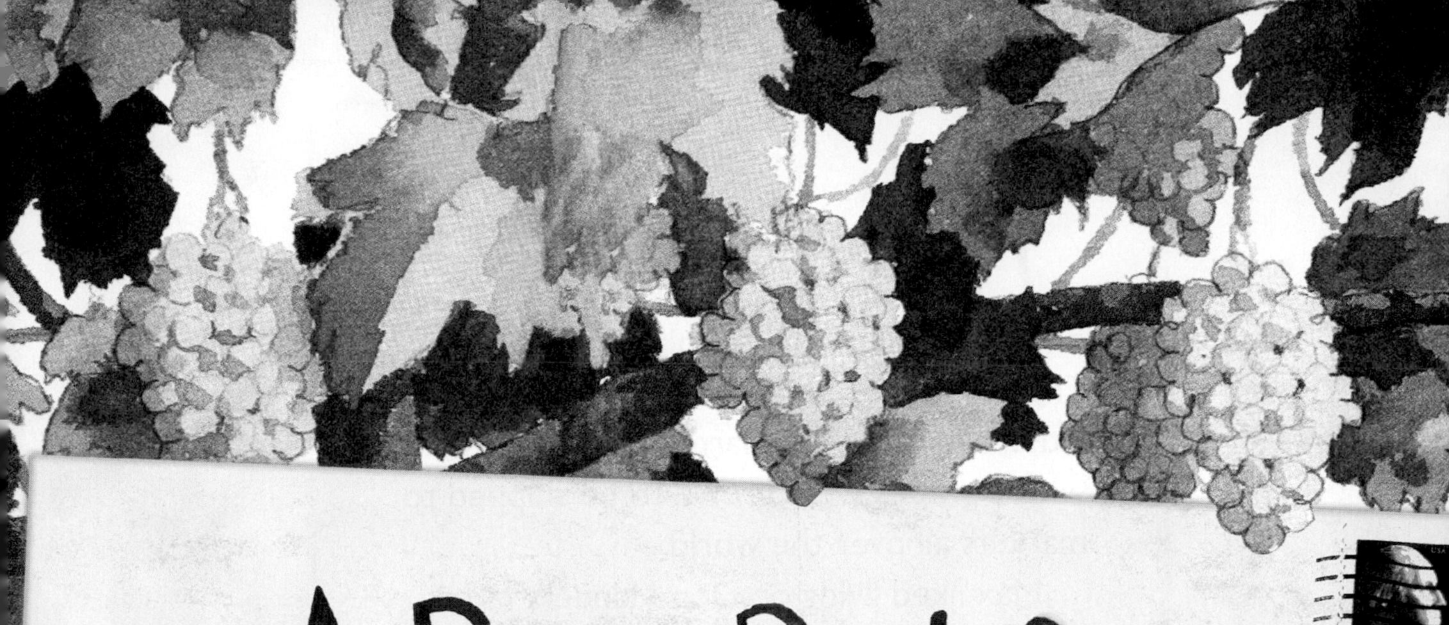

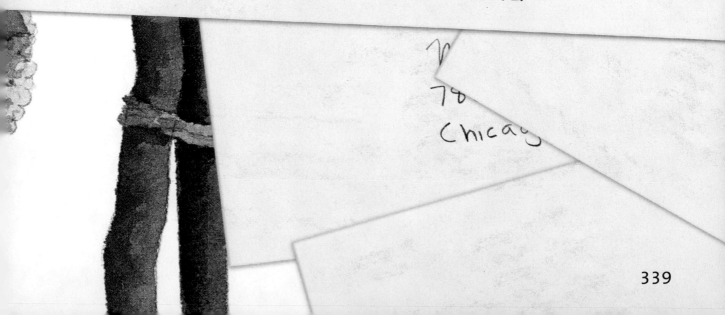

A Pen Pal for Max

by Gloria Rand

illustrated by Ted Rand

Maximiliano lived in a small house on a huge fruit farm in Chile, South America. The farm belonged to Don Manuel. Max's father worked in the farm's vineyard. That's where grapes were grown to be shipped to markets all over the world.

Max liked living on Don Manuel's farm. He had his own pony there and many friends nearby.

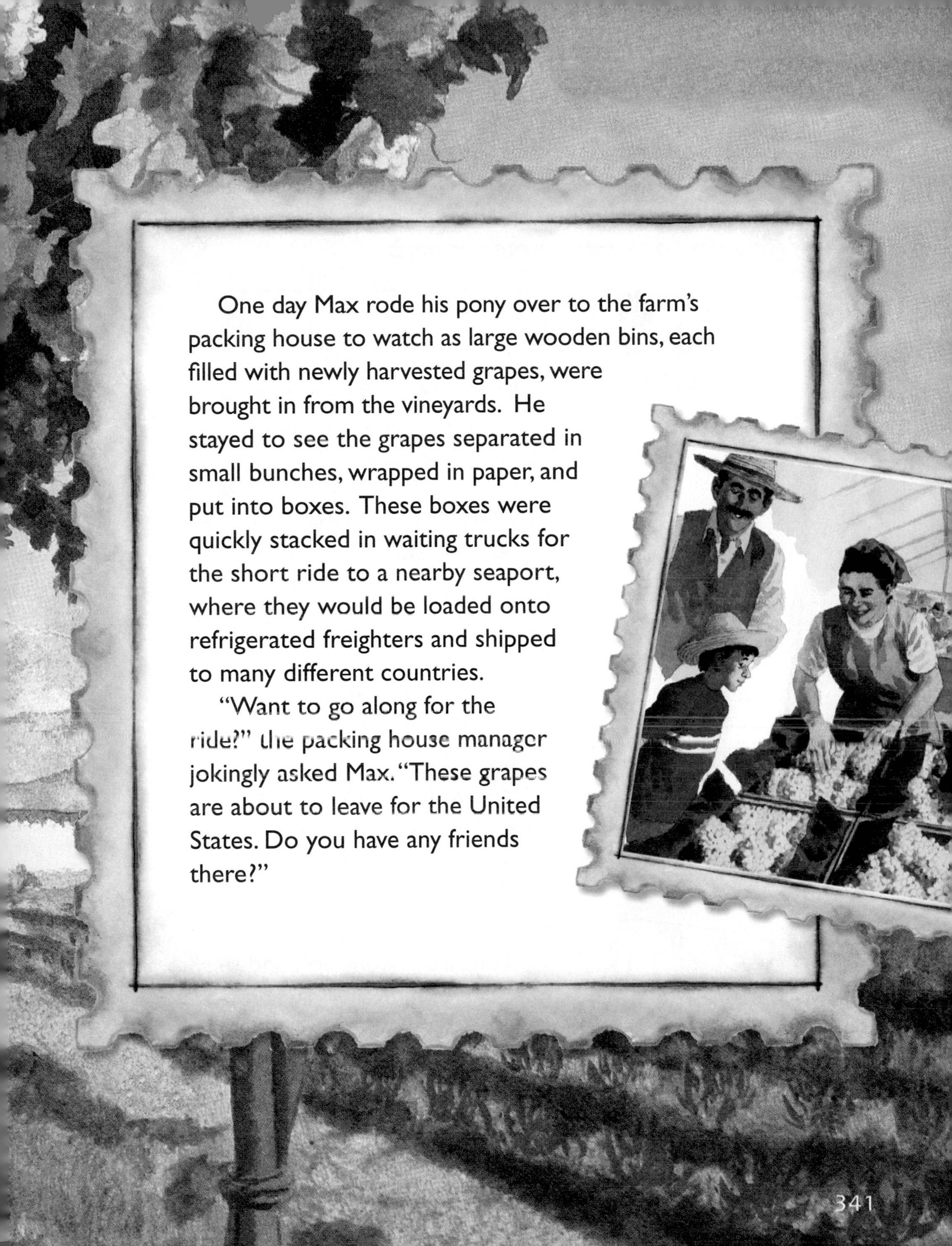

One day Max rode his pony over to the farm's packing house to watch as large wooden bins, each filled with newly harvested grapes, were brought in from the vineyards. He stayed to see the grapes separated in small bunches, wrapped in paper, and put into boxes. These boxes were quickly stacked in waiting trucks for the short ride to a nearby seaport, where they would be loaded onto refrigerated freighters and shipped to many different countries.

"Want to go along for the ride?" the packing house manager jokingly asked Max. "These grapes are about to leave for the United States. Do you have any friends there?"

Max had none. And that's when he got the idea that it would be fun to have a friend in a faraway place. Quickly he turned his pony around and headed home. As soon as he got there he secretly wrote this note:

Hola,

Mi nombre es Maximiliano Farias. Me gustaría ser tu amigo. Por favor, escríbame.

Maximiliano Farias
Casilla 74
El Monte, Chile

In English it read: "Hello, my name is Maximiliano Farias. I would like to be your friend. Please write to me." He signed his name and gave his address.

Max tucked the note into his shirt pocket and rode back to the packing house, where grapes were still being brought in and prepared for shipping. When no one was looking, Max slipped the note into a box of grapes.

"Maybe someone will find this," Max said to himself. "Maybe that person will write an answer to me and we can become friends."

Max told no one about the note, not even his little sister, but he often asked his mother, "Was there any mail for me today?"

"Are you expecting a letter?" his mother always asked.

"No, not really."

Weeks and weeks went by. Just when Max had about given up thinking that anyone would ever answer, a letter addressed to Maximiliano arrived at the house.

"Is this why you've been asking about the mail?" Max's mother looked puzzled as she handed him the envelope. "This is from someone in the United States. I can tell by the stamp. What in the world have you been up to, Max?"

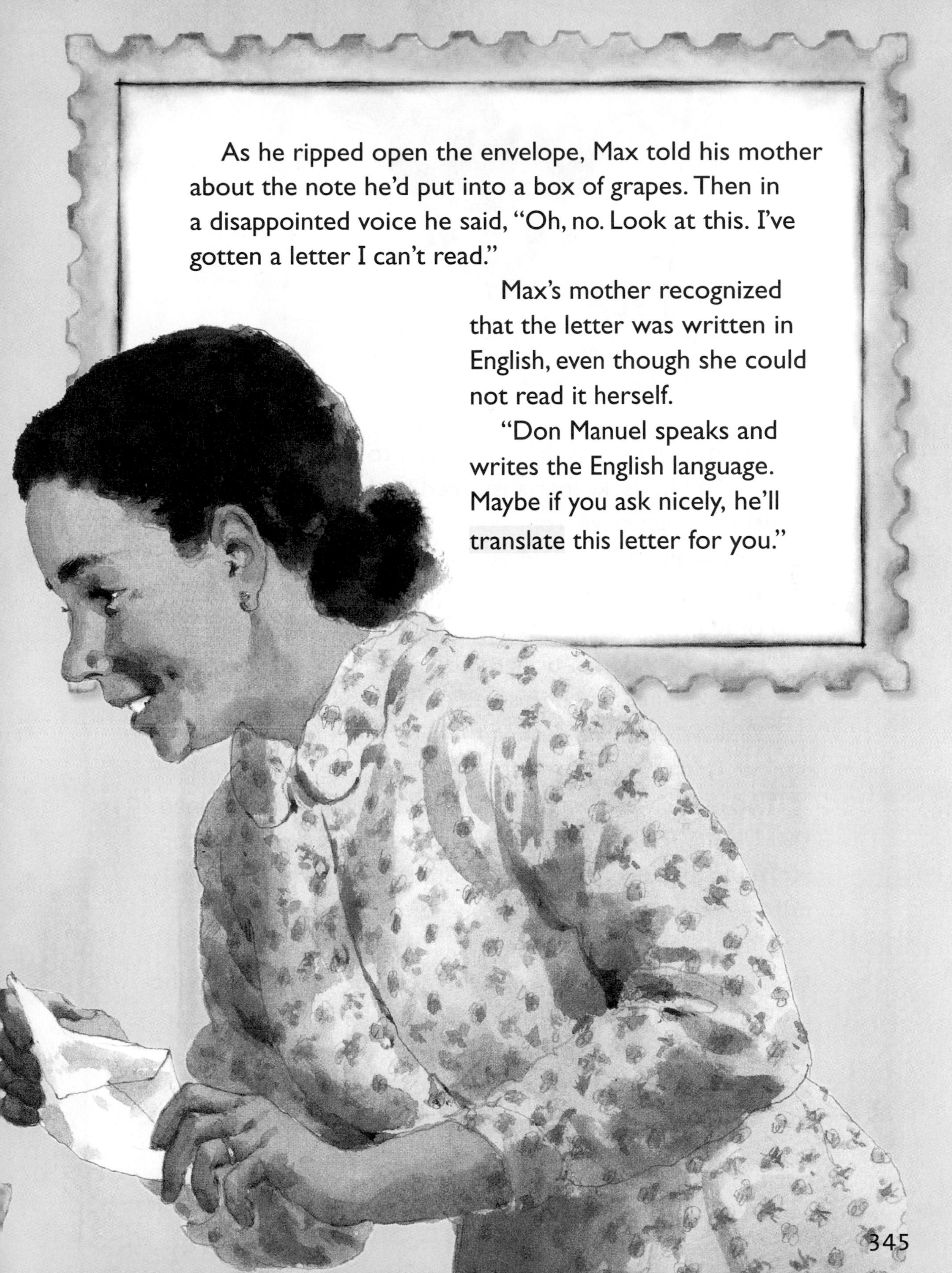

As he ripped open the envelope, Max told his mother about the note he'd put into a box of grapes. Then in a disappointed voice he said, "Oh, no. Look at this. I've gotten a letter I can't read."

Max's mother recognized that the letter was written in English, even though she could not read it herself.

"Don Manuel speaks and writes the English language. Maybe if you ask nicely, he'll translate this letter for you."

Max hurried down the dusty road to Don Manuel's house. The housekeeper answered his knock on the mansion's impressive front door.

"Come along," she said as she led Max into a grand room where Don Manuel was enjoying a late-afternoon cup of tea.

"Hello, Max. What brings you here?" Don Manuel asked.

Max explained about his secret note.

"Well, what an interesting thing to do." Don Manuel smiled. "Hand me the letter and I'll read it to you."

The letter was from a girl named Maggie. She explained that her father was the produce manager at a large grocery store in a big city in the United States. He'd found Max's note as he was opening up boxes of Chilean grapes.

"My father brought your note home and told me to take it to school. He was sure my teacher, Ms. Moore, who is also the school's Spanish teacher, could read it for me. Ms. Moore did, and she thinks you might be about my age. I'm ten years old," Maggie explained. "Are you ten years old, too? Write back."

That evening Max wrote to Maggie. Then Maggie wrote back to Max. They became regular pen pals. They wrote to each other often.

They wrote about school, soccer games, and their hobbies. They wrote about what they'd like to be when they grew up.

They wrote about the weather where they lived and how when it was summer in South America, it was winter in North America. They even wrote about how bothersome little brothers and sisters could be.

Don Manuel was always glad to translate for Max, and that's what he was doing one day when there was a loud rumbling sound and his big house began to shake. Furniture tumbled, vases and lamps crashed to the floor, tiles fell off the roof, and a cloud of dust rose up around everything. It was a terrible earthquake.

"Come on!" Don Manuel cried out as he grabbed Max's hand. Together they ran out into the garden, dodging falling parts of the old farm mansion.

"Here, hang on to me," Don Manuel yelled over the din of the quake, trying to stay on his feet out in the middle of a large lawn that was heaving up and down. "You'll be fine, just hang on. This shaking is sure to stop soon."

In the distance Max could see his pony running down the dirt road toward home. He wanted to run home, too, but Don Manuel said that wasn't a good idea. Debris was still crashing down everywhere.

"Stay right here until the earth quiets down," he told Max. "It won't be long."

As soon as the ground seemed to be moving less, Don Manuel said, "It's okay to go on home now. Your mother is probably worried sick. Hurry! Just don't get near any of the farm buildings in case more tiles fall from the roofs!"

Max reached his house in record time, just as his father was returning from the vineyards. His mother and sister, who had been at home during the whole horrible earthquake, hugged them both. They were all very happy to be together but still badly frightened by the force of the rumbling earth.

The next day Max learned that his school was closed because it had so many broken windows and large cracks in the walls. It would take weeks for the needed repairs to be made. Since the earth was still trembling and moving now and then, Max was glad to be home.

After a while the quake became only a scary memory, and Max went back to school.

"There's a nice surprise waiting for you here, Max," the school principal said as he pointed to a pile of boxes outside Max's classroom door. "These are all addressed to you and your classmates."

With the principal, the teacher, and the kids in his class helping, Max opened up box after box. They were filled with books, games, paper, pens, and even new clothes. In one box there was a picture of his friend Maggie and her classmates, along with a short letter.

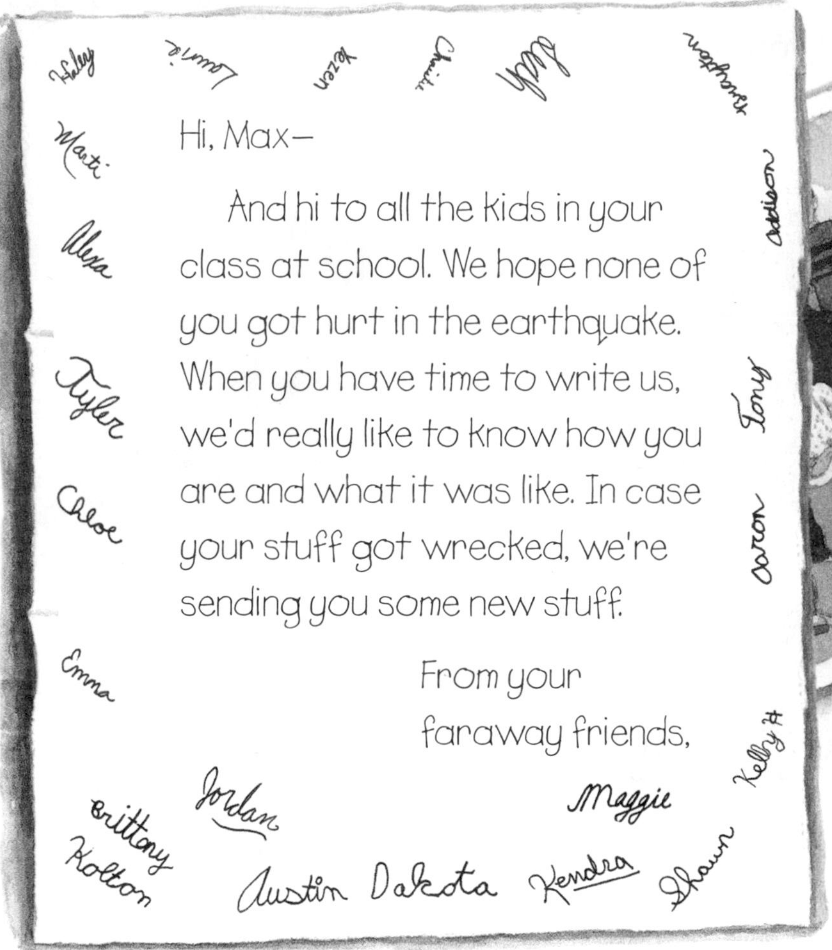

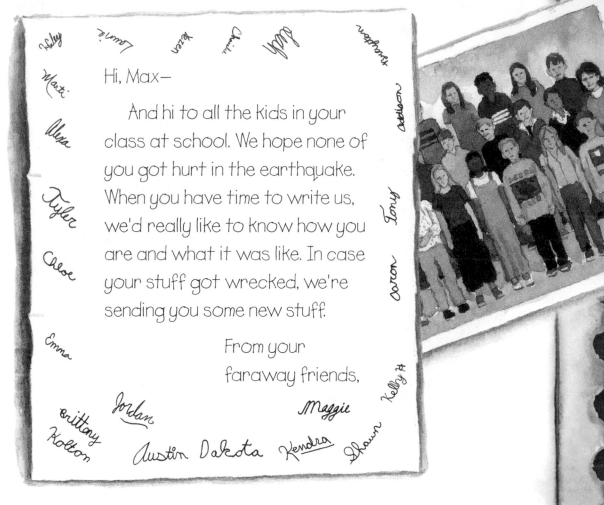

Hi, Max—

And hi to all the kids in your class at school. We hope none of you got hurt in the earthquake. When you have time to write us, we'd really like to know how you are and what it was like. In case your stuff got wrecked, we're sending you some new stuff.

From your
faraway friends,

Marti
Alexa
Tyler
Chloe
Emma
Tony
Aaron
Kelly
Jordan
Maggie
Brittony
Kolton
Austin
Dakota
Kendra
Shawn

Max was really pleased. The note he'd put into a box of grapes had found a faraway friend, not only for himself but for his whole class, too.

Think Critically

1. What problem does the earthquake cause at Max's school? What does Maggie do to help solve the problem? PLOT

2. How does Max feel when he opens the boxes from his pen pal? Why? CHARACTERS' EMOTIONS

3. Do you think Max chose a good way to find a friend? Why or why not? EXPRESS PERSONAL OPINIONS

4. How can you tell that the author thinks a pen pal in another country is a special kind of friend? DRAW CONCLUSIONS

5. **WRITE** What important events happened because Max put a letter in the box of grapes? SHORT-RESPONSE

LOUISIANA GRADE-LEVEL EXPECTATIONS—**3ELA-1-E4-08** identify story elements; **3ELA-1-E4-08(c)** identify character traits/feelings/motivation; **3ELA-1-E6-11** connect to prior knowledge; **3ELA-7-E1-17(c)** make inferences/draw conclusions; **3ELA-7-E2-18** explain chosen solutions to problems; **3ELA-7-E3-20** explain author's viewpoint; **3ELA-7-E4-21(c)** identify multiple causes/effects; **3ELA-2-E6-27** write for various purposes

Meet the Author

Gloria Rand

Gloria Rand has written many children's books. They have all been illustrated by her husband, Ted Rand. Most of her books are inspired by real events or by people she knows. The author says she enjoys everything about her work. She likes doing research and interviewing people for her stories. Best of all, she likes the children who read her books. She says, "If a young reader lets us know our books are okay, it makes us feel like winners in every way."

About the Illustrator

Ted Rand

Ted Rand illustrated all of his wife's books as well as children's books by other authors. He illustrated more than eighty books in all.

Ted Rand did not always illustrate books. In fact, he didn't start illustrating until he was in his sixties! He liked to add a lot of detail in his illustrations. Some people think his pictures are works of art.

Go online www.harcourtschool.com/storytown

POSTCARDS FROM AROUND THE GLOBE

Some pen pals stay in touch through letters or e-mails. These friends send postcards to their pen pals. They share interesting facts about the places where they live.

November 21

Dear Sara,

It's beautiful here in California. We grow a lot of tomatoes where I live. Some are shipped to stores. Most of the tomatoes we grow are made into things like juice and tomato sauce. You couldn't make pizza or spaghetti sauce without our yummy tomatoes!

Your friend,
Devon

Sara Jackson

123 Pine St.

Columbia, MO 65204

December 10

Dear Justin,

Hello from Costa Rica! The weather is very warm here all year. It's perfect for growing bananas. We send bananas all over the world. The next time you snack on a banana, remember that it may have been grown here in beautiful Costa Rica!

Sincerely,
Juan

Justin Manning

1255 Garden Ave.

New York, NY 10134

December 29

Dear Miguel,

Bonjour from Paris, France! This morning, my father and I went to a cheese shop. We learned that more than 400 kinds of cheese are made in France. The French have made cheese for a long time. In some parts of France, people were making cheese 1,000 years ago!

Write back,
Marie

Miguel Santos

445 Cardinal Dr.

Tampa, FL 33688

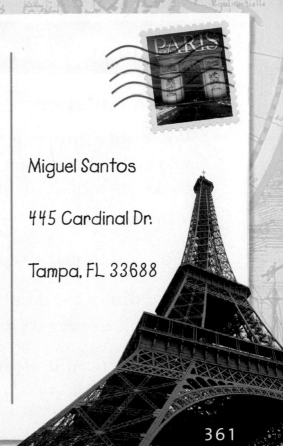

Connections

Comparing Texts

3ELA-7-E1-17(d)
3ELA-7-E4-21(e)

1. How are the pen pals in "A Pen Pal for Max" and "Postcards from Around the Globe" alike? How are they different?

2. Would you like to be pen pals with someone from another country? Explain.

3. What did you learn about Chile that you did not know before?

Vocabulary Review

3ELA-1-E1-06(b)

translate
repairs
heaving
bothersome
din
dodging

Rate a Situation

Work with a partner. Read aloud each sentence and point to the spot on the line that shows how you would rate each situation. Discuss your answers.

bothersome ———————————— enjoyable

- You had to make **repairs** to your bicycle.
- The **din** of the construction outside made it difficult to hear your friend.
- You practiced **dodging** during a soccer practice.

Fluency Practice 3ELA-1-E3-07

Partner Reading

Choose a section from "A Pen Pal for Max" that includes characters talking. Meet with a partner. Take turns reading aloud the sections you chose. Remember to read a character's words as a real person would speak.

Writing 3ELA-2-E6-27(a)

Write a Thank-You Note

Write a thank-you note to someone who has helped you. Describe what was done and why you appreciate it. Include the parts of a letter: the date, the greeting, the body, the closing, and the signature.

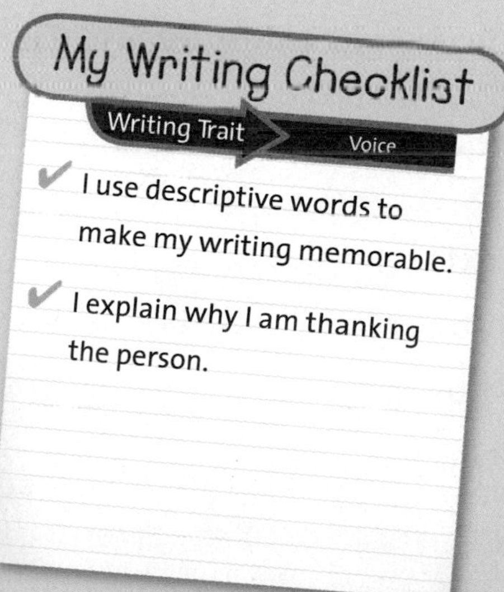

My Writing Checklist
Writing Trait
Voice
I use descriptive words to make my writing memorable.
I explain why I am thanking the person.

LOUISIANA GRADE-LEVEL EXPECTATIONS—3ELA-1-E1-06(b) use context clues; 3ELA-1-E3-07 adjust reading speed; 3ELA-7-E1-17(d) compare/contrast; 3ELA-7-E4-21(e) connect to real-life situations; 3ELA-2-E6-27(a) write informal letters

CONTENTS

Lesson 13

Genre: Expository Nonfiction
A TREE IS GROWING
by ARTHUR DORROS
illustrated by S. D. SCHINDLER
ANCIENT TREES SURVIVE IN CALIFORNIA'S MOUNTAINS
by April Pulley Sayre
Genre: News Feature

Phonics Skill

Words with Soft *c* and Soft *g*

The letter *c* can stand for the /s/ sound you hear in *city*. This happens when *c* is followed by *e* or *i*.

The letter *g* can stand for the /j/ sound you hear in *giant*. This often happens when *g* is followed by *e* or *i*.

Read the words in the chart, and listen for the soft sounds of the letters *c* and *g*.

Words with the soft *c* sound as in *city*	**Words with the soft *g* sound as in *giant***
cent	gem
ceiling	germ

Tip

The letter *g* can stand for the /j/ sound in *giant* or the /g/ sound in *get*. Try each sound to see which one makes sense.

Read the story and look at the chart. Tell which words have soft *c* as in *city* or soft *g* as in *giant.*

I had such a strange dream last night! I was walking in circles in a giant forest. I could smell spices like cinnamon and ginger. At the center of the forest, I met a man in a general's outfit. "Are you a citizen of this forest?" he asked.

"Gee, I don't think so," I said.

"Then we'd better get you back to the city," he said gently.

Words with the soft *c* sound as in *city*	**Words with the soft *g* sound as in *giant***

Try This!

Look back at the story. Add one sentence to tell more about the dream. Use a word that has soft *c* as in *city* or soft *g* as in *giant*.

www.harcourtschool.com/storytown

Vocabulary

Build Robust Vocabulary

- columns
- absorb
- protects
- rustling
- dissolve
- particles

Rain Forest Layers

Rain forests are made of four layers. The top layer is the emergent layer. Here, the trees are very tall. They stand like giant **columns** growing from the forest floor. Their leaves **absorb** the most sun. Animals such as eagles, monkeys, and bats live in this layer.

Next, the leafy canopy layer **protects** many animals. They can find food and water there and also hide from enemies.

Most rain forests of the world are in hot, wet climates.

It is difficult to see animals in the canopy layer, but the forest is full of their sounds. Monkeys leap from tree to tree, **rustling** the leaves as they search for fruit.

Below the canopy is the understory. Jaguars and leopards lie in wait on thick branches there.

The lowest level is the forest floor. It is difficult for plants to grow there in the dark. The heavy rains often **dissolve** the nutrients in the soil and wash them away. Snakes and insects live on the forest floor.

Earthworms in the forest floor break down soil into **particles**.

www.harcourtschool.com/reading

Word Detective

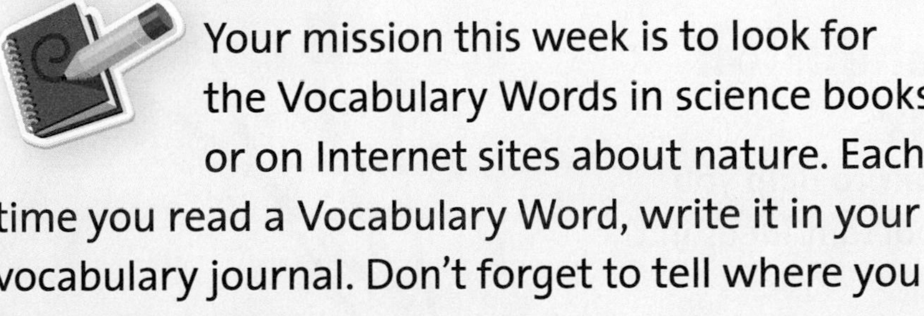

Your mission this week is to look for the Vocabulary Words in science books or on Internet sites about nature. Each time you read a Vocabulary Word, write it in your vocabulary journal. Don't forget to tell where you found the word.

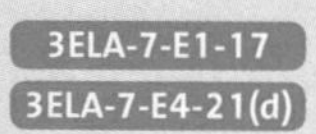

Genre Study

Expository nonfiction explains information and ideas. Look for

- illustrations and captions.
- facts and details to help you learn about a topic.

What I Know	What I Read	Author's Purpose

3ELA-7-E1-17
3ELA-7-E4-21(d)

Comprehension Strategy

Ask questions to help you explore important ideas in the selection.

LOUISIANA GRADE-LEVEL EXPECTATIONS—3ELA-6-E3-16 define characteristics of types of literature; 3ELA-7-E1-17 demonstrate understanding of information; 3ELA-7-E4-21(d) ask questions

A Tree Is Growing

by Arthur Dorros

illustrated by S. D. Schindler

A giant tree may look as if it has always been big. But even the biggest tree keeps growing and changing.

In the spring you can see that a tree is growing as you watch buds on the branches unfold into leaves.

Bristlecone pines are the oldest known living trees on earth. Some have been growing for five thousand years—since before the pyramids in Egypt were built.

Leaves can be skinny needles or big heart shapes. Whatever shape or size a leaf is, it makes food for the tree.

A kind of sugar is made in the leaves. Trees use the sugar as food.

The sugary water made in the leaves is mixed with other tree juices called sap. The food in the sap is carried throughout the tree. Where a branch breaks or where bark is cut, sap oozes out of a tree. The strong smells of some saps can keep insects from eating the trees they live on.

If you rub a sassafras leaf, the sap smells spicy.

Maple syrup is the boiled sap of sugar maple trees.

Baobab trees store water in the trunks. When a baobab tree trunk is swollen with water, it is round and fat. In dry weather, the tree gets water from the trunk. Then the trunk gets thinner.

A tree needs sunlight, air, soil, and water to grow.

Water travels through passages in the trunk and branches up to the leaves. The water moves up the trunk as if it is being sucked through a straw.

Sugary sap made in the leaves travels down other passages in the trunk, taking food to different parts of the tree.

A few kinds of trees drop roots from branches into the soil to gather water. Banyan tree roots grow into columns *all around the tree.*

Growing roots are strong. A root can lift a sidewalk or split a rock as it grows. By splitting the rock, it helps make soil.

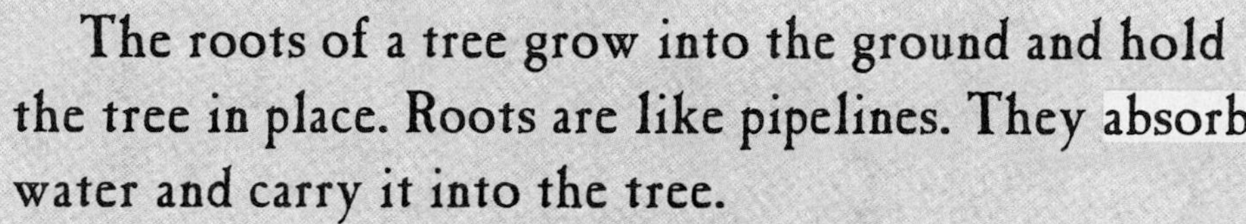

The roots of a tree grow into the ground and hold the tree in place. Roots are like pipelines. They absorb water and carry it into the tree.

A tree's roots spread out far underground. They usually grow out a little farther than the tree's branches.

Trees need minerals to grow. Minerals are tiny particles that are found in the soil. Salt is one kind of mineral. Like salt, other minerals dissolve in water. They are mixed in with the water that roots absorb and are carried throughout the tree.

Mushrooms growing among the roots of a tree can help it get minerals. And the mushrooms and plants growing near a tree get water brought by the tree's roots.

Bicolored boletus mushrooms

Flicker

Bark is the skin of a tree. The outer layer of bark protects the tree. When an oak tree is young, the bark is as smooth as a baby's skin. As the tree grows older, the bark becomes rough and cracked.

Polyphemus moth

Looking at the bark of a tree can help you know what kind of tree it is.

The cork used for bulletin boards is the peeled-off outer bark of a cork oak tree.

Honey locust bark has spines to help protect the tree.

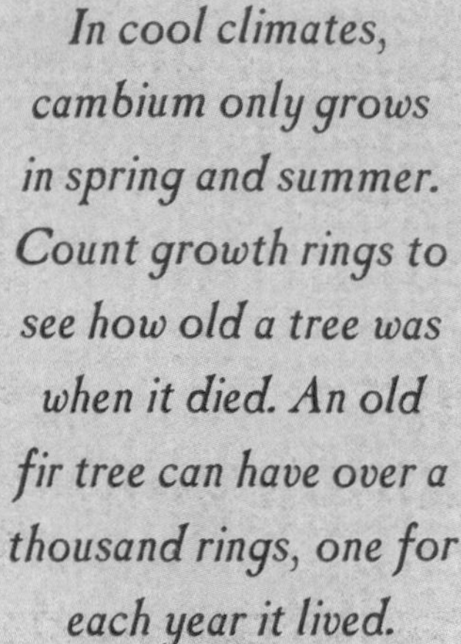

In cool climates, cambium only grows in spring and summer. Count growth rings to see how old a tree was when it died. An old fir tree can have over a thousand rings, one for each year it lived.

In tropical rain forest trees, the cambium grows all year and there are no rings. It is hard to tell the ages of those trees.

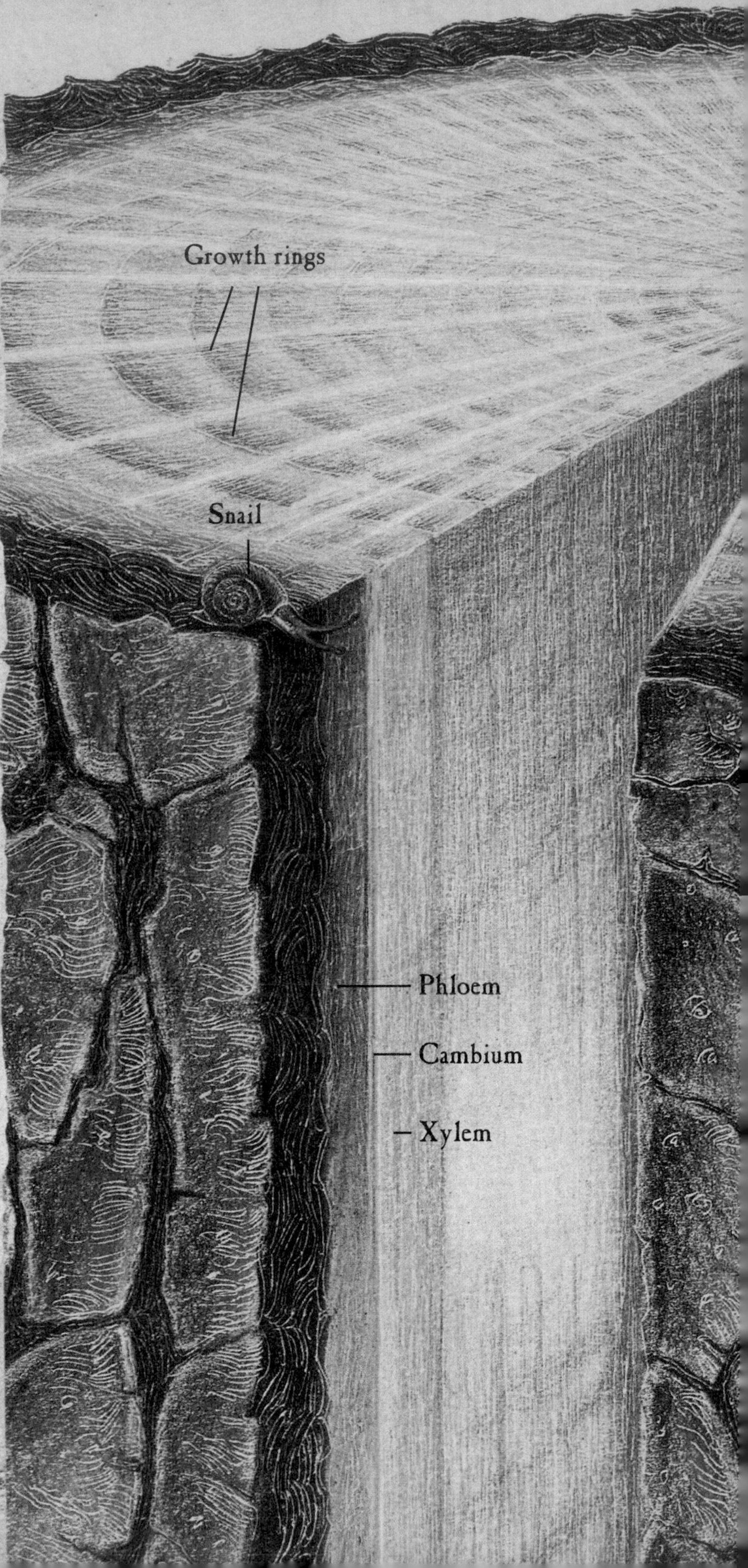

Growth rings

Snail

Phloem

Cambium

Xylem

Underwing moth

The bark you can touch and see is not growing anymore. Underneath it is a layer of growing bark, called *cambium*. Each year's cambium growth is a ring in the wood of a tree. As trees add new cambium, the trees become bigger around.

Next to the cambium are two layers called *xylem* and *phloem*. Water from the roots moves through the xylem, and sap from the leaves moves through the phloem.

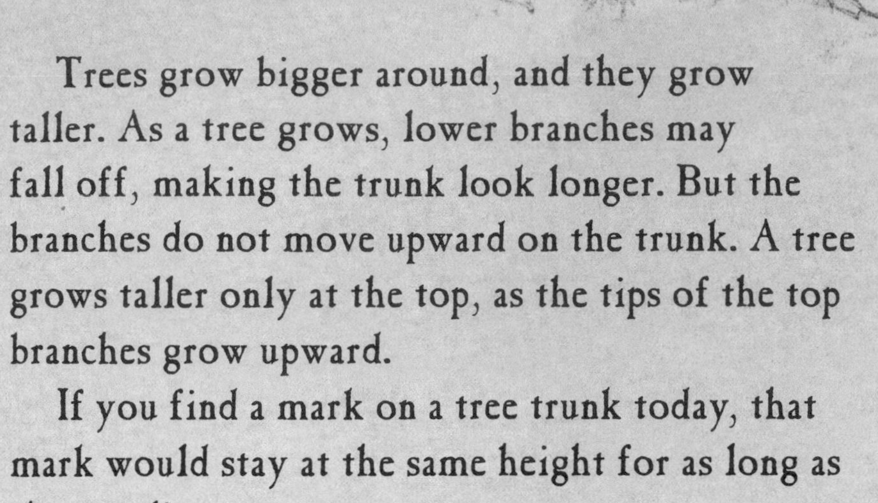

Trees grow bigger around, and they grow taller. As a tree grows, lower branches may fall off, making the trunk look longer. But the branches do not move upward on the trunk. A tree grows taller only at the top, as the tips of the top branches grow upward.

If you find a mark on a tree trunk today, that mark would stay at the same height for as long as the tree lives.

10 years

20 years

30 years

Wild turkey

Sequoias are some of the tallest trees in the world—over three hundred feet tall.
50 years
200 years

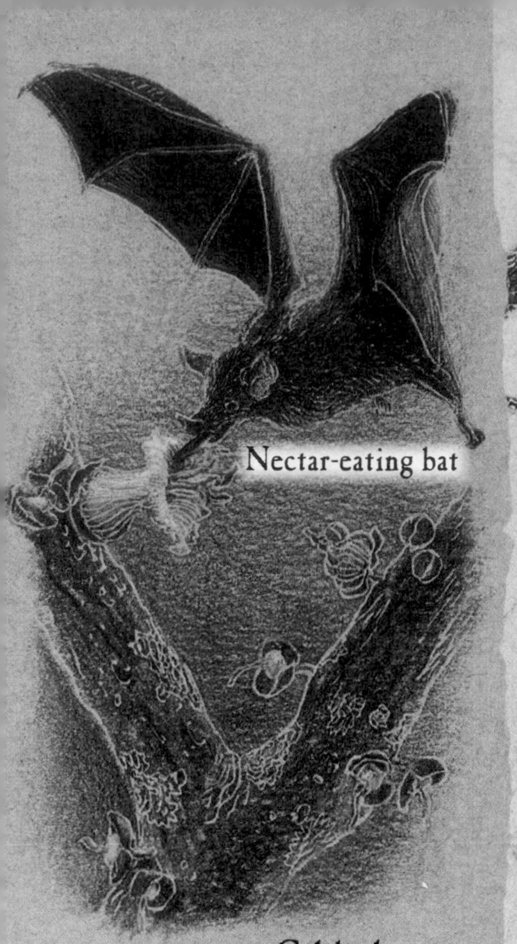

Birds, insects, and even bats are attracted to flowers to drink their sweet juices. When they brush the flowers, the animals get a powder called pollen on them. The animals carry the pollen to other flowers. When the pollen mixes with certain parts of the flowers, seeds grow. Wind also helps pollinate flowers.

In the spring, you can smell tree flowers. Tree flowers are found in many shapes and colors, and have many different smells. Parts of the flowers grow to become seeds. Oak trees have dangling clumps of flowers called catkins that help make acorns, the seeds of an oak tree.

An oak tree can drop more than fifty thousand acorns in one year. Only a few of them grow into oak trees. Most are eaten, are crushed, rot, or land in a place where they cannot take root.

Acorns can be carried away and dropped or buried by animals to grow in new places. Other kinds of seeds blow in the wind or float on water.

Different kinds of trees make seeds with different coverings. Nuts, cones, and fruits all have seeds inside.

Coconuts are seeds of a palm tree. A coconut can float across the ocean and sprout on a sandy beach.

Autumn is a great time to collect leaves. Each tree has its own special color.

Tulip poplar

Gingko

Big-tooth aspen

Sweet gum

Pin oak

In cool climates, trees stop growing in autumn. The leaves of many trees stop making sugary food for the tree, and they lose their green color. Then you can see the red, brown, yellow, and orange colors that are also in the leaves.

Pine trees and some other trees have needles or leaves that do not change color in autumn.

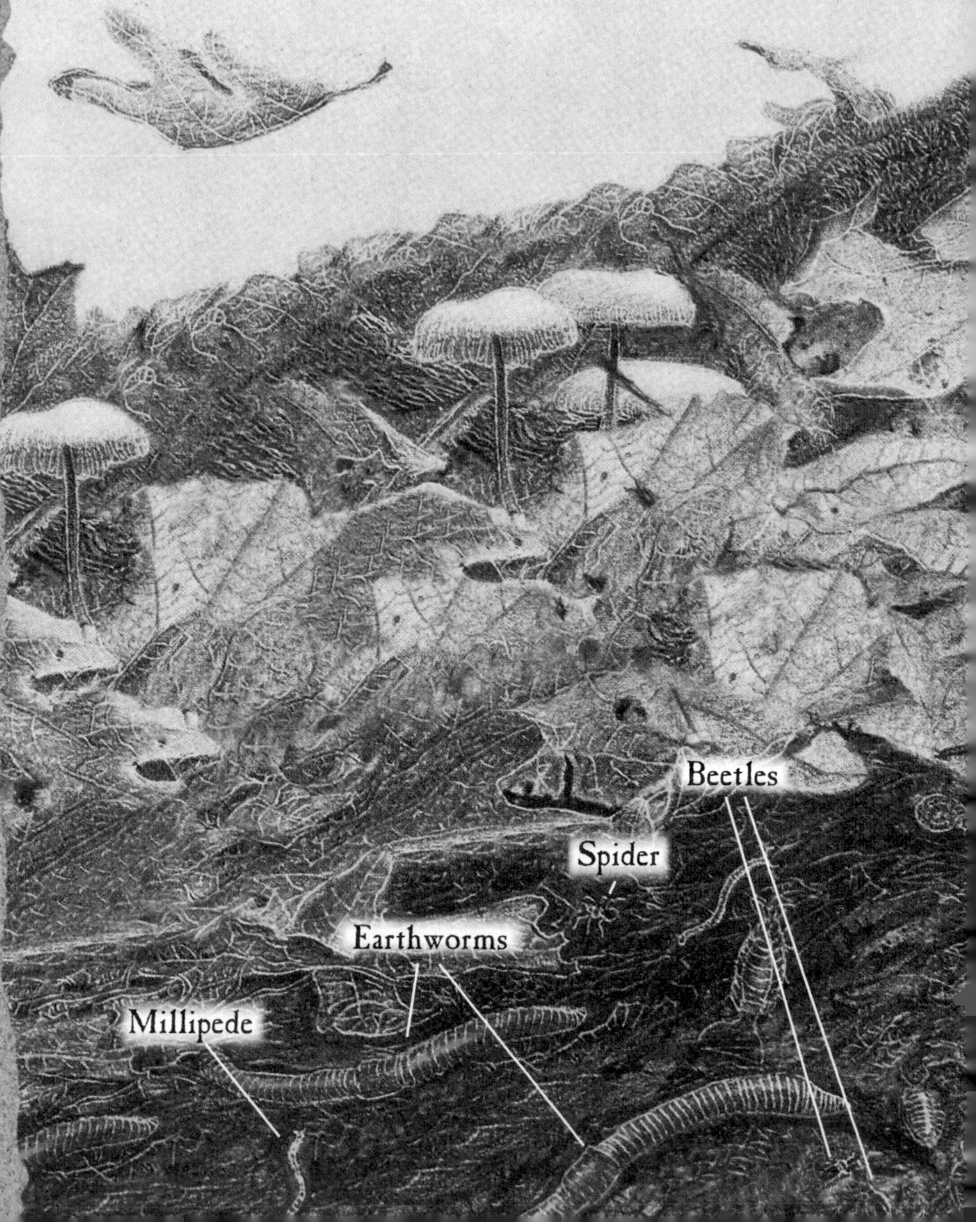

Beetles

Spider

Earthworms

Millipede

When leaves fall to the ground, insects and worms eat them. The chewed and eaten bits of leaves make the soil better for growing trees and other plants.

White oak

Trees rest in the cold of winter, and their branches are bare. They may look as if they are dead. But look closely and you can see small buds that will become leaves and flowers in the spring.

Horse chestnut

In the spring, listen to the wind rustling the leaves.

The trees are growing again.

White oak

Think Critically

1. What was the author's purpose for writing "A Tree Is Growing"? How do you know? Focus Skill AUTHOR'S PURPOSE

2. How do trees use the sugar made in the leaves? IMPORTANT DETAILS

3. What is the most interesting thing you learned about trees by reading the selection? EXPRESS PERSONAL OPINIONS

4. How can you tell that the author is interested in how trees change throughout the year? DRAW CONCLUSIONS

5. **WRITE** What changes happen to a tree as it grows? Use examples from the text to support your answer. EXTENDED RESPONSE

LOUISIANA GRADE-LEVEL EXPECTATIONS—3ELA-1-E6-11 connect to prior knowledge; 3ELA-7-E1-17 demonstrate understanding of information; 3ELA-7-E1-17(c) make inferences/draw conclusions; 3ELA-7-E3-19 identify author's purpose; 3ELA-7-E3-20 explain author's viewpoint; 3ELA-2-E1-22 write organized paragraphs

Meet the Author
Arthur Dorros

Arthur Dorros likes to write about the things that interest him. The author loves trees. When he was five, Arthur planted a maple seedling. The tree grew taller than a two-story house! He said it was almost as big as the tree in *A Tree Is Growing*.

Arthur Dorros believes that everyone has stories to tell. He encourages children all over the country to write. He tells them that if they read enough, they'll find out enough to help them write.

Meet the Illustrator
S. D. Schindler

S. D. Schindler began drawing and coloring when he was very young. When he was four, he won a red wagon in a coloring contest. In school, he was known as the class artist. His favorite pictures were of animals.

S. D. Schindler loves nature as much as he loves drawing. He used plants and animals from the woods near his home as models for the illustrations in *A Tree Is Growing*.

GO online www.harcourtschool.com/storytown

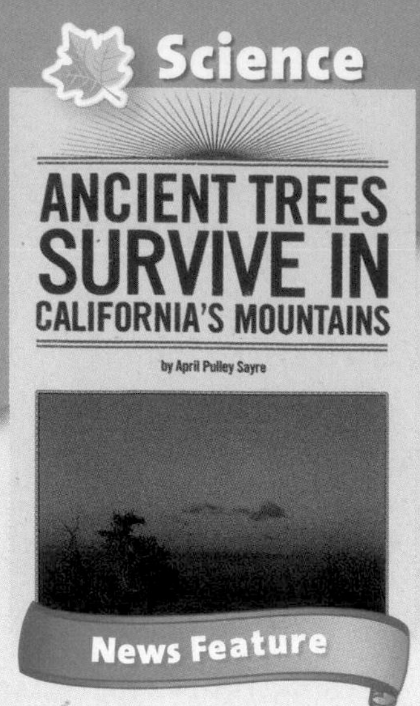

ANCIENT TREES SURVIVE IN CALIFORNIA'S MOUNTAINS

by April Pulley Sayre

Survivors

The world's oldest trees are the bristlecone pines that grow in California's White Mountains. Some of the trees are more than 4,000 years old. They started to grow at the time of the building of the Egyptian pyramids.

Bristlecones are survivors. Trees need water, soil, sunshine, and warmth; yet these trees live on dry, rocky, cold mountains. They get a lot of sunlight there, but little water, soil, or warmth.

Parts of the oldest trees may look as if they are dead. However, the trees still produce seeds.

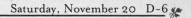

All trees need water to live. Since bristlecone pines live in dry areas, they stay alive by using very little water. They have narrow leaves called needles. Needles don't lose as much water as broad, flat leaves do.

In addition, these pines use very little energy. They are evergreens. This means that they keep their needles in winter. They always look green. However, even evergreens must drop old needles and grow new ones. This happens a few needles at a time, not all at once. White pine trees, for example, keep each needle for about two years. In contrast, bristlecone pines keep each needle for about 30 years! These trees save energy by not making new needles very often.

Bristlecone pine trees can remain standing for hundreds of years after they die.

The needles on a bristlecone pine provide energy to the tree.

Some young bristlecone pine cones are a purplish color.

Bristlecone pine trees can grow to be 60 feet tall.

Some of the bristlecones look dead, but they are still alive. On some, only a small strip of bark and xylem remain alive. Cells in the xylem carry water and soil nutrients up the tree.

It takes only a small strip of xylem to bring water and food to a single branch. That branch makes needles. It forms cones that hold seeds. Such a tree may look half dead, but it can live for thousands of years.

The Oldest Living Bristlecone Pine

The oldest living bristlecone pine is known as "the Methuselah tree." It is at least 4,700 years old. The Methuselah tree lives in the Ancient Bristlecone Pine Forest in California's White Mountains. You can visit the Ancient Bristlecone Pine Forest, but you will not easily find the Methuselah tree. It is not marked. The tree's identity is kept a secret so people will not get too close and harm the tree.

Stories from the Trees

These long-lived trees can help people learn about history. The trees cannot say what happened, but their tree rings hold information. Rainy or snowy years cause wider rings to form. Dry years result in narrow tree rings.

Scientists can drill a small sample from a tree. The sample is the size of a drinking straw. Scientists study the layers that show the rings. This way, they do not have to cut down the tree

to see its rings. By studying tree rings, scientists can learn more about the lives of plants, animals, and people that lived thousands of years ago. The ancient bristlecone pine trees hold stories for people who know how to read them!

Connections

Comparing Texts

3ELA-1-E6-11
3ELA-7-E1-17(d)
3ELA-7-E4-21(e)

1. How is the bristlecone pine tree in "Ancient Trees Survive in California's Mountains" like the oak tree in "A Tree Is Growing"? How is it different?

2. Now that you know more about trees, what will be your favorite season to look at them? Explain.

3. How does a tree make the world a better place?

Vocabulary Review

3ELA-2-E6-27

A tree's roots absorb particles of water.

Word Sort

Work with a partner. Sort the Vocabulary Words into two categories. Decide whether each word is an *action* or an *object.* Compare your sorted words with your partner's words. Take turns explaining why you put each word where you did. Then choose one word from each category and write a sentence that uses both words.

columns

absorb

protects

rustling

dissolve

particles

Fluency Practice 3ELA-1-E3-07

Repeated Reading

Choose a section from "A Tree Is Growing." Read the passage, letting your voice rise and fall naturally. Use a stopwatch to time your second reading. Repeat until you can read the passage with few or no errors.

Writing 3ELA-2-E3-24(b) 3ELA-2-E6-27

Write a Poem

Write a poem about a tree. Think about what you learned in "A Tree Is Growing" to help you get ideas. Use a graphic organizer to brainstorm interesting words and phrases. Your poem does not have to rhyme, but it should help the reader understand what you like about trees. You might even write your words to form the shape of a tree.

My Writing Checklist

Writing Trait → Sentence Fluency

- ✔ I use the graphic organizer to plan my poem.
- ✔ I elaborate on the ideas in my poem.

How trees look	How trees feel	How trees smell

LOUISIANA GRADE-LEVEL EXPECTATIONS—3ELA-1-E3-07 adjust reading speed; 3ELA-1-E6-11 connect to prior knowledge; 3ELA-7-E1-17(d) compare/contrast; 3ELA-7-E4-21(e) connect to real-life situations; 3ELA-2-E3-24(b) use prewriting strategies; 3ELA-2-E6-27 write for various purposes

CONTENTS

Lesson 14

Genre: Expository Nonfiction
One Small Place in a Tree
Be a Birdwatcher
Genre: Expository Nonfiction

Focus Skill

Author's Purpose

An **author's purpose** is his or her reason for writing.

- If an author is telling a story, the author's purpose is usually to entertain.
- An author's purpose for writing nonfiction is usually to give information.
- If the author is telling you what you should do or think, the author's purpose is to persuade.

To figure out the author's purpose, think about what you read and what you know about purposes for writing.

What I Know	What I Read	Author's Purpose

Tip

An author may also give some information while telling a story. To figure out the author's purpose, identify the main reason the author wrote the passage.

Read the passage below. Then use the chart to think about and tell the author's purpose. Tell which clues in the text helped you figure out the author's purpose.

Flying squirrels do not really fly. They glide or float through the air. The flying squirrel has a flap of skin on each side of its body. The flaps are joined to its front and back legs. When the squirrel wants to glide, it stretches its legs to open the flaps of skin. The flaps are like the wings of a glider. The squirrel steers by moving its front legs. A flying squirrel can glide for more than 100 feet!

What I Know	What I Read	Author's Purpose
Authors give many facts when they write to inform.		

Try This!

What if this author had written a fiction story about a squirrel that flies a plane? What would the author's purpose be then?

www.harcourtschool.com/storytown

LOUISIANA GRADE-LEVEL EXPECTATIONS—3ELA-7-E3-19 identify author's purpose

Vocabulary

Build Robust Vocabulary

suppose

roost

strikes

spears

glimpse

maze

The Everglades

If you were to visit the Florida Everglades, what do you **suppose** you would see? You might see flocks of birds that stop to **roost** in the treetops. Down below, there is plenty of food for birds.

There are areas with many pine trees. When lightning **strikes**, it can cause fires among the pines. These wildfires clear the land and let light in for young trees to grow.

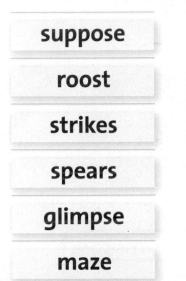

A great blue heron **spears** a fish with its sharp beak.

Another kind of tree you might see is the mangrove. These strange trees grow in places where fresh river water meets salty ocean water.

You might catch a **glimpse** of birds nesting in the mangroves' branches. Their tangled roots form a **maze**, in which fish can swim and hide.

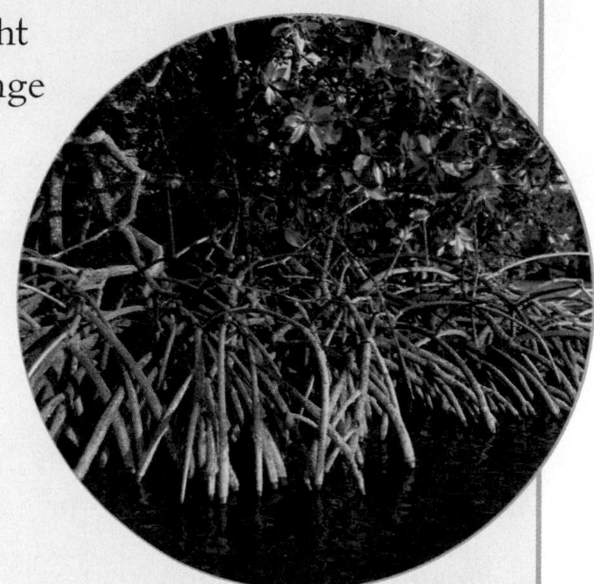

The roots of a mangrove keep the tree above the salty water.

www.harcourtschool.com/storytown

Word Champion

Your mission this week is to use the Vocabulary Words in conversation with family members or friends. For example, tell a family member about a bird that may roost in your area. Write in your vocabulary journal sentences that use Vocabulary Words.

LOUISIANA GRADE-LEVEL EXPECTATIONS—3ELA-2-E6-27 write for various purposes

3ELA-6-E3-16

Genre Study

Expository nonfiction explains information and ideas. Look for

- illustrations that support the facts.
- details to help you learn about a topic.

What I Know	What I Read	Author's Purpose

3ELA-7-E1-17
3ELA-7-E4-21(d)

Comprehension Strategy

Ask questions if you are confused about what you are reading.

LOUISIANA GRADE-LEVEL EXPECTATIONS—3ELA-6-E3-16 define characteristics of types of literature; 3ELA-7-E1-17 demonstrate understanding of information; 3ELA-7-E4-21(d) ask questions

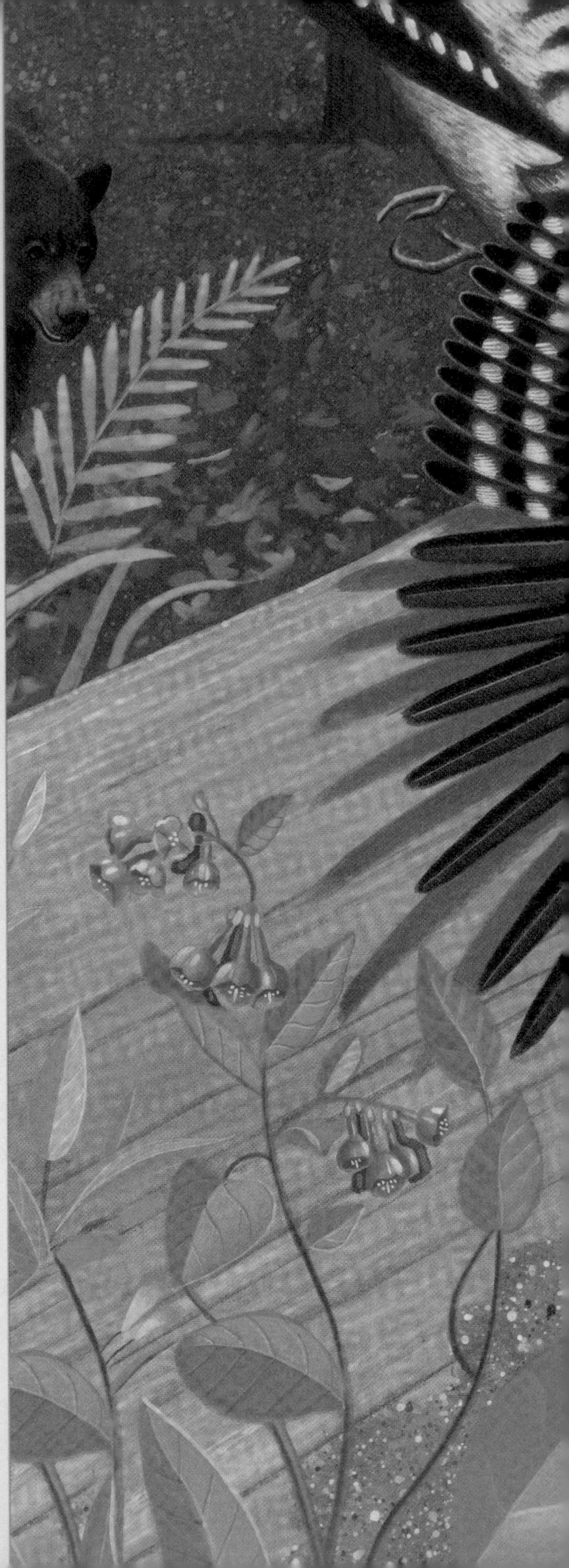

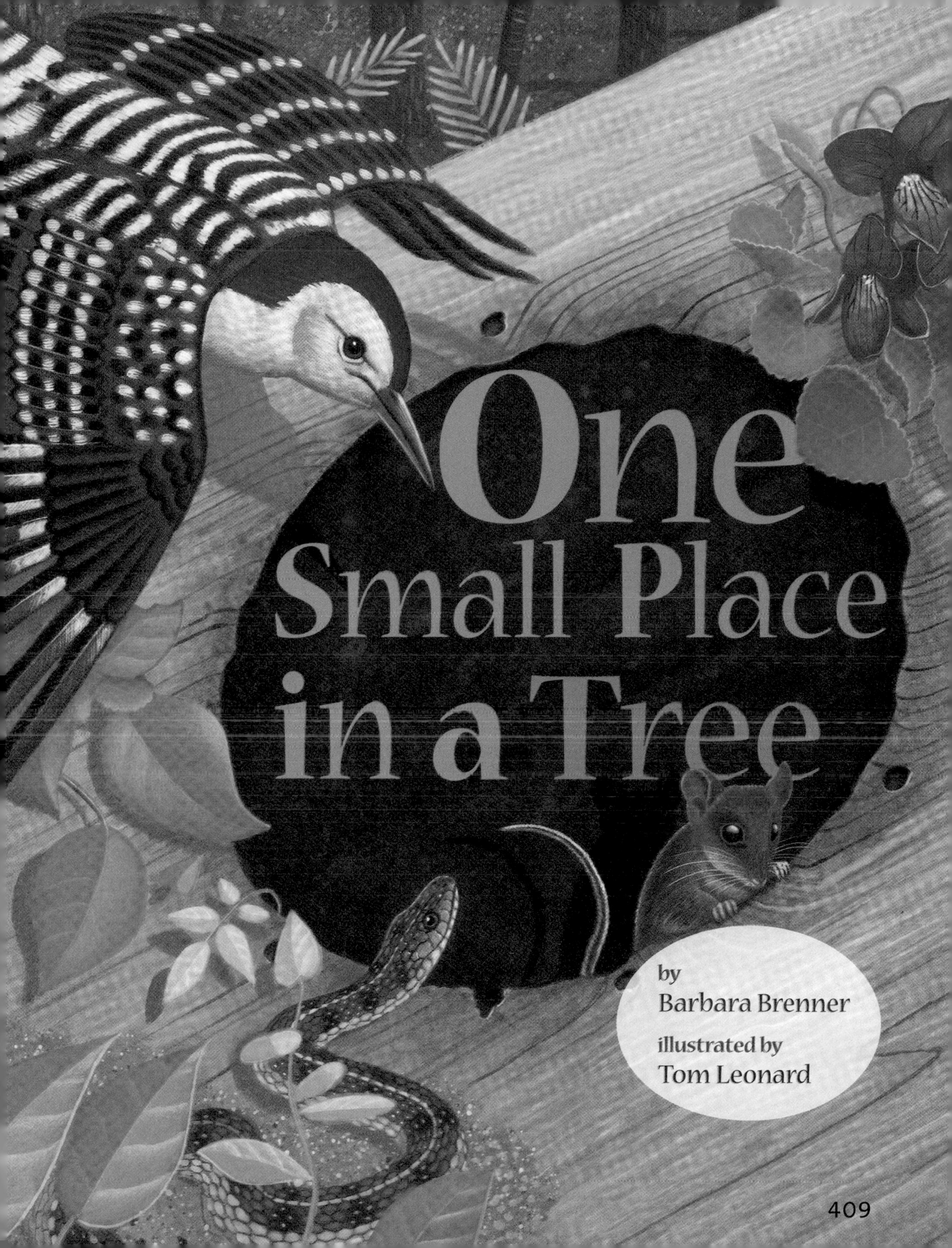

One Small Place in a Tree

by
Barbara Brenner

illustrated by
Tom Leonard

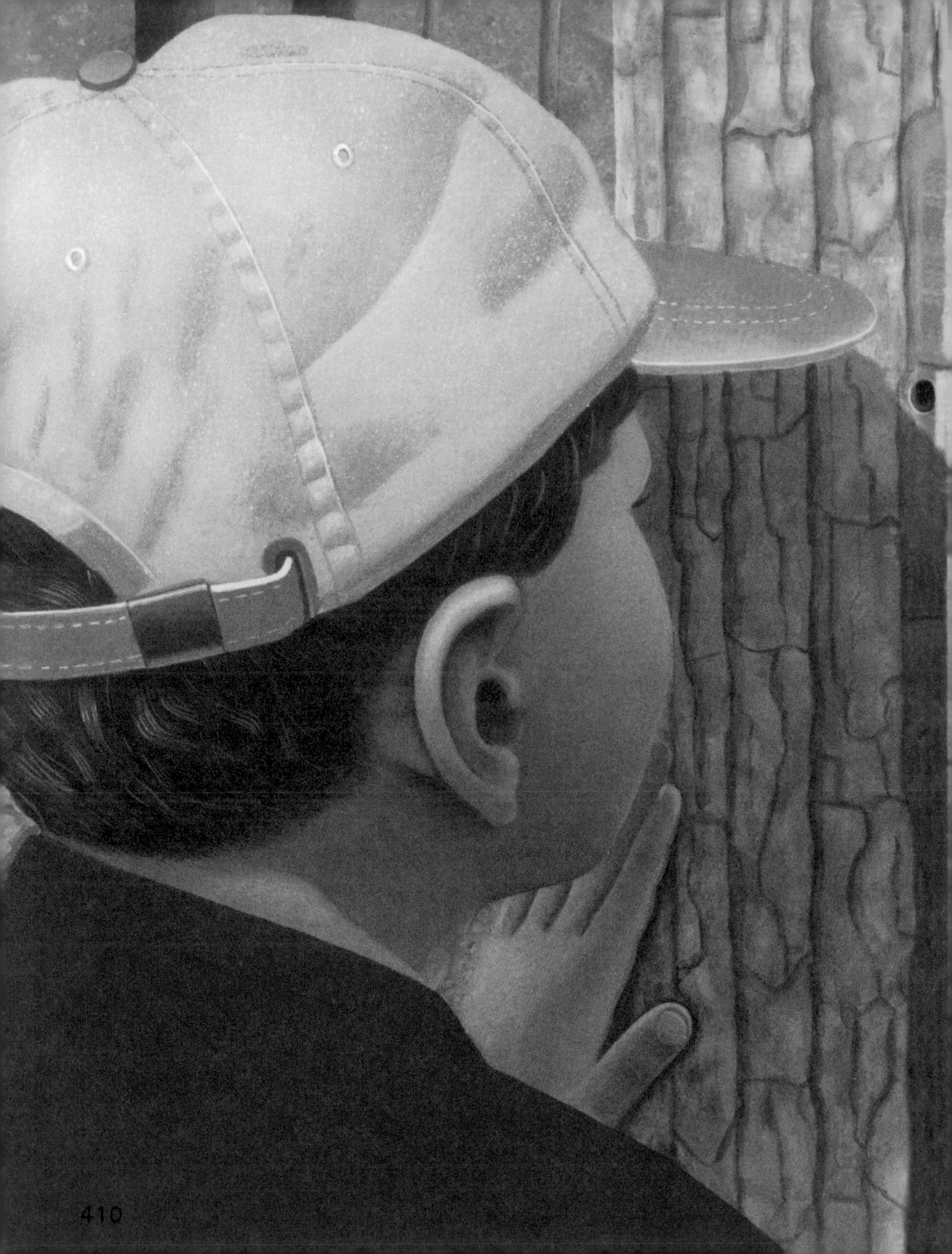

A tree hole. One small place in a tree. How does it get there? Who lives inside?

Suppose that you could watch a hole from its beginning. You might see something like this.

Here's one oak tree in a forest. It looks like the others, except—a black bear uses this one as a scratching post. Every time she goes by, the bear sharpens her claws on the trunk.

You're walking in the woods. You see the tree and notice the scratch marks on the bark. Maybe you even catch a glimpse of the bear!

After a while the scratching chips some pieces of bark off the tree. A cut forms in the bark. A hole in the tree is beginning.

Next time you're walking there, you see that tiny bugs have found the cut. They're timber beetles, and they're about to set up housekeeping.

The timber beetles get under the bark and bore into the tree. They make a maze of tunnels. They create spaces called cradles for their eggs. And they "plant" fungi for the colony to feed on. Imagine that you can look inside. You see something like this.

Soon the fungi spread and are growing all over the walls of the tunnels. The beetle eggs have hatched into grubs. The grubs are feeding on the fungi. The fungi are feeding on the soft wood inside the tree.

The beetle grubs become full-grown timber beetles.

They eat their way out of the chambers and make more holes in the tree.

On your next visit you count more than ten holes. But the first one is the largest.

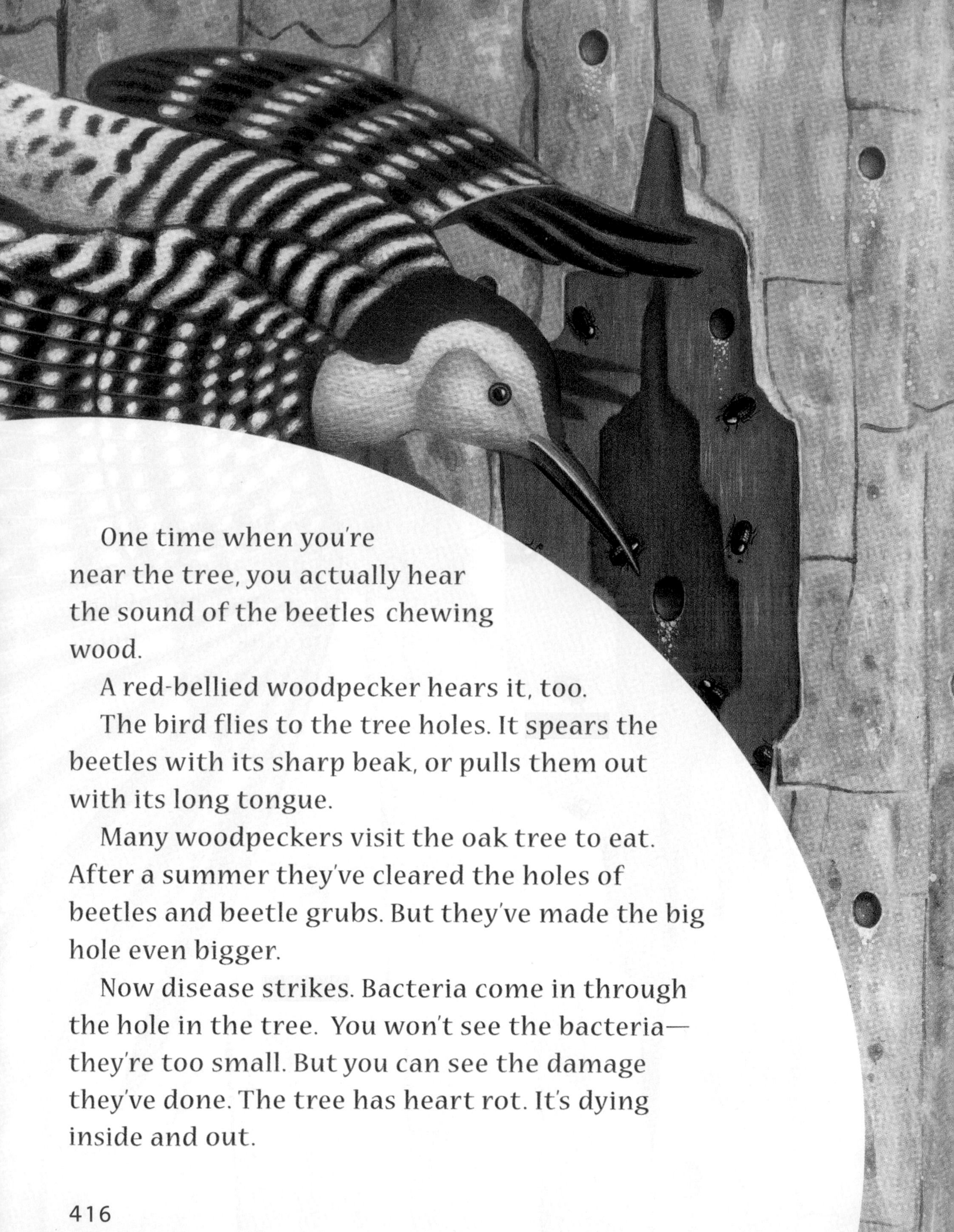

One time when you're near the tree, you actually hear the sound of the beetles chewing wood.

A red-bellied woodpecker hears it, too.

The bird flies to the tree holes. It spears the beetles with its sharp beak, or pulls them out with its long tongue.

Many woodpeckers visit the oak tree to eat. After a summer they've cleared the holes of beetles and beetle grubs. But they've made the big hole even bigger.

Now disease strikes. Bacteria come in through the hole in the tree. You won't see the bacteria—they're too small. But you can see the damage they've done. The tree has heart rot. It's dying inside and out.

Bark begins to loosen and fall off. The hole is now so large that you can actually see inside.

It has become a hollow place that looks as if it could be home for something.

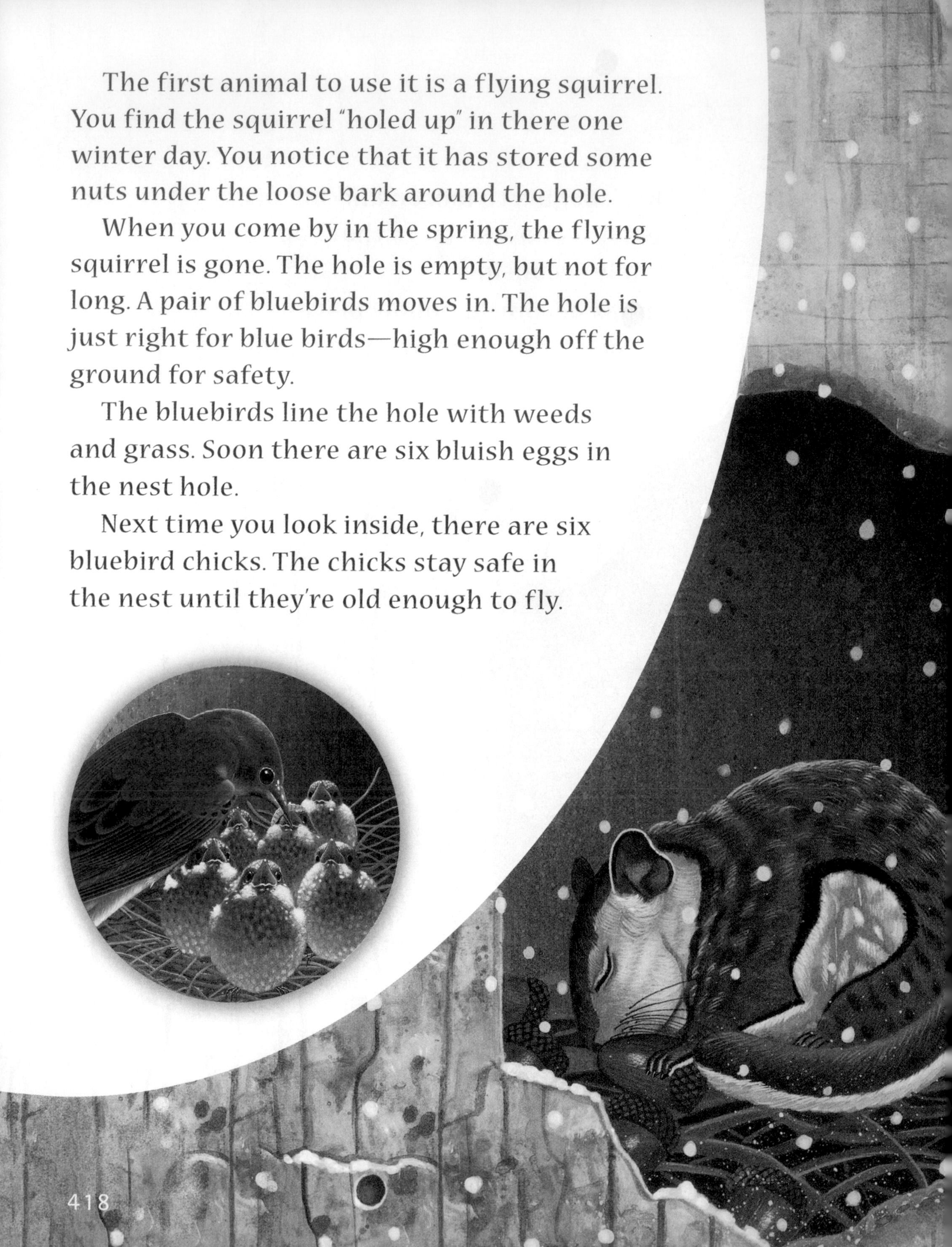

The first animal to use it is a flying squirrel. You find the squirrel "holed up" in there one winter day. You notice that it has stored some nuts under the loose bark around the hole.

When you come by in the spring, the flying squirrel is gone. The hole is empty, but not for long. A pair of bluebirds moves in. The hole is just right for blue birds—high enough off the ground for safety.

The bluebirds line the hole with weeds and grass. Soon there are six bluish eggs in the nest hole.

Next time you look inside, there are six bluebird chicks. The chicks stay safe in the nest until they're old enough to fly.

By this time the oak tree is no longer sending out leaves. Almost all of its bark is gone. But the hole-dwellers don't seem to care.

For the next three springs, the hole in the tree is a nest for the same pair of bluebirds.

For the next three winters, it's home to a family of white-footed mice.

In all those three years, the tree hasn't grown at all. This oak tree is dead. But—the hole is full of life.

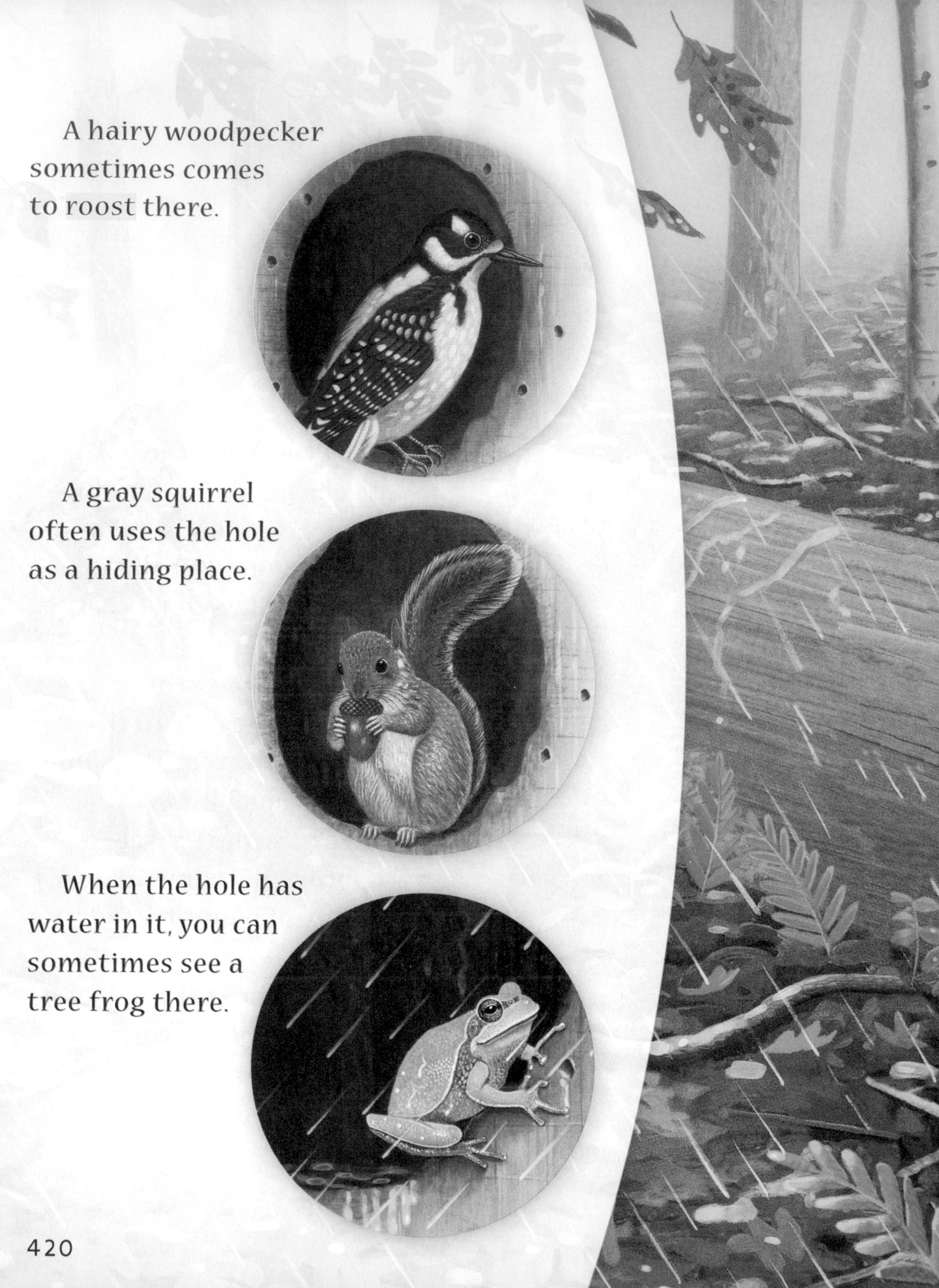

A hairy woodpecker sometimes comes to roost there.

A gray squirrel often uses the hole as a hiding place.

When the hole has water in it, you can sometimes see a tree frog there.

One day lightning, or a high wind, or heavy rain, or snow will bring this dead tree down. Many years later all that may be left will be a log with a hole in it.

But the hole will still be a place for living things. A small garter snake may cool off in there.

A redback salamander may lay its eggs there.

Or maybe a hammock spider will make a web across the hole to catch swarming insects.

Living trees are important. But so are dead and dying trees. A dead tree often has a hole—one small place that is usually home for something.

Think Critically

1. What do you think was the author's purpose in writing "One Small Place in a Tree"? AUTHOR'S PURPOSE

2. What important events happen after the bear scratches the tree? SEQUENCE

3. What information surprised you most as you read the selection? EXPRESS PERSONAL OPINIONS

4. How can you tell that the author thinks trees are useful, even when they are dead? DRAW CONCLUSIONS

5. **WRITE** How is the tree helpful to other living things? Give examples from the story to support your answer. SHORT RESPONSE

LOUISIANA GRADE-LEVEL EXPECTATIONS—3ELA-1-E6-11 connect to prior knowledge; 3ELA-7-E1-17(a) sequence events; 3ELA-7-E1-17(c) make inferences/draw conclusions; 3ELA-7-E3-19 identify author's purpose; 3ELA-7-E3-20 explain author's viewpoint; 3ELA-2-E4-25 write paragraphs with description/narration

Barbara Brenner

Barbara Brenner loves everything in nature, especially reptiles. She once got a snake as a birthday present. Later, she had 23 reptiles and amphibians as pets! She used to bring her pet boa with her when she visited schools.

When Barbara Brenner needs an idea for a new book, she thinks about books she has read and about things that interest her. She likes to write books about science that have more than just facts. She says that mixing stories with science makes science even more interesting.

Meet the Illustrator

Tom Leonard

Tom Leonard has been drawing pictures since he was a boy. He started by drawing the characters from his favorite cartoon strips. After he went to art school, he had jobs drawing for newspapers and magazines. Then he began to illustrate children's books.

Before Tom Leonard begins work on the pictures for a book, he spends a lot of time doing research. His illustrations are known for being realistic and colorful. Someday he would like to write and illustrate his own books.

GO online www.harcourtschool.com/storytown

Science

Expository Nonfiction

Be a Birdwatcher

by Beverly J. Letchworth

Do you want to be a birdwatcher and solve some bird mysteries? You can by paying attention to the details.

First, learn to identify the birds you see. Look for birds in your own backyard. Then ask yourself these questions:

- ☞ What color is the bird?
- ☞ How big is it?
- ☞ What does the tail look like? The beak?
- ☞ How does the bird move? Some birds, such as crows and grackles, walk. Others, such as sparrows, hop.
- ☞ Does the bird have other color markings on it?

Describe the bird's behavior. Nuthatches creep head-first down a tree trunk. Eastern phoebes wag their tails when perched on a branch.

Is the bird singing? What does the song sound like?

Now it's time to find out the name of your mystery bird. Look through a bird field guide and match your clues to a picture of the bird you saw.

Did you find it? Great!

Case solved!

Nuthatch

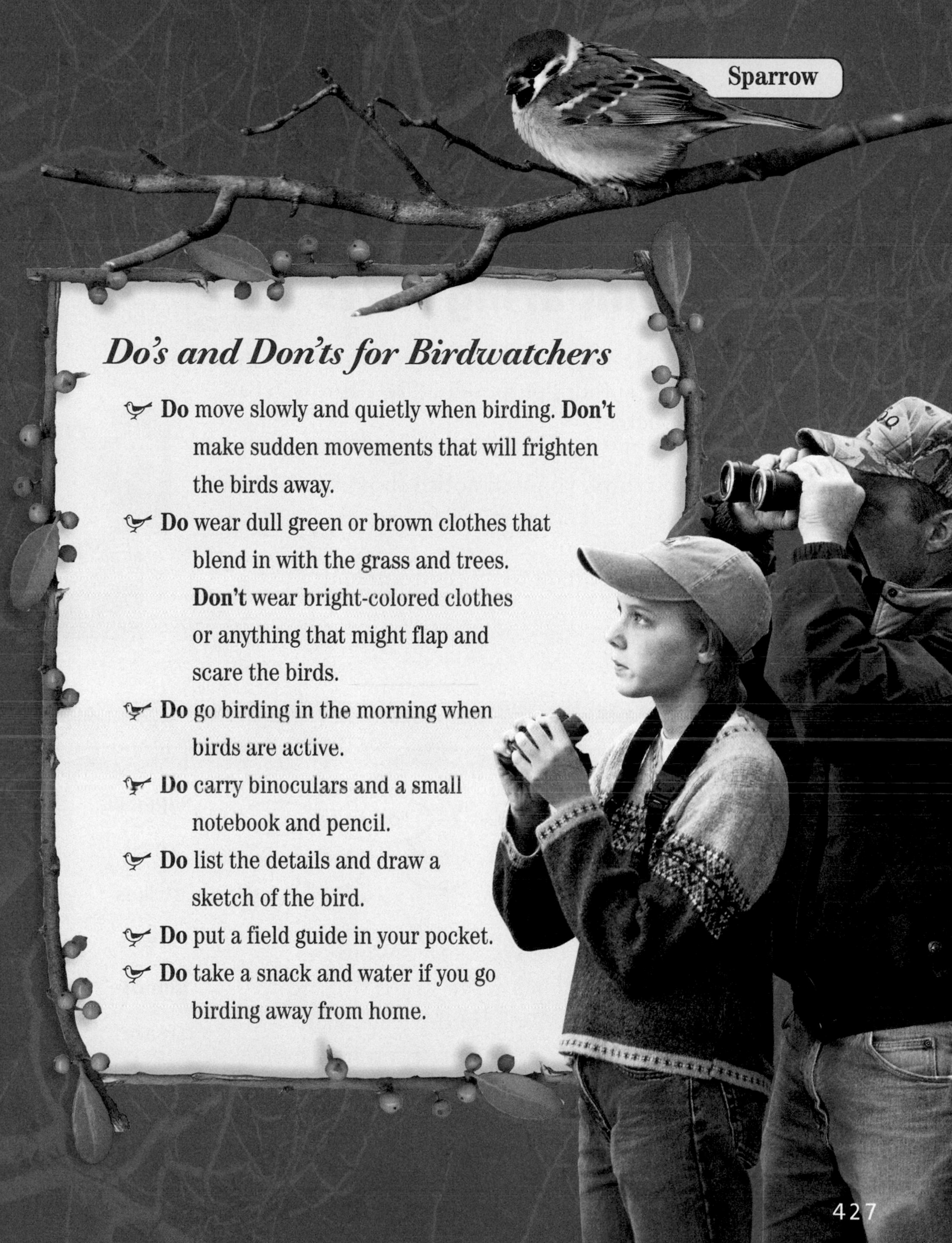

Do's and Don'ts for Birdwatchers

- **Do** move slowly and quietly when birding. **Don't** make sudden movements that will frighten the birds away.
- **Do** wear dull green or brown clothes that blend in with the grass and trees. **Don't** wear bright-colored clothes or anything that might flap and scare the birds.
- **Do** go birding in the morning when birds are active.
- **Do** carry binoculars and a small notebook and pencil.
- **Do** list the details and draw a sketch of the bird.
- **Do** put a field guide in your pocket.
- **Do** take a snack and water if you go birding away from home.

Connections

Comparing Texts

3ELA-1-E6-11
3ELA-7-E1-17(d)
3ELA-7-E3-19
3ELA-7-E4-21(e)

1. How is the author's purpose in "One Small Place in a Tree" like the author's purpose in "Be a Birdwatcher?" How is it different?

2. What do you think you will notice about the next tree you see?

3. Why is a tree important to its environment?

Vocabulary Review

Word Webs

nest — roost

Work with a partner. Choose two Vocabulary Words and create a word web for each word. Put the Vocabulary Word in the center of your web. Then write words that are related to the Vocabulary Word in the web. Share your word web with your partner. Explain how each word in your web is related to the Vocabulary Word.

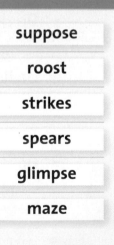

Fluency Practice 3ELA-1-E3-07

Partner Reading

Choose a section from "One Small Place in a Tree." Meet with a partner. Take turns reading aloud. Let your voice rise and fall naturally. Have your partner give you feedback about your reading.

Writing 3ELA-1-E5-10 3ELA-2-E3-24(b) 3ELA-2-E4-25

Write a Summary

Write a paragraph that summarizes "One Small Place in a Tree." Include key ideas from the selection. Share your paragraph with a partner.

My Writing Checklist

Writing Trait → Sentence Fluency

- ✔ I elaborate to give my reader enough information about the tree.
- ✔ I use a graphic organizer to plan my writing.

What I Know	What I Read	Author's Purpose

LOUISIANA GRADE-LEVEL EXPECTATIONS—3ELA-1-E3-07 adjust reading speed; 3ELA-1-E5-10 summarize main events/ideas/details; 3ELA-1-E6-11 connect to prior knowledge; 3ELA-7-E1-17(d) compare/contrast; 3ELA-7-E3-19 identify author's purpose; 3ELA-7-E4-21(e) connect to real-life situations; 3ELA-2-E3-24(b) use prewriting strategies; 3ELA-2-E4-25 write paragraphs with description/narration

CONTENTS

READERS' THEATER

Advice Column

Build Fluency

- Read with expression to show characters' feelings.
- Use intonation to show whether someone is asking a question or making a statement.

Build Vocabulary

- Read, write, and learn the meanings of new words.

Review Vocabulary

- Read theme vocabulary words in a different context.

Realistic Fiction

Use Story Structure

- Review how to use story structure to think about what you read.

Ask Questions

- Review how to monitor comprehension by asking questions about what you read.

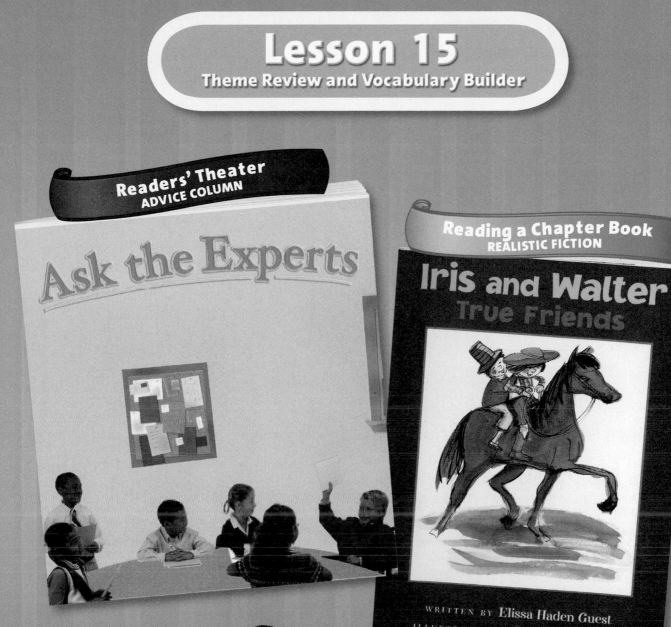

Lesson 15

Theme Review and Vocabulary Builder

Readers' Theater
ADVICE COLUMN

Ask the Experts

Reading a Chapter Book
REALISTIC FICTION

Iris and Walter
True Friends

WRITTEN BY Elissa Haden Guest
ILLUSTRATED BY Christine Davenier

READERS' THEATER

issue

advice

consult

recommend

sensible

devise

3ELA-1-E3-07 Reading for Fluency

When you read a script aloud,

- read with feeling, the way a person would speak.
- let your voice rise and fall naturally to show the character's feelings.

LOUISIANA GRADE-LEVEL EXPECTATIONS—
3ELA-1-E3-07 adjust reading speed

Ask the Experts

Roles

Corey	Friend Lee
Taylor	Book Buddy
Healthy Heart	Smarty Jackson

Place: The editors' offices of *What Should I Do?* magazine

Corey: Okay, quiet, everyone! I can't hear above the din of rustling papers in this room.

Taylor: I hope everyone has had a glimpse of our huge pile of letters, e-mails, and Web postings to discuss for our next issue of the magazine. We have a lot of work to do.

Corey: Lots of children have been writing to us.

Taylor: It's encouraging to see that so many people want our expert advice. As the editors of this advice magazine, Corey and I chose the best letters. Now we'll consult with you, our experts, to answer them. Let's get started.

Corey: First, let's hear from Healthy Heart, our health expert.

Healthy: Thanks, Corey. This brief letter comes from a girl in Florida. I'll read it to you:

Dear Healthy Heart,

Are video games a good form of exercise?

Sincerely,

Video Girl

Taylor: All right, Healthy. What is your answer?

Healthy: I wrote this reply.

Dear Video Girl,

While video games can be fun to play, they are not a good form of exercise. You need to move your body and release a lot of energy. Activities that are safe and fun, such as jumping rope, playing soccer, or riding bikes with your friends, are great!

Yours in health,

Healthy Heart

Taylor: That's good advice, Healthy.

Corey: The next letter is about friendship.

Taylor: Friend Lee is our friendship expert.

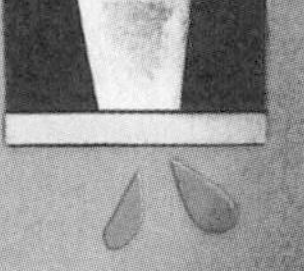

Friend Lee: This is an e-mail sent to us.

Dear Friend Lee,

Help! My father just got a new job on the other side of the United States. Now my family has to move. I'll miss my friends so much when I leave! Also, I'm afraid that I won't have any friends in our new town. What should I do?

Your worried friend,
Sad About Moving

Fluency Tip

Make your voice rise and fall to show the letter writer's feelings.

Corey: That's so sad!

Taylor: Moving to a new town is hard.

Fluency Tip

Friend Lee is giving kind words of advice. Use a smooth, calm voice to read these lines.

Friend Lee: The problem isn't really so hard to solve. Here's my advice:

Dear Sad About Moving,

Don't worry too much. Talk to your parents about how you feel. They are probably sad about moving, too. Let your friends know you'll miss them. You could have a good-bye party with them.

In your new town, joining groups will help you meet other kids. You'll make new friends in no time!

Good luck,
Friend Lee

Corey: That's good advice.

Taylor: The next letter asks for some reading advice.

Corey: Book Buddy is our reading expert.

Buddy: This is a question I get asked a lot. It's from a boy in California.

Dear Book Buddy,

I like to read, but I have a hard time choosing books to read. Do you have any suggestions?

Sincerely,
Reid A. Lott

Taylor: I'd like to know the answer to this. I need a new book to read, too.

Buddy: Here's what I wrote:

Dear Reid,

When you choose a new book to read, start by thinking about what you enjoy. Choose a book that sounds interesting to you. Try reading both fiction and nonfiction books. Also, try asking your friends what books they like. Maybe they will recommend *a book for you.*

Keep reading!
Book Buddy

Taylor: That's sensible advice, Book Buddy.

Corey: Next, we have a letter about homework.

Taylor: Smarty Jackson is our homework expert.

Smarty: This next letter was posted on the *What Should I Do?* website. It's from a girl in Ohio.

Dear Smarty,

What is the best time to do my homework? I usually wait until bedtime. Is that a good idea?

Sincerely,
Harriet

Corey: What should she do?

Smarty: Here is what I wrote.

Dear Harriet,

I think you might be dodging your work! You should start your homework earlier. Many students find that the best time to do homework is right after they get home from school. Other students find that they work best right after dinner. You need to devise *a plan that will give you plenty of time to finish your assignments each night. Don't wait until bedtime!*

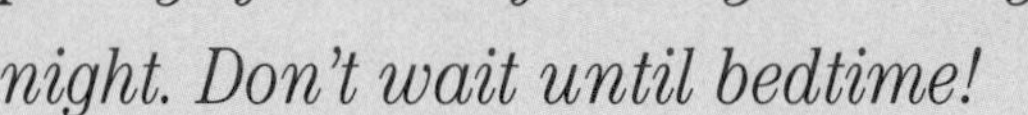

Happy studying,
Smarty Jackson

Corey: Well, that's all the letters we have.

Taylor: Which ones should we put in the magazine?

All: Let's put them all in! They're all good questions.

Corey: That's what I was thinking.

Taylor: Me, too! I suppose our meeting is over.

Corey: Wait a second. I've found one last letter. It's from a student in Washington, D.C.

> *Dear* What Should I Do? *Editors,*
>
> *What's your best advice about taking advice from other people?*
>
> *Sincerely,*
>
> *Need Some Advice*

Fluency Tip

Think about how you would speak if you were giving advice to a friend.

Taylor: What would you say, Corey?

Corey: I'd say that the best advice about taking advice is to be careful where you get it. Always make sure the person giving the advice knows what he or she is talking about.

Taylor: Good job, everyone. This issue of *What Should I Do?* will be our best one yet!

COMPREHENSION STRATEGIES

Review

Reading a Chapter Book

Bridge to Reading Longer Fiction A chapter book is a long story divided into smaller sections called chapters. The notes on page 441 show some of the features of a chapter book. Before you read, scan a book for these features.

Review the Focus Strategies

You can also use the strategies you learned in this theme to help you read chapter books.

Use Story Structure

Use what you know about how stories are arranged to help you understand a chapter book. Think about the problem in each chapter. Think about the plot of the book as a whole and how it changes as you read each chapter.

Ask Questions

Ask yourself questions before, while, and after you read. What is happening in each chapter? How do the characters behave? What will happen next?

As you read two chapters from *Iris and Walter, True Friends* on pages 441–445, think about where and how to use the comprehension strategies.

TITLE
The title of the chapter book usually gives clues to what the book will be about.

CHAPTER NUMBER AND TITLE
Chapters may begin with a number, a title, or both.

1. DREAMING OF RAIN

Iris dreamed of riding Rain over green meadows, down a path of pines, straight into the sparkling stream.

"You can't ride Rain," said Walter.

"Why not?" asked Iris.

"Because," said Walter, "Rain is fast and wild."

But Iris *wanted* to ride Rain.

The next day, Iris put on her cowgirl boots. She put on her cowgirl hat. Then she and Walter went to see Rain. "Yoo-hoo, Rain. Come here!" shouted Iris. But Rain only snorted and stamped her hoof, then galloped away.

"Why doesn't she come?" asked Iris.

"Because," said Walter, "horses don't like shouting."

"Oh," said Iris.

The next day, Iris brought Rain a present. "Come here, Rain," said Iris. "I brought you Grandpa's special cookies."

But Rain did not come.

"Why doesn't she come?" asked Iris.

"Because," said Walter, "horses can be shy."

"Walter, what do horses like?" asked Iris.

"Horses like clucking and carrots and gentle hands," said Walter.

"Hmm," said Iris.

PLOT
A chapter book has a plot that continues throughout the book. Look for smaller problems and solutions within chapters.

Apply the Strategies Read these two chapters from *Iris and Walter, True Friends*. As you read, stop and think about how you are using comprehension strategies.

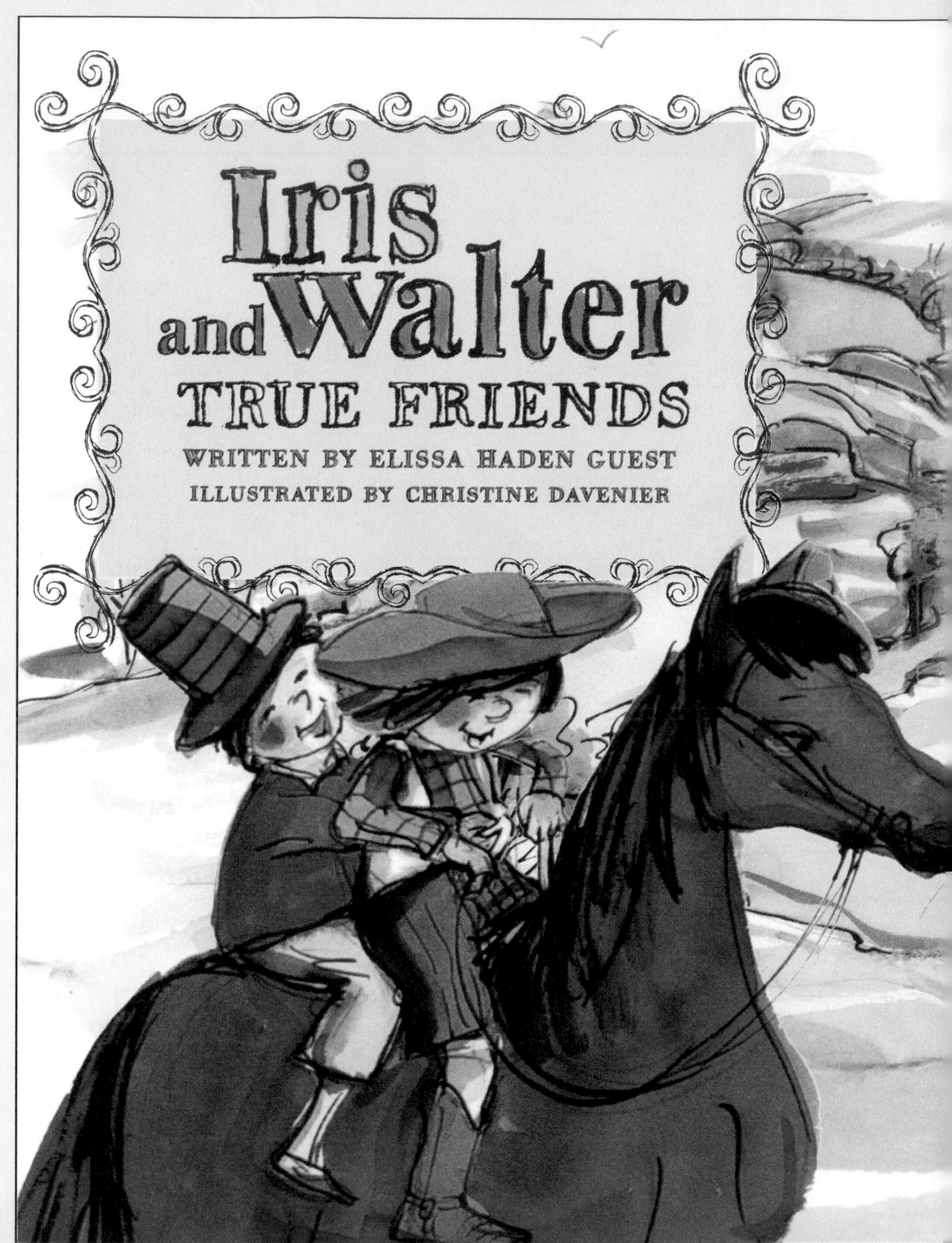

Stop and Think

Think about the **story structure** in this chapter. What is the problem in this chapter?

1. DREAMING OF RAIN

Iris dreamed of riding Rain over green meadows, down a path of pines, straight into the sparkling stream.

"You can't ride Rain," said Walter.

"Why not?" asked Iris.

"Because," said Walter, "Rain is fast and wild."

But Iris *wanted* to ride Rain.

The next day, Iris put on her cowgirl boots. She put on her cowgirl hat. Then she and Walter went to see Rain. "Yoo-hoo, Rain. Come here!" shouted Iris. But Rain only snorted and stamped her hoof, then galloped away.

"Why doesn't she come?" asked Iris.

"Because," said Walter, "horses don't like shouting."

"Oh," said Iris.

The next day, Iris brought Rain a present. "Come here, Rain," said Iris. "I brought you Grandpa's special cookies."

But Rain did not come.

"Why doesn't she come?" asked Iris.

"Because," said Walter, "horses can be shy."

"Walter, what do horses like?" asked Iris.

"Horses like clucking and carrots and gentle hands," said Walter.

"Hmm," said Iris.

2. RIDING RAIN

The next day, Iris and Walter went to see Rain. They had carrots. They had hope. They had a plan.

Iris held out a carrot. "Come here, Rain," she said. But Rain did not come.

"Why doesn't she come?" asked Iris.

"Try clucking," said Walter.

So Iris clucked and clucked. Rain moved backwards. Rain moved sideways. But still, Rain did not come.

"Maybe Rain doesn't like me," said Iris.

"Maybe Rain is scared of you," said Walter.

"Don't be scared of me, Rain," said Iris.

Every day, Iris and Walter went to see Rain. Every day, Iris clucked and clucked—and held out a carrot.

Then one day, Rain walked slowly, slowly over to Iris. Iris felt Rain's hot breath on her hand. Rain stared at Iris. Then *chomp*—she ate the carrot!

"Oh," said Iris.

Stop and Think

What **questions** do you have so far? How does knowing about **story structure** help you keep track of the events?

Day after day, Iris and Walter went to see Rain. They fed her carrots. They stroked her neck. They sang sweet songs in her ear.

Then one fine day, Iris climbed up on Rain's back. "Hold on, Iris. Hold on tight," said Walter. "Whatever you do, don't let go!"

And then Rain took off! Away Iris rode, over green meadows, down a path of pines, straight into the sparkling stream.

"Oh, Walter! Did you see me? Did you see me riding Rain?" asked Iris.

"Yes, you are very brave, Iris," said Walter.

"Thank you, Walter," said Iris.

"May I have a turn now?" asked Walter.

"You bet!" said Iris.

Using the Glossary

Like a dictionary, this glossary lists words in alphabetical order. To find a word, look it up by its first letter or letters.

To save time, use the guide words at the top of each page. These show the first and last words on the page. Look at the guide words to see if the word falls between them alphabetically.

Here is an example of a glossary entry:

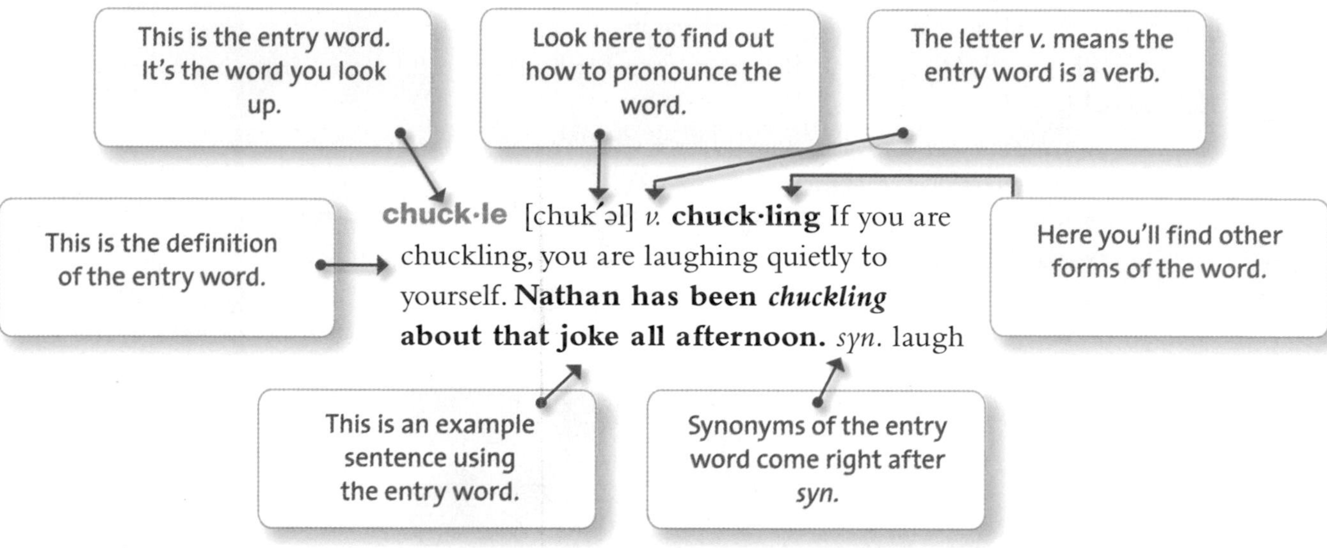
This is the entry word. It's the word you look up.
Look here to find out how to pronounce the word.
The letter v. means the entry word is a verb.
This is the definition of the entry word.
chuck·le [chuk′əl] v. chuck·ling If you are chuckling, you are laughing quietly to yourself. Nathan has been chuckling about that joke all afternoon. syn. laugh
Here you'll find other forms of the word.
This is an example sentence using the entry word.
Synonyms of the entry word come right after syn.

Word Origins

Throughout the glossary, you will find notes about word origins, or how words got started and have changed. Words often have interesting backgrounds that can help you remember what they mean.

Word Origins

uniform This word comes from the Latin word *uniformis*, meaning "one form." So if everyone wears only one form of clothing, they are wearing a uniform.

Pronunciation

The pronunciations in brackets are respellings that show how the words are pronounced.

The pronunciation key explains what the symbols in a respelling mean. A shortened pronunciation key appears on every other page of the glossary.

PRONUNCIATION KEY

a	add, map	m	move, seem	u	up, done
ā	ace, rate	n	nice, tin	û(r)	burn, term
â(r)	care, air	ng	ring, song	yo͞o	fuse, few
ä	palm, father	o	odd, hot	v	vain, eve
b	bat, rub	ō	open, so	w	win, away
ch	check, catch	ô	order, jaw	y	yet, yearn
d	dog, rod	oi	oil, boy	z	zest, muse
e	end, pet	ou	pout, now	zh	vision, pleasure
ē	equal, tree	o͝o	took, full	ə	the schwa, an
f	fit, half	o͞o	pool, food		unstressed vowel
g	go, log	p	pit, stop		representing the
h	hope, hat	r	run, poor		sound spelled
i	it, give	s	see, pass		*a* in *above*
ī	ice, write	sh	sure, rush		*e* in *sicken*
j	joy, ledge	t	talk, sit		*i* in *possible*
k	cool, take	th	thin, both		*o* in *melon*
l	look, rule	th̸	this, bathe		*u* in *circus*

Other symbols:
- • separates words into syllables
- ʹ indicates heavier stress on a syllable
- ʹ indicates lighter stress on a syllable

Abbreviations: *adj.* adjective, *adv.* adverb, *conj.* conjunction, *interj.* interjection, *n.* noun, *prep.* preposition, *pron.* pronoun, *syn.* synonym, *v.* verb

A

ab·sorb [əb·zôrb′] *v.* Something absorbs a liquid if it soaks up the liquid. **The towel will *absorb* the water.** *syn.* take in

> **ACADEMIC LANGUAGE**
>
> **accuracy** When you read with *accuracy,* you read without any mistakes.

ad·vice [ad·vīs′] *n.* If you give someone advice, you tell what you think the person should do. **Lauren's *advice* was to choose the game that was the most fun to play.** *syn.* recommendation

> **ACADEMIC LANGUAGE**
>
> **advice column** An *advice column* gives suggestions for how to solve a problem and is found in a newspaper or magazine.

a·gree·a·ble [ə·grē′ə·bəl] *adj.* Something that is agreeable is pleasing to the senses. **The smell of an apple pie baking was very *agreeable.*** *syn.* pleasant

a·lert [ə·lûrt′] *v.* If you alert people to something, you get their attention and let them know to be careful. **The smoke alarm will *alert* you to the fact that fire is present.** *syn.* notify

ap·ply [ə·plī′] *v.* When you apply for a job, you are asking for work. **Kiarra will call the company to *apply* for a job.** *syns.* request, ask

as·sem·bly [ə·sem′blē] *n.* An assembly is a group of people who have gathered for a reason. **The school will hold an *assembly* to honor the reading contest winners.** *syns.* meeting, gathering

au·to·graph [ô′tə·graf′] *v.* **au·to·graphed** If you autographed something, you signed your name on it. **Adam's friends *autographed* his yearbook.** *syn.* sign

autograph

B

ban·quet [bang′kwit] *n.* If you are going to a banquet, you are going to a special meal that will have a large amount of food. **There will be a lot of food at the *banquet.*** *syn.* feast

banquet

> **ACADEMIC LANGUAGE**
>
> **biography** A *biography* is the story of a person's life, written by another person.

both·er·some [both′ər·səm] *adj.* When something is bothersome, it bothers you and causes problems. **The broken zipper on my boot is *bothersome*!** *syn.* annoying

brief [brēf] *adj.* If something is brief, it does not take much time. **The class will take a *brief* break before continuing the test.** *syn.* short

cam·ou·flage [kam′ə·fläzh′] *n.* When something has camouflage, it blends into its surroundings. **An arctic hare has white fur in winter as *camouflage* against the snow.**

Word Origins

camouflage *Camouflage* comes from the Italian *camuffare,* which means "disguise or trick." This word got its start during World War I, when soldiers practiced hiding objects from the enemy.

cer·tain [sûr′tən] *adj.* A certain thing is one particular thing. **Cole wants a *certain* kind of candy.** *syn.* specific

chat·ter [chat′ər] *v.* When animals chatter, they repeat their sounds quickly. **I heard the squirrels *chatter* outside.** *syn.* talk

chore [chôr] *n.* **chores** Chores are small jobs that you need to do but may not enjoy. **Julia has to do her *chores* at home every day.** *syn.* duty

chuck·le [chuk′əl] *v.* **chuck·ling** If you are chuckling, you are laughing quietly to yourself. **Nathan has been *chuckling* about that joke all afternoon.** *syn.* laugh

co·in·ci·dence [kō·in′sə·dəns] *n.* A coincidence is when two things happen that seem to fit together but are not connected. **It was a *coincidence* that Sophia and Mackenzie wore identical shirts today.**

col·lapse [kə·laps′] *v.* **col·lap·ses** When something collapses, it falls down because it is not well supported. **"Run out of the tent before it collapses!" I yelled.**

col·umn [kol′əm] *n.* **col·umns** A column is a tall, circular structure that holds up part of a building. **The roof of the porch is held up by *columns*.** *syn.* pole

column

com·mu·ni·cate [kə·myo͞o′nə·kāt′] *v.* When two people or animals communicate, they share information. **One way people *communicate* is by talking.**

Word Origins

communicate *Communicate* comes from the Latin *communicatus,* which means "share."

con·ceal [kən·sēl′] *v.* **con·cealed** Something that is concealed is covered up so it can't be seen. **Malik wanted to surprise his dad, so he *concealed* the gift under the couch.** *syn.* hide

a add	e end	o odd	o͞o pool	oi oil	th this	ə = *a* in *above*
ā ace	ē equal	ō open	u up	ou pout	zh vision	*e* in *sicken*
â care	i it	ô order	û burn	ng ring		*i* in *possible*
ä palm	ī ice	o͝o took	yo͞o fuse	th thin		*o* in *melon*
						u in *circus*

con·fess [kən·fes′] *v.* When you confess, you tell the truth about something you did wrong. **It can be hard to *confess* that you have made a mistake, but it is best to tell the truth.** *syn.* admit

con·sult [kən·sult′] *v.* When you consult someone, you ask him or her for information. **Daniel wanted to *consult* his coach about how he could jump higher.**

cul·ture [kul′chər] *n.* A culture is made up of a group's customs and traditions. **In North American *culture*, people shake hands when they meet.**

cu·ri·os·i·ty [kyo͝or′ē·os′ə·tē] *n.* Something that is called a curiosity is something odd or unusual that interests people. **The flower's blooming in winter was a *curiosity*.** *syn.* oddity

D

dazed [dāzd] *adj.* If you are dazed, you are confused and cannot think properly. **The winner was *dazed* by the surprise announcement and didn't know what to say.**

dem·on·strate [dem′ən·strāt′] *v.* When you demonstrate something, you show how it works or how it is done. **Adrianne will *demonstrate* a basketball trick.** *syn.* show

demonstrate

de·vise [di·vīz′] *v.* To devise is to figure out a way to do something. **Emma needed to *devise* a way to get her chores finished.** *syn.* invent

din [din] *n.* If there is a din, there is so much noise that it is hard to hear anything over it. **The *din* of the crowd made it hard to hear my friend talk.** *syn.* racket

dis·ap·poin·ted [dis′ə·point′ed] *adj.* You are disappointed if you are unhappy about the way something turned out. **Elijah was *disappointed* that his team lost the game.** *syns.* saddened, upset

dis·miss [dis·mis′] *v.* To dismiss is to give permission to leave. **Savannah hopes the teacher will *dismiss* the class early for recess.**

dis·solve [di·zolv′] *v.* When something dissolves, it mixes completely with a liquid. **The powder will *dissolve* if you stir it into water.**

dodge [doj] *v.* **dodg·ing** When you are dodging something, you avoid something that is coming toward you. **Fast runners are usually good at *dodging* the ball.** *syn.* avoid

do·nate [dō′nāt′] *v.* **do·nat·ed** Something that has been donated has been given away for free. **Many parents *donated* flowers to be planted in front of the school.**

E

el·e·va·ted [el′ə·vā′ted] *adj.* Something that is elevated is lifted up. **The *elevated* walkway lets people cross the street by walking above it.** *syn.* raised

em·bar·rass [im·bar′əs] *v.* If you embarrass someone, you make that person feel uncomfortable or ashamed. **Courtney will *embarrass* herself if she forgets her lines in the play.**

en·cour·ag·ing [in·kûr′ij·ing] *adj.* Something that is encouraging gives someone hope or confidence. **The coach's speech before the championship game was *encouraging*.** *syn.* hopeful

ex·pert [ek′spûrt] *n.* An expert is someone who knows a lot about a certain subject. **The quarterback is an *expert* at throwing a football.**

> **ACADEMIC LANGUAGE**
>
> **expository nonfiction** *Expository nonfiction* explains information and ideas.
>
> **expression** Reading aloud with *expression* means using your voice to match the action of the story and the character's feelings.

> **ACADEMIC LANGUAGE**
>
> **fable** A *fable* is a short story that teaches a lesson about life. A fable often uses animals that act like people.

fa·mine [fam′in] *n.* When there is famine, there is not enough food to feed everyone. **Hot, dry weather for a long period of time can cause *famine* in an area.**

flick [flik] *v.* When you flick something, you move it or snap it quickly. **The frog can *flick* its tongue to catch a bug.** *syn.* snap

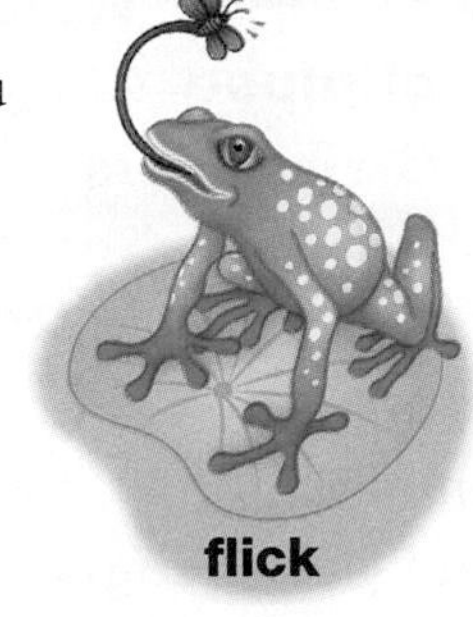
flick

> **ACADEMIC LANGUAGE**
>
> **folktale** A *folktale* is a story that has been passed down through time.

gaze [gāz] *n.* A gaze is a long look at something. **Gabriella's *gaze* was directed at the sky.** *syn.* stare

gen·er·ous [jen′ər·əs] *adj.* People who are generous are happy to share with others. **Justin was *generous* when he shared his lunch after Desiree forgot hers.** *syn.* giving

> **ACADEMIC LANGUAGE**
>
> **genre** *A genre* is a kind of writing, such as fiction or nonfiction.

a add	e end	o odd	o͞o pool	oi oil	th this	ə =	a in *above*
ā ace	ē equal	ō open	u up	ou pout	zh vision		e in *sicken*
â care	i it	ô order	û burn	ng ring			i in *possible*
ä palm	ī ice	o͝o took	yo͞o fuse	th thin			o in *melon*
							u in *circus*

glimpse [glimps] *n.* When you get a glimpse of something, you get only a quick peek at it. **Anthony got a *glimpse* of his birthday cake in the box.** *syn.* peek

Word Origins

glimpse *Glimpse* comes from the German word *glim* which meant "to shine softly" or "to see a soft flash."

groom [gro͞om] **1.** *v.* **grooms** When an animal grooms itself, it makes itself neat and clean. **Angelica's cat *grooms* itself by licking its fur.** *syn.* clean **2.** *n.* A groom is a man who is being married or was just married. **The *groom* stood quietly as the wedding music began.**

heave [hēv] *v.* **heav·ing** Heaving means throwing something heavy with great effort. **Davion needs help *heaving* this heavy bag onto the truck.** *syn.* throw

hin·der [hin′dər] *v.* When you hinder someone, you make it difficult or impossible for them to do something. **Tiana's sore ankle won't *hinder* her from finishing the race.** *syn.* stop

ACADEMIC LANGUAGE

historical fiction *Historical fiction* is a made-up story that is set in the past with people, places, and events that did happen or could have happened.

in·de·pen·dent [in′di·pen′dənt] *adj.* A person who is independent is someone who does things on his or her own. **Learning to tie his shoes made my little brother more *independent*.**

ACADEMIC LANGUAGE

intonation *Intonation* is the rise and fall of your voice as you read aloud.

in·ven·tion [in·ven′shən] *n.* An invention is something completely new that someone has made. **The scientist's *invention* will make life easier for everyone.**

in·ves·ti·gate [in·ves′tə·gāt′] *v.* When you investigate something, you try to find out the truth about it. **Tyler had to *investigate* the disappearance of his lunch box.**

is·sue [ish′o͞o] *n.* An issue is an edition of a newspaper or magazine. **Carlos was excited when the latest *issue* of his favorite magazine came in the mail.**

ACADEMIC LANGUAGE

journal A *journal* is a personal record of daily events.

lab·o·ra·to·ry [lab′rə·tôr′ē] *n.* A place where experiments are done is a laboratory. **The scientist bought some brand-new equipment for his *laboratory*.**

> **ACADEMIC LANGUAGE**
>
> **legend** A *legend* is a story from the past that is often partly true.

loy·al [loi′əl] *adj.* Someone who is loyal stands by you in good times and bad. **Caleb's dog is *loyal* to him.** *syn.* faithful

> **ACADEMIC LANGUAGE**
>
> **magazine article** A *magazine article* is a short selection that appears in a magazine and gives information about a topic.

maze [māz] *n.* A maze is a winding set of paths that is like a puzzle. **Finding my way around town was like being lost in a *maze*.**

midst [midst] *n.* If you are in the midst of something, you are in the middle of it. **Andrew and Marissa were in the *midst* of discussing their project.**

mo·del [mod′əl] *v.* **mo·deled** If you modeled something, you showed it so that others could see it. **Francisco *modeled* his costume for the class.** *syn.* show, present

mur·mur [mûr′mûr] *v.* **mur·mured** When people murmur, they speak so softly that they can hardly be heard. **Trevor could not hear what Nia *murmured* to herself.** *syn.* mumble

> **ACADEMIC LANGUAGE**
>
> **mystery** In a *mystery,* something strange happens that is not explained until the end of the story.

> **ACADEMIC LANGUAGE**
>
> **news feature** A *news feature* gives information—about a person or topic—in a newspaper or magazine.
>
> **newsletter** A *newsletter* presents information about an organization to a person or group of people.
>
> **news script** A *news script* is a text that is read aloud and gives information about important events.
>
> **nonfiction** *Nonfiction* gives facts and information about people, places, or things.

a	add	e	end	o	odd	o͞o	pool	oi	oil	th	this
ā	ace	ē	equal	ō	open	u	up	ou	pout	zh	vision
â	care	i	it	ô	order	û	burn	ng	ring		
ä	palm	ī	ice	o͝o	took	yo͞o	fuse	th	thin		

ə = *a* in *above*, *e* in *sicken*, *i* in *possible*, *o* in *melon*, *u* in *circus*

o·bey [ō·bā′] *v.* When you obey, you do what you are told to do. **Good citizens *obey* the law.**

> **ACADEMIC LANGUAGE**
>
> **online information** *Online information* is found on an Internet website.

> **ACADEMIC LANGUAGE**
>
> **pace** Reading at an appropriate *pace* means reading at the right speed.

par·ti·cle [pär′ti·kəl] *n.* **par·ti·cles** Tiny pieces of something are called particles. **Cody wiped the dust *particles* off the computer screen** *syn.* bit

patch·work [pach′wûrk′] *n.* Patchwork is cloth made by sewing together small pieces of different fabrics. **The quilt Grandma made is a *patchwork* of pieces cut from the family's old clothing.**

patchwork

pa·trol [pə·trōl′] *v.* People patrol an area to watch over and guard it. **Police *patrol* a neighborhood to keep it safe.** *syns.* tour, watch, guard

> **ACADEMIC LANGUAGE**
>
> **photo essay** A *photo essay* presents information mostly with photographs and with some text.
>
> **phrasing** *Phrasing* is the grouping of words into small "chunks," or phrases, when you read aloud.

pleas·ant [plez′ənt] *adj.* Something that is pleasant is enjoyable and makes you happy. **The weather is *pleasant* today.**

plen·ty [plen′tē] *n.* If you have plenty of something, you have more than enough. **There are *plenty* of toys for everyone.**

> **ACADEMIC LANGUAGE**
>
> **poetry** *Poetry* uses rhythm and imagination to express feelings and ideas.
>
> **postcards** *Postcards* can be mailed without an envelope and usually have a picture on one side.

praise [prāz] *v.* **praised** If you have praised someone, you have told that person that he or she did something well. **The teacher *praised* the students for their fine drawings.**

pro·tect [prə·tekt′] *v.* **pro·tects** When you protect something, you keep it safe. **Amir *protects* his head by wearing a bicycle helmet.** *syns.* guard, defend

> **Word Origins**
>
> **protect** *Protect* comes from the Latin word *prōtegere*. The prefix *pro-* means "in front" and the root word *tegere* means "cover." So when you protect someone, you cover him or her from the front like a shield.

ACADEMIC LANGUAGE

punctuation Paying attention to *punctuation,* such as commas and periods, will help you read a text correctly.

R

ACADEMIC LANGUAGE

reading rate Your *reading rate* is how quickly you can read a text correctly and still understand what you are reading.

realistic fiction *Realistic fiction* is a story that could happen in real life.

re·cite [ri·sīt′] *v.* **re·ci·ted** If you recited something, you memorized it and then spoke it aloud. **Ali *recited* the names of all 50 states without looking at a map.**

rec·om·mend [rek′ə·mend′] *v.* When you recommend something, you tell someone that you think it is good. **Alexis asked her teacher to *recommend* a book to read.**

re·pair [ri·pâr′] *n.* **re·pairs** When something needs repairs, it needs to be fixed. **Cynthia needs to make *repairs* to her bike before the race.**

re·search [ri·sûrch′ or rē′sûrch′] *n.* Research involves getting information about a question or topic. **Isabel has done *research* on desert animals for her report.** *syn.* study

re·source [ri·sôrs′ *or* rē′sôrs′] *n.* **re·sour·ces** Resources are materials, money, and other things that can be used. **Water *resources* are important to cities.** *syn.* supply

roost [ro͞ost] *v.* Birds roost, or perch, when they sleep in trees at night. **Many birds *roost* in the tree outside my window each night.**

rus·tle [rus′əl] *v.* **rust·ling** When objects are rustling, they are moving and making soft sounds. **Please stop *rustling* those papers.**

S

scent [sent] *n.* A scent is the smell of something. **Carol loves the *scent* of spring flowers.** *syns.* odor, smell

scent

sen·si·ble [sen′sə·bəl] *adj.* Someone who is sensible makes good decisions and judgments. **Jennifer is a *sensible* eater who chooses fruits as treats.** *syn.* wise

shab·by [shab′ē] *adj.* Shabby things look old and worn out. **This *shabby* coat will be fine for working in the garden.**

sig·nal [sig′nəl] *n.* A signal is a sound or an action that sends a message. **The green light is a *signal* to go.** *syn.* sign

a	add	e	end	o	odd	o͞o	pool	oi	oil	th	this	ə = *a* in *above*
ā	ace	ē	equal	ō	open	u	up	ou	pout	zh	vision	*e* in *sicken*
â	care	i	it	ô	order	û	burn	ng	ring			*i* in *possible*
ä	palm	ī	ice	o͝o	took	yo͞o	fuse	th	thin			*o* in *melon*
												u in *circus*

sob [sob] *v.* **sobbed** Someone who sobbed cried very hard. **Brenda *sobbed* when she lost her favorite book.** *syn.* cry

sooth·ing [so͞oth′ing] *adj.* Something that is soothing makes you feel calm. **Jazmine thinks the sound of rain is *soothing.*** *syn.* calming

spear [spir] *v.* **spears** If someone spears something, he or she sticks something sharp through it. **Steven *spears* the green beans with his fork.** *syn.* stab

squirm [skwûrm] *v.* **squirmed** If you squirmed in your seat, you kept wriggling around as if you were uncomfortable. **The puppy *squirmed* when Savion tried to pick it up.** *syn.* wriggle

strike [strīk] **1.** *v.* **strikes** If something strikes something else, it hits it. **Rod *strikes* a nail with his hammer.** *syn.* hit **2.** *n.* In baseball, a strike is a pitch that the batter misses. **After the third *strike,* Edward had to walk off the baseball field.**

strike

sup·pose [sə·pōz′] *v.* When you suppose something, you think it is true. **What do you *suppose* will happen tomorrow?** *syn.* believe

sur·vive [sər·vīv′] *v.* To survive is to remain alive, even after great difficulties. **Living things need food, water, air, and shelter to *survive.*** *syn.* live

sus·pect [sə·spekt′] *v.* When you suspect someone of doing something, you think that person has done it. **Knowing her brother made Emily *suspect* that he had eaten all the cookies.**

ACADEMIC LANGUAGE

syllable A *syllable* is the smallest part of a word that contains a single vowel sound.

T

tal·ent·ed [tal′ən·tid] *adj.* A talented person has the special ability to do something very well. **Serena is a very *talented* drummer.** *syns.* skilled, gifted

ACADEMIC LANGUAGE

textbook A *textbook* is a book that is used in schools to teach a subject.

time line A *time line* is a line that shows dates of past events in the order in which they happened.

trans·late [trans·lāt′] *v.* If you translate something, you say or write it in another language. **Can Kimberly *translate* this letter into English?** *syn.* interpret

tu·tor [to͞o′tər] *n.* A tutor is someone who helps another person with schoolwork. **César has a math *tutor* to help him after school.** *syns.* teacher, instructor

u·ni·form [yo͞o′nə·fôrm′] *n.* **u·ni·forms** Uniforms are clothes that all the people in a group wear so that they are dressed alike. **Ian could tell his teammates by their *uniforms*.**

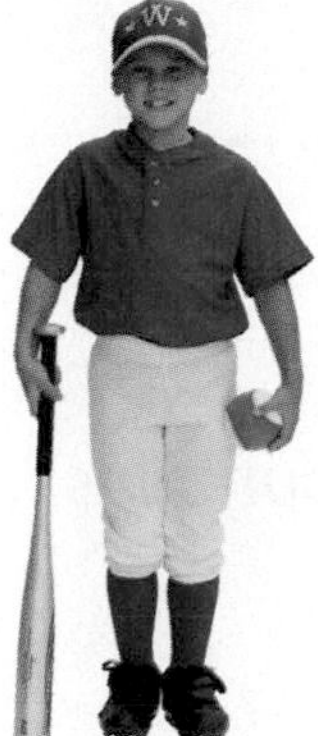

uniform

Word Origins

uniform This word comes from the Latin word *uniformis* meaning "one form." If everyone wears only one form of clothing, they are wearing a uniform.

var·i·ous [vâr′ē·əs] *adj.* When there are various objects, there are objects of different types. **The box was full of *various* items that students had lost.** *syn.* assorted

view·er [vyo͞o′ər] *n.* **view·ers** Viewers are people who watch something. **The host of the show told stories that were interesting to his *viewers*.**

wan·der [wän′dər] *v.* **wan·ders** A person who wanders travels without planning where he or she is going. **The tourist *wanders*, stopping at places of interest around town.**

whine [hwīn] *v.* **whined** If someone or something whined, it gave a long, high cry. **The toddler *whined* when his mother would not buy the toy.** *syn.* whimper

a	add	e	end	o	odd	o͞o	pool	oi	oil	th	this	ə = *a* in *above*
ā	ace	ē	equal	ō	open	u	up	ou	pout	zh	vision	*e* in *sicken*
â	care	i	it	ô	order	û	burn	ng	ring			*i* in *possible*
ä	palm	ī	ice	o͝o	took	yo͞o	fuse	th	thin			*o* in *melon*
												u in *circus*

Index of Titles and Authors

Page numbers in green refer to biographical information.

Acknowledgments

For permission to reprint copyrighted material, grateful acknowledgment is made to the following sources:

Aladdin Paperbacks, an imprint of Simon & Schuster Children's Publishing Division: From *Loved Best* by Patricia C. McKissack, cover illustration by Felicia Marshall. Text copyright © 2005 by Patricia C. McKissack; cover illustration copyright © 2005 by Felicia Marshall.

Boyds Mills Press, Inc.: From *Aero and Officer Mike: Police Partners* by Joan Plummer Russell, photographs by Kris Turner Sinnenberg. Text copyright © 2001 by Joan Plummer Russell; photographs copyright © 2001 by Kris Turner Sinnenberg. Published by Caroline House, an imprint of Boyds Mills Press.

Curtis Brown, Ltd.: "Good Books, Good Times!" from *Good Books, Good Times!* by Lee Bennett Hopkins. Text copyright © 1990 by Lee Bennett Hopkins. Published by HarperCollins Publishers.

Children's Book Press, San Francisco, CA, www.childrensbookpress.org: "Keys to the Universe/Las llaves del universo" from *From the Bellybutton of the Moon/Del Ombligo de la Luna* by Francisco X. Alarcón, illustrated by Maya Christina Gonzalez. Text copyright © 1998 by Francisco X. Alarcón; illustrations copyright © 1998 by Maya Christina Gonzalez.

DK Publishing: "The Shepherd Boy and The Wolf" from *The Lion and the Mouse: And Other Aesop's Fables,* retold by Doris Orgel, cover illustration by Bert Kitchen. Text copyright © 2000 by Doris Orgel; cover illustration copyright © 2000 by Bert Kitchen.

Harcourt, Inc.: The Babe & I by David A. Adler, illustrated by Terry Widener. Text copyright © 1999 by David A. Adler; illustrations copyright © 1999 by Terry Widener. From *Iris and Walter: True Friends* by Elissa Haden Guest, illustrated by Christine Davenier. Text copyright © 2001 by Elissa Haden Guest; illustrations copyright © 2001 by Christine Davenier. "A Beagle Speaks of Noses" and "Guide Dog" from *It's About Dogs* by Tony Johnston. Text copyright © 2000 by The Living Trust of Tony Johnston.

HarperCollins Publishers: One Small Place in a Tree by Barbara Brenner, illustrated by Tom Leonard. Text copyright © 2004 by Barbara Brenner; illustrations copyright © 2004 by Tom Leonard.

Heinemann-Raintree, Chicago, IL: From *Schools Around the World* by Margaret Hall. Text copyright © 2002 by Heinemann Raintree Library, a division of Reed Elsevier Inc.

Henry Holt and Company, LLC: A Pen Pal for Max by Gloria Rand, illustrated by Ted Rand. Text copyright © 2005 by Gloria Rand; illustrations copyright © 2005 by Ted Rand.

Beverly J. Letchworth: From "Be a Birdwatcher" by Beverly J. Letchworth in *US Kids* Magazine, March 2000.

Margaret K. McElderry Books, an Imprint of Simon & Schuster Children's Publishing Division: From *The Day Eddie Met the Author* by Louise Borden, cover illustration by Adam Gustavson. Text copyright © 2001 by Louise Borden; cover illustration copyright © 2001 by Adam Gustavson.

Beverly McLoughland: "Surprise" by Beverly McLoughland. Originally appeared in *Cricket* Magazine, 1985.

National Geographic Society: From *How Animals Talk* by Susan McGrath. Text copyright © 1987 by National Geographic Society.

Random House Children's Books, a division of Random House, Inc.: "The Singing Marvel" from *Birds Do the Strangest Things* by Leonora and Arthur Hornblow. Text copyright © 1965 by Random House, Inc.; text copyright renewed 1993 by Leonora and Arthur Hornblow and Random House, Inc.

The Rosen Publishing Group, Inc.: From *I Live in a Town* by Stasia Ward Kehoe. Text copyright © 2000 by The Rosen Publishing Group, Inc.

Scholastic Inc.: A Tree Is Growing by Arthur Dorros, illustrated by S. D. Schindler. Text copyright © 1997 by Arthur Dorros; illustrations copyright © 1997 by S. D. Schindler. *Stone Soup,* retold and illustrated by Jon J Muth. Copyright © 2003 by Jon J Muth. *Ruby the Copycat* by Peggy Rathmann. Copyright © 1991 by Margaret Rathmann.

Photo Credits

Placement Key: (t) top; (b) bottom; (l) left; (r) right; (c) center; (bg) background; (fg) foreground; (i) inset

18 (cr) Royalty-Free/Corbis; 54 (bl) PhotoDisc; 109 (c) The Image Bank; 112 (bl) PhotoDisc; 113 (tr) NASA; 114 (bl) Bill Howe/Alamy; 114 (cr) NASA-DFRC; 117 (c) NASA or National Aeronautics and Space Administration; 119 NASA/JPL/Phil Degginger/www.color-pic.com; 125 (c) Image by © CORBIS; 126 (tr) NASA or National Aeronautics and Space Administration; 126 (bc) Photo By Nasa/Getty Images; 127 (tc) NASA Johnson Space Center; (NASA-JSC); 128 (bc) NASA/The Image Works; 130 (cl) NASA/Photo Researchers, Inc; 131 (bc) NASA/Handout/Getty (editorial); 132 (c) © NASA/CORBIS SYGMA; 133 (bc) Photo By Nasa/Getty Images; 134 Index Stock/Alamy; 137 (tr) NASA-KSC; 157 (cr) Photonica; 158 (bl) Ryan McVay/Getty; 189 (cr) The Granger Collection; 196 (t) Ioan Nicolae; RF/Shutterstock; 198 (t) Natalia Bratslavsky/Shutterstock; 218 (t) Cindy Jenkins; RF/Shutterstock; 221 (cr) Royalty-Free/Corbis; 226 (bl) Peter Arnold, Inc./Alamy; 227 (tr) Digital Stock, Corbis Corporation; 246 (tc) Tom Brakefield/CORBIS; 247 (tr) Purestock/Alamy; 247 (tl) Stone; 247 (br) Tom Brakefield/CORBIS; 247 (inset) Tom Brakefield/CORBIS; 247 (tc) Visual&Written SL/Alamy; 249 (cr) Digital Stock, Corbis Corporation; 279 (cr) Keren Su/CORBIS; 302 (bl) Richard Lewisohn/Getty; 303 (tr) Omni Photo Communications, Inc/Index Stock Imagery; 304 (bc) David Young-Wolff/PhotoEdit; 305 (tr) Royalty-Free/Corbis; 326 (t) Ariel Skelley/Corbis; 334 (bl) Daniel Fort/Index Stock Imagery; 336 (cr) Photographer's Choice RF; 336 (b) The Image Bank/Getty; 368 (br) SMITH, NIGEL J.H./Animals Animals–Earth Scenes—All rights reserved.; 369 (tr) STEPHEN DALTON/Minden Pictures; 396 (cr) Galen Rowell/CORBIS; 397 (inset) D. Robert & Lorri Franz/CORBIS; 397 (br) Richard Olsenius/National Geographic Image Collection; 397 (tr) Tom Till/Alamy; 398 (t) Altrendo; 399 (bc) W. Perry Conway/CORBIS; 401 (cr) Photodisc Red; 404 (bl) Joe McDonald/CORBIS; 405 (tr) Joe McDonald/CORBIS; 406 (t) Anastasiya Maksymenko; RF/Shutterstock; 407 (tr) Theo Allofs/CORBIS; 429 (cr) Photodisc Red; 447 (tr) Corel Stock Photo Library.

All other photos © Harcourt School Publishers. Harcourt photos provided by Harcourt Index, Harcourt IPR, and Harcourt Photographers: Weronica Ankarorn, Eric Camden, Doug DuKane, Ken Kinsie, April Riehm and Steve Williams.

Illustration Credits

Cover Art; Laura and Eric Ovresat, Artlab, Inc.

1. Fountas & Pinnell
2. Comprehension Questions -> differentiating factor
3. Anaya is at level L (mid 2nd) (NOP is 3)
4. Reading is phenomenal. Comprehension needs work
5. Climbing High -> Grade 3.
6. Summer Reading Program
   Shrewsbury Public Library
   Barnes & Noble
7. ERIN McCAUGHLIN.